W9-DEC-772

THE CHILD FROM
THREE TO EIGHTEEN

THE CHILD FROM THREE TO EIGHTEEN

Olle Jane Z. Sahler, M.D.

Assistant Professor of Pediatrics and Psychiatry,
Division of Biosocial Pediatrics/Adolescent Medicine,
Department of Pediatrics, University of Rochester School of Medicine,
Rochester, New York

Elizabeth R. McAnarney, M.D.

Associate Professor of Pediatrics, Psychiatry, Medicine, and Nursing;
Director, Division of Biosocial Pediatrics/Adolescent Medicine;
Department of Pediatrics, University of Rochester School of Medicine,
Rochester, New York

The C. V. Mosby Company

ST. LOUIS • TORONTO • LONDON   1981

MOSBY

1906 **75** 1981
YEARS

A TRADITION OF PUBLISHING EXCELLENCE

Copyright © 1981 by The C. V. Mosby Company

All rights reserved. No part of this book may be reproduced
in any manner without written permission of the publisher.

Printed in the United States of America

The C. V. Mosby Company
11830 Westline Industrial Drive, St. Louis, Missouri 63141

Library of Congress Cataloging in Publication Data

Sahler, Olle Jane Z   1944-
    The child from three to eighteen.

    Bibliography: p.
    Includes index.
    1. Child development. 2. Pediatrics—
Psychological aspects. 3. Children—Diseases—
Social aspects. I. McAnarney, Elizabeth R., joint
author. II. Title. [DNLM: 1. Adolescence.
2. Adolescent psychology. 3. Child behavior dis-
orders. 4. Child development. 5. Growth.
WS 350.6 S131c]
RJ131.S23   155.4   80-27126
ISBN 0-8016-4290-6

C/D/D 9 8 7 6 5 4 3 2 1   02/A/209

To three individuals,
each of whom influenced some aspect of our growth and development
so uniquely that remembering or honoring them with
this book seems most appropriate:

Raymond J. Zagraniski, *physician and father*

Mary and Kiki McAnarney, *understanding teachers*

Foreword

Progress is achieved neither smoothly nor rapidly; *The Child from Three to Eighteen* is a milestone on the road of progress for all professional workers caring for children, as well as for parents and children.

Let me illustrate what I mean. As long ago as 1951, the American Board of Pediatrics took cognizance of what is presented in this text as biosocial pediatrics with the following*:

The Board does not believe that pediatricians should be less adequately trained in the care of the sick infant and child. It does believe, however, that a study of growth and developmental processes can be advantageously incorporated into such training. . . . It becomes obvious, therefore, that pediatric training centers must increasingly assume the responsibility for the day-to-day teaching of growth and development in a clinical setting. This means a practical evaluation of the total development of each patient and its meaning to parents and physicians. It also means that some opportunity to observe presumably well infants and children become part of the training program where it is not at present.

One of the pioneers in such teaching, Dr. Milton Senn, wrote in that same year†:

In formulating a treatment program or one of prevention, the physician and nurse need to know the potentialities for growth and change which are inherent within the human being, and which need to be mobilized for overcoming ill health of any kind and in maintaining good health. Under the stimulation of teachers who have an understanding of the dynamic concepts of personality development and of behavior, students in a meaningful way may acquire knowledge of biological and psychological patterning, and of the developmental characteristics of the human organism.

Yet, it was not until 1978 in the recent report of the Task Force on Pediatric Education that a consensus on the need for such education and training and its applications in clinical care developed. This report said‡:

Biosocial and developmental problems, such as early family adjustment difficulties and school failure, adversely affect the health of many children and adolescents. These problems are serious and very wide-spread. All pediatricians should have the skills to cope with them.

*From American Board of Pediatrics. 1951. Statement on training requirements in growth and development, *Pediatrics* 7:430-432.
†From Senn, M. J. E. 1951. The contribution of psychiatry to child health services, *American Journal of Orthopsychiatry* 21:138-147.
‡From Task Force on Pediatric Education. 1978. *The future of pediatric education*. Denver, Hirschfield Press, p. IX.

In the long perspective of history, almost 30 years does not seem too long a wait for a professional discipline to broaden its orientation. This new orientation is not fortuitous or the consequence of persuasiveness on the part of a few enthusiasts. Rather, in my view, it is the consequence of two major developments:

1. The remarkable improvement in the health of children—the result, in no small measure, of the applications of outstanding research contributions to our knowledge. Over the past several decades the incidence of many childhood diseases in this country has been sharply reduced. These advances are illustrated by a constantly declining infant mortality rate, the worldwide eradication of smallpox, the striking reduction in occurrence of all acute infectious diseases of childhood, and the control of many metabolic disorders. The decline in morbidity and mortality rates has freed much professional time for attention to the psychological and social development of the child and the family. A personal note illustrates this point. During my house staff training in pediatrics, more than half my time was spent caring for children with acute infectious diseases that current medical students in the United States will not see during their education and training.

2. The major sociological changes in American society that have had such a significant impact on children and families have created new types of problems for us in our efforts to foster the greatest potentialities for our children's growth and development. These changes are too numerous to be detailed here. They include the urbanization of our society, which has resulted in greater mobility; changes in traditional sex roles; large numbers of women with young children now entering the work force; and a significant increase in the number of single-parent families. Accompanying these societal changes has been a renewed interest in issues such as child abuse, developmental disabilities, and learning and behavioral disorders.

In modern society parents expect professionals in child health and child care to help them address these new problems. Fortunately this expectation occurs at a time when our knowledge base on developmental issues has been expanding. An incorporation of biosocial pediatrics into practice involves a conceptual shift. We must learn to incorporate a knowledge of the *processes* of growth and development along with our understanding of *abnormal conditions* and *disease*. We should welcome this shift that, although not entirely new, represents a significant enrichment for pediatrics and pediatric education.

The appearance of this book and an increasing literature in biosocial pediatrics indicate that pediatrics is better prepared than ever before to deal with the challenges posed in caring for the health of this nation's children. It is particularly encouraging to me to see that a new generation of pediatric educators is now able to add its expertise in biosocial pediatrics to other areas of pediatric training and to pass on its knowledge to a new generation of pediatricians, child psychiatrists, and other professionals concerned with the health and well-being of children.

Julius B. Richmond, M.D.

Assistant Secretary for Health and Surgeon General of the United States, July 1980

Preface

Developmental considerations impact on all phases of comprehensive care of the child. No medical or psychological text is complete without reference to the differences in cause, manifestation, or management of a given disorder when it occurs in an infant, child, or adolescent who has not attained full adult physiological or psychological functioning. Thus, the providers of health care for children—physicians, nurses, psychologists, social workers—must have a unique appreciation for and understanding of the principles of human development and their relationship to health and disease.

Biosocial pediatrics is the branch of pediatric medicine that emphasizes the behavioral component of two major areas of dysfunction in children: symptom formation and illness. Perhaps in no other subspecialty is knowledge of the maturational process as critical or of such continuing importance as it is in the study, interpretation, and management of behavioral problems.

Certain aspects of biosocial care have been practiced throughout the history of pediatrics. Unlike other subspecialty disciplines, however, biosocial pediatrics has neither had formal title or organizational structure nor focused on any explicit body of knowledge that distinguished it as a separate entity within the general field of pediatric medicine. Such lack of definition has been beneficial in some ways, since it has attracted persons with widely diverse interests who have pioneered work in a variety of related biosocial areas. On the other hand, to the interested but uninitiated, this apparent lack of a unified thrust has made the field seem too broad for adequate mastery.

This lack of structure is changing rapidly. The movement to formalize biosocial pediatrics has received its major impetus in response to new demands from the consumer public: parents and children who find it difficult to cope with our highly technological and uncertain world in which divorce, mobility, dissolution of the extended family, and abnegation of formal belief systems have removed many of the traditional support structures of society. Many families appear to be attempting to recapture some of their lost social stability through stronger and more varied ties with their health providers, to whom they are now looking for advice in parenting and child rearing as well as the management of disease. Recognizing this trend, the recent Task Force on Pediatric Education has clearly stated new priorities in medical education to help practitioners meet the demands of present and future generations of children and their families: "There should be increased emphasis [in residency training] on the biosocial aspects of pediatrics and adolescent health care."*

The Child from Three to Eighteen reflects our training, investigation, and clinical experience in traditional pediatric medicine and developmental/behavioral pediatrics, including study in the related fields of developmental psychology and child psychiatry. As pediatricians, we recognize that emotional responses to real or perceived situational stresses can assume the guise of physical illness or interfere with treatment of a previously diagnosed disease. Thus it is only as expected that children and their parents seek help from the health care provider as a first step in finding a solution to their underlying problem.

We have participated in the education of medical, nursing, and psychology students; social workers; house officers; and fellows in a general pediatric and adolescent medicine program for a number of years. Aware of the many pressures trainees face in trying to master the basic principles of health care, we have consciously attempted to make the understanding of children's behavior in health and disease pragmatic and relevant to clinical practice. We have been most successful when we have been able to incorporate the principles of normal growth and development into explanations of problem behaviors and their treatment. Such an approach has two advantages: it reinforces basic principles and teaches a reasoned approach to diagnosis and care. The topics and discussions in this text are the result of what we have learned at the bedside and found most exciting and helpful to our students in the classroom.

This book is designed as a first step toward helping both the student and the established practitioner incorporate a more conscious biosocial approach in their clinical practice based on a clear understanding of the developmental issues, both theoretical and observed, that influence the behavior presented as the primary complaint by the child or his† parents. By providing the clinician with such information, we hope that developmental theory can be comfortably integrated into meaningful answers to the practical questions about emotions and behavior asked by today's children, adolescents, and parents.

In Part One, we have reviewed normal physiological growth and psychological development of the child from 3 to 18 years of age: the school-aged child. We have concentrated on three specific theories of psychological development: *psychoana-*

---

*From Task Force on Pediatric Education. 1978. *The future of pediatric education*. Denver, Hirschfield Press.
†Throughout this text, we have chosen to use the masculine form to designate the universal individual for ease in reading and to avoid cumbersome sentence structure.

lytic (Freud and Erikson), *cognitive-intellectual* (Piaget and Kohlberg), and *learning*. It is extremely important to recognize that a host of factors impact on the growing child. Some of these have formed the bases for other theories of development, and some are just beginning to be appreciated for their importance. However, although we realize that our selectivity precludes a full and complete discussion of the field of developmental psychology that will satisfy the natural curiosity and skepticism of all readers, the three theories chosen seem to us to form a good basic foundation for understanding behavior and to be the most applicable to the diagnosis and management of behavioral problems in private practice settings.

In Part Two, we have integrated the pertinent features of specific stages in both physiological and psychological development into practical evaluation and treatment schemes of children and adolescents who have such contemporary biosocial problems as disturbed family relationships, school difficulties, and physical illness. We hope that the vignettes we use to illustrate developmental principles as they relate to observed behavior will provide the reader with diagnosis and management strategies that have broad applicability in a wide variety of situations.

As should be apparent from the clinical examples, careful attention to the biosocial aspects of care can be integrated into regular practice schedules. Even apparently complex and overwhelming problems lend themselves to the kind of differential diagnostic and investigative planning common to all branches of medical care. As in any other subspecialty, some of the investigation and treatment may require the help of specially trained professional or ancillary personnel.

The time required to manage biosocial problems can range from trivial to substantial. The perception that inordinate amounts of time may be demanded stems less from reality than from sporadic experiences with poorly constructed interventions that have no definite goals. Like all aspects of health care, successful biosocial care requires practice and a resolution not to be defeated by one or two misadventures.

To be most fair, we must acknowledge that biosocial care demands patience and a certain amount of organizational skill to develop successful diagnosis and treatment plans. The presentation of symptoms is seldom well or objectively articulated by people caught in an emotional crisis. Appropriate treatment usually requires a level of energetic support and direction comparable, on the average, with that provided to a new diabetic patient and his family.

Many practitioners have chosen to offer purely biosocial consultations at times of low office overhead (evenings, for example), since the need for assistance or laboratory facilities is rare, once the diagnosis is made. In some practices, some or most of the formal biosocial care is provided by nonphysician personnel, such as skilled nurse practitioners or social workers. In other practices, pediatric-psychiatric or general pediatric–biosocial pediatric liaisons have been established so that consultation or direct care is provided by referral to another professional in a separate practice or agency. Although any of these alternatives is consistent with good care, it remains imperative that the primary practitioner possess the expertise to recognize behavioral problems as such and facilitate the patient's or family's search for treatment.

As pediatricians, we know that some of our patients will experience cardiac, neurological, or infectious illnesses or diseases. However, we also know that, with few exceptions, all of our patients will grow and develop. The knowledge that we have played some role in maintaining optimal physical health for these children is an outstanding reward for our efforts. The fact that we have helped these same children achieve the most independent, emotionally healthy, and productive maturity of which they are capable provides us with the satisfaction of having positively influenced the growth and development of generations of children yet to come.

We are indebted to a number of individuals who played significant roles in the preparation of *The Child from Three to Eighteen:* Valerie A. Wheeler, our research assistant, for sharing her excellent knowledge of developmental psychology, careful attention to detail, and unfailing enthusiasm; Alfred L. Baldwin, Christopher H. Hodgman, Robert A. Hoekelman, Robert W. Chamberlin, and Barbara B. Keller for their valuable criticisms and recommendations, a number of which we have been able to incorporate in the finished text; the Fellows in General Academic Pediatrics at the University of Rochester for some cogent suggestions about the organization of the manuscript; the Rochester-area pediatricians who reviewed our initial outline for their insightful recommendations about specific content areas of most relevance and concern to clinicians; Kathy Schafer, Susan A. Brightman, Tammy Lynn Sherman, Lyn Neary, and Carole M. Berger for secretarial assistance; and our families and friends for patience and encouragement. We also wish to acknowledge Psychiatric Pediatric Liaison Training Grant NIMH: 1 T01 MH 15275-01 for partial support during the preparation of this manuscript.

Olle Jane Z. Sahler
Elizabeth R. McAnarney

Contents

PART ONE

THEORIES OF GROWTH AND DEVELOPMENT

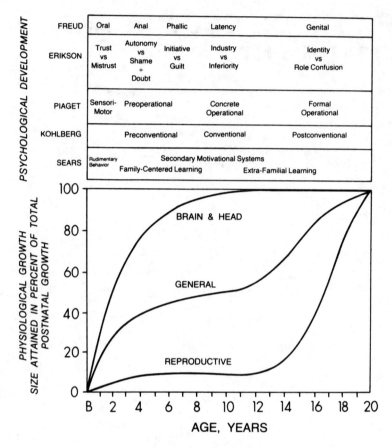

PHYSIOLOGICAL AND PSYCHOLOGICAL GROWTH
AND DEVELOPMENT

Bottom, Modified from Tanner, J. M. 1962. *Growth at adolescence* (2nd ed.). Oxford, England: Blackwell Scientific Publications Ltd.

Chapter 1

Overview of growth and development

Although the terms **growth*** and **development** are often used synonymously, it is appropriate for our purposes to distinguish between them. We shall use *growth* to designate an increase in size, a phenomenon most conveniently measured in terms of such parameters as length, weight, or breadth. The term can therefore refer, for example, to physical size or the magnitude of knowledge or experience of an individual. We shall use *development* to designate maturation or differentiation, a phenomenon most conveniently measured by assessing complexity of functioning or degree of performance skill. Development can describe, therefore, the evolution of physiological or psychological functional capacity. Although growth and development are related and interdependent, they are separate processes that can proceed to some extent independently of one another.

DETERMINANTS OF GROWTH AND DEVELOPMENT

Individual growth and development are determined by **heredity** (the inherent **nature** of the individual) and **environment** (the physical, social, and cultural milieu; the external sources of **nurturance** or training).

Heredity

Heredity, or genetic endowment, defines, within broad limits, an individual's basic overall potential and predisposition. **Genotype** refers to actual gene composition as determined by deoxyribonucleic acid (DNA) sequencing. **Phenotype** refers to the morphological and physiological characteristics of a given individual as determined by the expression or suppression of certain gene compositions or combinations. Two of the major characteristics determined by genetic endowment and often implicated in differential growth and development are sex and race.

Temperament is the apparently innate characteristic or habitual inclination or mode of emotional response to stimuli idiosyncratic to an individual. First displayed in early infancy, temperament might be considered the psychological component of phenotype.

---

*Terms in boldface type are defined in the Glossary at the end of the text.

Environment

The tenor of the environment, or the degree of nurturance the individual receives from the physical and psychological milieu in which he grows and develops, can either limit or potentiate genetic endowment. The broad category of environment can be divided into (1) the physical environment, including such intrauterine and extrauterine conditions as temperature or climate, nutrition, and prevalence of disease, and (2) the psychological environment, the total social context of an individual, including the influences of the family, school, peer group, and community.

Certain factors have a direct impact on these two environments. For example, **socioeconomic status** often determines the extent to which an individual will have access to environmental protection and/or enrichment. **Culture,** the characteristics or customs peculiar to the group of people of which the individual is a member, can produce a bias toward or away from particular traits, habits, and personal goals.

PROCESSES OF GROWTH AND DEVELOPMENT

The overall progression of growth and development is affected by a number of phenomena.

Variation

No two individuals are exactly alike. To understand how similar or different they are from each other and the population as a whole, we often rely on statistical analysis. The concept of **normal variation,** in particular, is frequently used in conjunction with measurements of physiological and psychological parameters.

Statistical and clinical uses of the adjective "normal" are substantially different but are often confused. The statistical definition of normal variation involves the assumption that measurable characteristics are symmetrically distributed around the population mean in a **bell-shaped curve.** The value of the particular characteristic under consideration is designated to fall "within normal limits" if it lies within two standard deviations of the population mean. Thus, by design, approximately 5% of all naturally occurring values will fall symmetrically outside the upper and lower limits of normal.

Being outside normal limits in the statistical sense is not, by itself, a sufficient criterion to define the presence of a *clinically abnormal* (pathological) condition. However, the finding that the value of a certain parameter for a particular individual falls outside these defined boundaries implies that further clinical investigation may be warranted to accept or reject the statistical suggestion of abnormality.

This concept of normality of variation is applicable to both populations and individuals. For example, there is a wide variation in height among all children or adolescents at a given age; similarly, a wide variation exists in the velocity of height growth from one age to the next in a given child (Tanner, 1978).

The widest variations among populations and within individuals occur during

transitional periods from one stage of growth and development to another. This point is made clearer by considering transitional periods as intervals of time during which growth or developmental changes emerge. Thus, during early adolescence, it is not uncommon for some girls to have almost full breast development and others no development whatsoever despite their same chronological age; in addition, some girls experience notable asymmetry in breast budding, a naturally occurring and common variation in the breast development of an individual.

Acceleration/deceleration

Acceleration refers to the overall process of further or continued growth and development. **Deceleration,** on the other hand, refers to a decline in size (e.g., height loss with advanced age), a decrease in certain abilities, or an unlearning of formerly appropriate responses that have become inappropriate. Deceleration is a normal part of the growth and development continuum.

"Critical" or "sensitive" periods

There appear to be circumscribed periods of time during which some organisms display intense responsivity to particular environmental stimuli. The work of Lorenz (1935) emphasized the importance of **critical periods** for the formation of primary social bonds (imprinting) in young birds. McGraw (1946) was among the first to suggest that critical periods for optimal learning of motor skills may exist in human infants as well. Subsequent investigation has extended the notion of "critical" or "sensitive" periods for the formation of basic social relationships, for infantile stimulation, and for learning (Scott, 1962; Tanner, 1978).

This notion of "sensitive" periods was incorporated into the educational theory of Maria Montessori. Montessori (1964a,b) hypothesized that there are times when a child is most "ready" to acquire certain skills or abilities and will spontaneously practice such skills repetitively and at great length (e.g., activities involving pouring substances from one container to another in the 3-year-old).

The concept of critical periods implies a time of maximal receptivity or greatest ease in acquiring or modifying a particular function. The concept does not imply that a particular skill cannot be acquired at some other time, although the individual's capacity for doing so may be diminished. For example, the optimum age for beginning the continuous learning of a second language appears to occur within the span of 4 through 8 years of age with superior performance expected at ages 8 through 10 years (Levenson and Kendrick, 1967). Although nonaccented fluency can certainly be achieved at a later age, the task is more difficult because of a decreased ability to mimic sounds and intonations and to manipulate language patterns.

The existence of critical periods is not universally accepted among researchers in human development. However, the concept is a helpful one if used as a flexible guideline for the introduction of certain activities at particular points along the developmental continuum. A rigid interpretation of critical periods does not do justice to the greater plasticity and adaptability of the human organism as compared with lower forms of life.

Change

Physical growth is accomplished in one or both of two ways: increase in cell size and/or number. Associated with growth is the phenomenon of **cell replacement,** whereby older, injured, or nonfunctional cells are replaced by new cells. Physical development is accomplished by **cell maturation,** whereby new or different functions are performed on a molecular level by alterations in existing cells.

An example of maturation is menarche. The mechanism of action for this particular maturational phenomenon is poorly understood but was thought to result from hormonal changes triggered by a critical body weight of approximately 47 kg (Frisch, Revelle, and Cook, 1971). More recent research indicates that the ratio of lean body weight to fat and the metabolic rate per kilogram may actually be more important determinants of sexual maturation (Frisch, 1974; Crawford and Osler, 1975).

Environmental factors also appear to play a role in growth by providing or not providing adequate substrata, thus modifying individual genetic potential. An example of inadequate substrate availability is the amenorrhea associated with **anorexia nervosa.**

Psychological growth and development are analogous to physiological growth and development. Changes occur, however, at the level of the entire organism rather than at the level of the individual cell. For example, psychological responses or skills increase in magnitude and number, inappropriate or nonfunctional responses or skills are replaced by new responses or skills, and more complex functions are performed through modification of existing response or skill structures.

Whether nature (the genetic makeup of the individual) or nurture (the environment) is the preeminent impetus to change has been a source of serious debate among psychologists for some time. A current view, that the individual and his environment form a transactional pair in which each is an important partner, underscores the dynamic equilibrium that exists between these two forces. As stated by Sameroff (1975), the child "is actively engaged in attempts to organize and structure his world. . . [he] is in a [perpetual] state of active reorganization and cannot be properly regarded as maintaining inborn characteristics as static qualities. In this view, the constants in development are not some set of traits, but rather the *processes* by which these traits are maintained in the transactions between organism and environment." For example, when the environment initiates a change, the child adapts to the environment and in so doing changes his impact on the environment, which in turn accommodates, and so forth. This mutuality of change perpetuates further change and results in the acquisition of new experiences and new skills that ensure continuous development. Such a transactional model gives equal weight to the contributions of the organism and the environment, a viable concept except under conditions of extreme physical or psychological deprivation or incompetence.

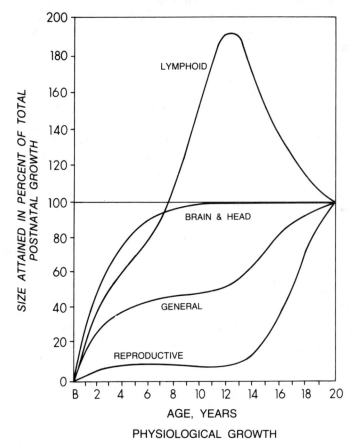

PHYSIOLOGICAL GROWTH

From Tanner, J. M. 1962. *Growth at adolescence* (2nd ed.). Oxford, England: Blackwell Scientific Publications Ltd.

Chapter 2

Physiological growth and development

The basic organizational structures of physiological growth and development follow an orderly sequence that parallels, but does not strictly adhere to, chronological age. This is as expected, since, as mentioned previously, growth and development proceed at variable rates under the influence of several factors, whereas chronological age is the result of the evenly measured passage of time.

INFLUENCE OF HEREDITY

Growth entails alterations in size, shape, and rate of change. In general, genetic control of growth rate appears to be independent of genetic control of body size or shape. Shape appears to be more rigorously controlled than size "presumably because shape represents chiefly how the cells are distributed while size represents more the sum of sizes of various cells" (Tanner, 1978, p. 121).

We will consider each aspect of growth separately, using the well-investigated parameter of height to illustrate size, various body-part measurements to illustrate shape, and menarche to illustrate change. We will also give examples of race-related and sex-related differences in these various categories.

Height. Under adequate environmental conditions, total variation in adult height is about 25 cm for most male populations, 16 cm for siblings, and 1.6 cm for monozygotic twins reared together. Because of the bell-shaped, or normal, distribution of height in the population, height is generally, although not conclusively, thought to be controlled by many small-effect genes, or polygenes, located apart from "major" gene sites on chromosomes (Tanner, 1978).

Both parents appear to contribute equally to the height characteristics of offspring (Susanne, 1975), although genes governing tall stature show some dominance over genes governing short stature. That is, the mating of a tall and a short parent appears to result in offspring who are taller than the average of the heights of the parents. This phenomenon is known as hybrid vigor in animals and as "heterosis" in man (Tanner, 1978).

SEX DIFFERENCES. Before puberty boys tend to be slightly taller than girls. From about age 11 to 14 years, the average girl is taller than the average boy because of the earlier female growth spurt. However, the adult male is about 15 cm taller than the female (Tanner, 1978).

RACIAL DIFFERENCES. Under similar environmental conditions, Asiatic children are distinctly shorter than either European or Afro-American children (Eveleth and Tanner, 1976).

Shape. Very little is known about genetic control of body shape. Some body measurements show higher adult intrafamilial correlations than do others. For example, for biacromial or shoulder width measurements the best intrafamilial correlation is between mothers and daughters. For facial measurements, interpupillary breadth is most closely correlated between fathers and daughters (Susanne, 1975). Thus different measurements show different patterns of familial resemblance, and our knowledge at this point is too rudimentary to explain observed differences accurately.

SEX DIFFERENCES. The distribution of subcutaneous tissue is one of the most obvious sex-related differences in individual body shape, or habitus. At birth, girls have slightly more total fat than do boys, and the difference increases gradually during childhood. In adolescence, limb fat in males decreases, as does the rate of gain of body fat, although there is no actual loss. In females, the rate of limb fat gain decreases, and trunk fat shows a steady increase into adulthood (Tanner, 1978).

The most marked sexual dimorphism of the skeleton, which occurs at puberty, involves the hips and shoulders. Higher levels of circulating estrogen in females result in a particularly large increase in hip width. Males have a marked increase in shoulder width secondary to differential cartilage cell sensitivity to androgen, particularly testosterone, stimulation (Tanner, 1975).

RACIAL DIFFERENCES. Racial differences in body proportion are more striking than any other growth parameter. For example, Australian aborigines have a much lower sitting height for leg length (longer legs) than do Africans, who have longer legs than do Europeans (Eveleth and Tanner, 1976).

Rate of growth. The genetic influence on growth rate is dramatically exemplified by age at menarche. In 1935, Petri reported that there was an average difference of 2.8 months in the age at menarche for monozygotic twins, 12.0 months for dizygotic twins, 12.9 months for sisters, and 18.6 months for unrelated women. Both parents are thought to contribute equally to growth rate.

SEX DIFFERENCES. Girls mature, enter puberty, and cease to grow earlier than do boys. At birth, girls are 4 to 6 weeks more mature and at early adolescence are up to 2 years more mature than boys. Sex differences are apparent in the earlier permanent tooth eruption and earlier skeletal ossification seen in girls. Deciduous (milk) teeth, however, appear at the same age in both sexes.

RACIAL DIFFERENCES. The African newborn has greater skeletal and motor maturity than does the European neonate. The child maintains this advance throughout life, including earlier dental development and menarche, if such environmental factors as nutrition and socioeconomic status are similar for both groups (Tanner, 1978).

INFLUENCE OF ENVIRONMENT
Physical environment

Intrauterine environment. A defect in the fertilized ovum, placental insufficiency, or disease or starvation of the mother can each lead to a small-for-gestational age infant. The majority of these infants eventually grow within the normal percentiles, but most do not fulfill their genetic potential as defined by their parents' heights.

Climate. Except for the larger chest circumference and lung capacity found among Quechua children living in the Peruvian *altiplano* (4,000 meters above sea level) as compared with Quechua children living on the coast, the differences in growth resulting from ecological conditions have been the result of selection over many generations. The close correlation between adult weight per unit height and average annual temperature of the area in which the individual lives or from which he migrated serves as an example: the long-limbed African dissipates more heat per unit volume than does the European, and the thickset body and short limbs of the northern Asiatic are adaptive to the Arctic region where conservation of body heat is necessary (Tanner, 1978).

Seasonal variations in growth velocity are striking, at least among Western European children. From 7 to 10 years of age, children grow maximally during spring and summer. Growth velocity during the 3 months of greatest gain averages three times the growth velocity during the months of smaller gain (Marshall, 1971).

The exact mechanism of this phenomenon is unknown. However, since animal breeding cycles appear to be related to the amount of light or radiation falling on the eyes, Marshall and Swan (1971) studied the differential growth rates of blind and sighted children. Growth variations exist in totally blind children, but are independent of the seasons. This finding gives some validity to the theory that exposure to sunlight is a regulatory function of growth in sighted children who show seasonal variation.

In tropical countries, the amount of rain appears to influence seasonal variations in growth.

Nutrition. Nutritional influences on growth have been clearly demonstrated by the effects of war conditions on children's height. For example, a study of German children from 1911 to 1953 showed a decrease in average height at any given age associated with the famines of both world wars (Tanner, 1962). Whereas malnutrition of short duration and mild to moderate severity may be completely reversible, chronic malnutrition throughout most or all of childhood, especially between the ages of 1 and 5 years, usually results in smaller adults.

Growth rate appears to be affected earlier and more frequently than is final size or shape. Thus, poorly nourished children experience a period of slow growth followed by "catch-up" growth when nutritional conditions are more favorable. Final adult size is affected more frequently than is overall shape (e.g., leg length), which is only insignificantly affected by undernutrition (Tanner, 1978).

The concept of catch-up growth under favorable nutritional conditions was substantiated in a study by Richardson (1975) in Jamaica. Children who were chronically poorly nourished and required an acute hospitalization for malnutrition had the same somatic growth at school age as did nutritionally, socially, and biologically matched controls who had not been so hospitalized. However, children with an early acute episode of malnutrition who were more disadvantaged in all parameters than their comparison group generally demonstrated smaller somatic growth at school age, although complete catch-up growth was still possible.

Illness. Illness appears to be closely linked with nutrition. However, minor, self-limited infections in otherwise well-nourished children exert minimal effects on growth.

In children who are less adequately nourished, minor illness can lead to periods of poor growth followed by "catch-up" growth after recovery. Chronic minor illnesses can lead to small size, but the contribution of poor diet and economic depression may be as significant or more significant than the illness itself.

Major disease can affect stature directly as in growth hormone deficiency, hypothyroidism, precocious puberty, achondroplasia, or hypochondroplasia or indirectly as in malabsorption and heart and kidney disease. Psychological illness, which may include the effects of both starvation and/or secondary growth hormone deficiency as seen in children with so-called **nonorganic failure to thrive,** is discussed next. A return to normal growth may or may not be possible depending upon the severity of the illness, the potential for correction of the nutritional or endocrinological disorder, and the child's age at diagnosis.

Psychological environment

The social context of the individual can influence physiological growth and development in a variety of ways. For example, nonorganic failure to thrive is the term used to describe poor growth in children in the absence of a medical disorder sufficient to account for the observed growth deficiency. Psychosocial investigation of these children shows them to be suffering from a lack of adequate appropriate social stimulation, most commonly resulting from maternal neglect. Endocrinological studies have demonstrated that many of these children have a functional hypopituitarism, manifested by deficiencies in adrenocorticotropic hormone (ACTH) and growth hormone. This syndrome has been termed **psychosocial dwarfism.** The reversibility of this particular growth failure without any specific therapy except removal of the child from the disturbed environment is highly suggestive of a psychologically mediated effect on release of pituitary tropic hormone by the central nervous system (Powell, Brasel, and Blizzard, 1967; Powell, Brasel, Raiti, and Blizzard, 1967).

Socioeconomic status and culture

As discussed previously, two other factors, socioeconomic status and culture, have an effect on growth and development. In studies based on socioeconomic status, American children, ages 6 to 11 years, whose fathers are in the professional or managerial class have been shown to be 3 cm taller than children whose fathers are manual laborers (Hammil, Johnson, and Lameshow, 1972). On the other hand, among urban Swedish children, no differences in height were found recently among children ages 7 to 17 years regardless of the father's occupation (Lindgren, 1976). Interestingly, within families, firstborn British children tend to be taller than later-born children, but full adult height does not differ systematically according to birth order (Goldstein, 1971).

The discrepancies among these studies deserve comment. Although paternal occupation has traditionally been used as the primary measure of socioeconomic status, both the standard of living (a function of socioeconomic status) and the child-centeredness of the home (a culturally related phenomenon) are probably operative factors in the differences and similarities in size and rate of growth seen in children of different classes. This interrelationship between socioeconomic status and culture should be kept in mind even when comparing economically defined groups within what appears to be a culturally homogeneous population unless one can be completely certain that subcultural differences such as religion, geographical location, and race or ethnic extraction have been controlled. For example, even in a relatively small midwestern American town, the middle-class value systems of families of English descent can differ from those of families of Italian descent and ultimately impact on physiological growth and development.

In addition to height, other parameters of body size and shape are affected by socioeconomic status and culture. For example, the incidence of obesity is inversely related to social class except for families that are consistently below the poverty level, whose children are relatively thinner (Forbes, 1978). Feeding practices, the value placed on food as a sign of good mothering, and the desirability of a particular habitus, as well as the obvious effect of food availability, can influence the incidence of obesity.

Another cultural factor that affects body size and shape is perceived peer group pressure, which can lead, for example, to massive body building programs or face or breast reconstructions. In addition, social or religious customs such as foot binding or skull molding can result in physiologically abnormal sizes or shapes of body parts.

Somatic growth and development

Somatic, or body, growth is a process that proceeds regularly and with predictability. The well-studied parameter of height serves as a guide to and an easily measured and visualized example of general physical growth (p. 8).

Between 3 and 5 years of age, the average annual increase in height is 7.6 cm; between 5 and 10 years of age, 6.0 cm. This increase is in contrast to a peak velocity during the adolescent growth spurt of 10.3 cm per year for males (average age of peak velocity, 14 years) and of 9.0 cm per year for females (average age of peak velocity, 12 years).

Most tissues and parts of the body follow the general height growth curve. The face, for example, undergoes a sizable adolescent spurt, especially in the mandible of males, resulting in a longer and more projecting jaw, a straighter profile, and a more pointed chin. Similarly, a small but definite spurt occurs in head length and breadth caused by thickening of the skull bones and the scalp and the development of air sinuses. The eye appears to undergo a slight adolescent growth spurt that is more prominent in the axial than the vertical dimension. Such a differential rate of growth may help to explain the increase in myopia that occurs in females at 11 to 12 years of age and males at 13 to 14 years of age.

Exceptions to the general growth curve exist, however. For example, the brain and skull reach 80% of adult size at about 4 years of age. If the brain has an adolescent growth spurt, it appears to be quite small. The reproductive organs, on the other hand, have a very slow growth rate until early adolescence, when dramatic changes in size and function occur. The growth curve of the lymphoid tissues is also substantially different from the general growth curve. Lymphoid tissue is almost double final adult size in early adolescence and declines steadily until late adolescence. This decline in size is thought to be directly influenced by sex hormones.

Important sex differences occur in the timing of growth and the final adult size of various body parts. The growth spurt in girls occurs about 2 chronological years earlier than in boys. Muscle growth is primarily under the influence of androgenic stimulation, which results in greater muscle mass and strength in the mature male than in the mature female. Another somatic change influenced by male sex hormones, particularly testosterone, is that involving red blood cell mass. During adolescence, males develop a higher hematocrit than do females.

Motor development

Increase in body size, including the differential rates of growth of various parts, and maturation of neuronal pathways, among other factors, contribute to the child's and adolescent's increasing ability to perform complex motor functions. For example, the child of 3 years can balance on one foot for 5 seconds, the child of 5 can balance for 10 seconds, and the child of 10 can balance for 15 seconds or more.

The child of 5 can catch a bounced ball, whereas a child of 10 can catch a fly ball. At 3, a child can copy a circle; at 5, a square; and at 8, a diamond, all of which require increasing ability to discriminate form and coordinate hand and eye movements.

Large muscles develop before small muscles. Therefore, younger children are more skillful in activities that involve gross motor movements than in those requiring fine motor coordination. In early adolescence, however, differential bone and muscle growth may result in a transient awkwardness, particularly in gross motor functioning. During middle to late adolescence, the characteristic decrease in growth rate and the development of more stable body proportions result in a gradual correction of this motoric awkwardness. Some examples of fine and gross motor "milestones," through midadolescence, are presented in Table 1.

Table 1. Motor development

Age (years)	Gross motor	Fine motor
3	Stands on one foot Walks upstairs alternating feet	Has bilateral handedness Can build tower of 9 or 10 blocks
4	Pedals tricycle Runs smoothly Throws ball overhand	Pours without spilling Right-handedness predominates Cuts straight line with scissors

5	Walks downstairs
	  alternating feet
	Skips
	Marches with rhythm
	Catches bounced ball
		Hand-eye coordination incomplete,
		  often spills reaching beyond
		  arm's length
		Copies square

6	Hops Jumps	Holds pencil with fingertips Ties a bow
7	Pedals bicycle	Letters aligned horizontally Uses table knife for cutting
8	Has good body balance	Spaces words when writing Writes with slanting letters Copies diamond

9	Engages in vigorous
	  bodily activities,
	  especially team sports
		Has good hand-eye coordination

10	Balances on one foot 15 seconds Catches fly ball	

12	Motor awkwardness secondary
	  to uneven bone and muscle
	  growth	

15	Gradual correction of motor awkwardness	

Sexual growth and development

At birth, pituitary follicular-stimulating hormone (FSH) and luteinizing hormone (LH) levels are negligible. During infancy and childhood the central nervous system inhibits the activation of the hypothalamic–pituitary gonadotropin–gonadal apparatus. Gonadotropin secretion occurs only intermittently. Slight growth of both the internal and external genitalia parallels increases in body size, but the genitalia retain their infantile appearance and function.

The changes that occur as part of adolescence are related to endocrine function and can be divided into three stages: prepubescence (prepuberty), puberty, and postpubescence. In the prepubertal state the concentration of sex steroids and gonadotropins remains low. The hypothalamic "gonadostat" is functional, but still highly sensitive to low levels of sex steroids. During this time the individual begins to acquire the characteristics of physical and sexual maturity: physical growth, changes in body proportion, and appearance of **secondary sexual characteristics.**

At puberty, there is decreased sensitivity of the hypothalamus to negative feedback by sex steroids, increased release of luteinizing hormone releasing factor (LRF), and enhanced secretion of gonadotropins. Gonadotropin and sex steroid concentrations rise progressively toward adult levels. During puberty, the reproductive organs (**primary sexual characteristics**) become capable of functioning, and the secondary sexual characteristics become more evident.

Postpubescence includes a 1- to 2-year period of reproductive sterility. During this time skeletal growth is almost completed, and the new biological functions become established (Grumbach et al., 1974; Grumbach, 1975).

Several concepts are important when considering the physical changes that occur in males and females between 10 and 18 years of age:
1. The exact timing and duration of pubertal growth vary from individual to individual.
2. Young people grow at a faster rate during adolescence than at any other time except for infancy.
3. Females, on the average, begin and complete their growth 2 years before males.
4. Males, on the average, are taller and heavier than are females upon completing their physical growth.
5. Growth occurs at an earlier age today than it did a hundred years ago (**secular trend**), although evidence exists that this progressive decrease in age at puberty has reached a plateau.
6. Sexual changes in males and females usually proceed according to a predictable pattern (**sequencing**).

Secular trend

Secular trend is an epidemiological term referring to changes in population characteristics observed over a period of time. This term has been used extensively

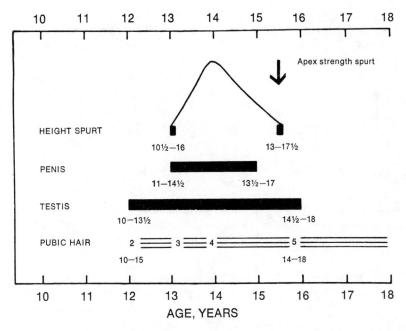

Fig. 1. Sequence of events at adolescence in males. (From Tanner, J. M. 1962. *Growth at adolescence* [2nd ed.]. Oxford, England: Blackwell Scientific Publications Ltd.)

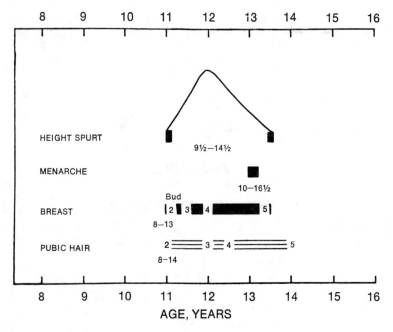

Fig. 2. Sequence of events at adolescence in females. (From Tanner, J. M. 1962. *Growth at adolescence* [2nd ed.]. Oxford, England: Blackwell Scientific Publications Ltd.)

in adolescent medicine to describe the observation that the young people of today reach sexual maturity earlier than did their relatives of past generations. Although this phenomenon is true for both males and females, it is most dramatically illustrated by the decrease in the age of menarche by approximately 3 to 4 months per decade over the last hundred years. For reasons that are not yet clear, this gradual decrease in the age at puberty has reached an apparent plateau during the past decade.

Sequencing

Sequencing, as it applies to physical development in adolescents, refers to the predictable order of appearance of secondary sexual characteristics. This sequence of sexual development appears to follow a similar pattern from generation to generation and culture to culture. It can, therefore, be used to stage development in a variety of situations, despite the wide range in the age of appearance of certain characteristics, as indicated in Figs. 1 and 2.

Following is the sequence of sexual change in *males:*
1. Growth of the testes and changes in the texture and color of the scrotum
2. Initial penile growth
3. Pubic hair development
4. Accelerated penile growth and continued growth of the testes and scrotum
5. Growth of the seminal vesicles and prostate gland
6. Peak height velocity
7. Full facial hair
8. Voice change

The adolescent height spurt and other body dimension changes usually begin approximately a year after the testes begin to grow. Peak height velocity is reached about a year later, after pubic hair begins to develop. The median age for the onset of nocturnal emissions is between $12^{1}/_{2}$ and 14 years. Mature spermatozoa usually appear between 14 and 16 years of age. The growth of facial and full body hair and voice change are late-occurring events.

The sequence of sexual change in *females* is as follows:
1. Broadening of the bony pelvis
2. Breast development
3. Development of the uterus, vagina, labia, and clitoris
4. Pubic hair development
5. Maximum height spurt
6. Menarche

Menarche is a late occurrence and follows the maximum height spurt. The average age of menarche is between 12.8 and 13.2 years (Tanner, 1978).

FREUD	Oral	Anal	Phallic	Latency	Genital	
ERIKSON	Trust vs Mistrust	Autonomy vs Shame + Doubt	Initiative vs Guilt	Industry vs Inferiority	Identity vs Role Confusion	
PIAGET	Sensori-Motor	Preoperational		Concrete Operational	Formal Operational	
KOHLBERG		Preconventional		Conventional	Postconventional	
SEARS	Rudimentary Behavior	Secondary Motivational Systems				
		Family-Centered Learning		Extra-Familial Learning		

B 2 4 6 8 10 12 14 16 18 20

AGE, YEARS

PSYCHOLOGICAL DEVELOPMENT

Chapter 3

Psychological growth and development

For the purposes of our discussion, we will consider psychology as the science of affect (emotion), the mind (cognitive function), and social conduct (behavior).

The two major elements, heredity (nature) and environment (nurture), influence psychological development. These elements interact to determine **individuality,** the characteristics that distinguish one person from another and that appear to be both innate and learned behaviors or responses.

Influence of heredity

Heredity, or genetic endowment, appears to play a role in defining both temperament and **intelligence.**

TEMPERAMENT

In studying psychological individuality, Thomas and associates (1964) found that idiosyncratic differences in responsiveness exist in infants and young children *even before* the effects of experience or learning might be expected to play a role in modifying behavior. Nine categories for assessing individuality in behavioral functioning, or temperament, were defined:

1. Activity level
2. Rhythmicity
3. Approach or withdrawal from a new stimulus
4. Adaptability
5. Intensity of reaction
6. Threshold of responsiveness
7. Mood
8. Distractibility
9. Attention span and persistence

Because of the young child's unique blend of individual traits, not all children will necessarily react the same way to a given stimulus. Interestingly, however, Thomas discovered that "most of the children were regular rather than irregular, highly adaptable rather than unadaptable, and preponderantly positive in mood" (Thomas et al., 1964, p. 87). Such reactions among newborns and infants greatly enhance their chances of survival by facilitating parent-infant interactions and therefore helping to ensure appropriate caregiving responses. It also appears that these individually identifiable states of reactivity are persistent features of a given child's behavior at least throughout the first 2 years of life and probably form the basis for such early parental perceptions of their child as "easygoing" or "hard to handle."

Sex differences

Preliminary data suggest that male infants may be more irritable and more difficult to calm than female infants. Firstborn boys may be more irritable than second-born boys (Moss, 1974). It is not known whether such behavioral differences are the result of the greater somatic (neurological) maturity of the female at birth or of the higher incidence of birth complications among infant males (Bell, 1960).

INTELLIGENCE

Intelligence is the capacity to perceive and understand facts and propositions and their relations and to reason about them. Although it is impossible to separate completely the relative contributions of heredity and environment to individual intelligence, so many studies have focused on sex and racial differences that we shall include our discussion of intelligence in this section concerning genetic influences on psychological development.

Intelligence is a composite of a number of specific abilities, including verbal ability (use of language), quantitative ability (use of numbers), spatial ability (discriminating relationships of objects and space), disembedding (separating an element from its background), analytic ability (problem solving), concept mastery, and reasoning (formulating and testing hypotheses).

Intelligence is measured by functional ability on formal, standardized tests such as the Stanford-Binet Intelligence Scale, the Wechsler Intelligence Scale for Children (WISC), or the Wechsler Adult Intelligence Scale (WAIS). The behaviors elicited under such conditions are then systematically analyzed, studied, and interpreted.

Intelligence is often expressed in terms of the **intelligence quotient** (IQ) identified as the ratio of **maturational age** (the functional ability of the individual as compared with the normative functional ability of other individuals at specified ages) to chronological age multiplied by 100 ($IQ = MA/CA \times 100$). Thus, an IQ of 100 indicates a maturational age equal to chronological age. For example, if a child of 5.0 years of age has a maturational age (functional ability in the testing situation) of a child of 6.0 years, the IQ is computed as follows: $IQ = 6.0/5.0 \times 100 = 120$. Although test interpretations vary somewhat, the IQ range of 90 to 110 is generally considered average.

Intelligence tests (ideally defined as measures of innate capability or the ability to learn something new) should be distinguished from **achievement tests** (measures of learned capability or knowledge), which are normally focused on a range of subject matter for which training has been given. Despite the fact that these two categories of tests are designed to measure different capabilities, in fact they correlate with each other to about the same extent that different intelligence tests intercorrelate (Humphreys, 1972). The reasons for these correlations are unclear and may reflect genetic or environmental factors. Regardless, a significant discrepancy between an individual's IQ score and an achievement test score may represent **underachievement** or **overachievement** for ability and deserves further investigation and evaluation.

Aptitude tests represent yet another category of assessment tools. These scales define areas of natural talent or facility rather than measure ability or knowledge and should be carefully distinguished from either intelligence or achievement tests.

Sex differences

Global intelligence testing attempts to equalize the contribution of each of the component abilities in arriving at an overall score. However, if we direct our attention to each specific ability, it has been fairly established that (1) females have a greater verbal ability than males: this difference is inconsistently seen in early life and is most marked in adolescence when females score higher on both "high-level" verbal tasks (creative writing, analogies, and comprehension of written material) and "low-level" verbal tasks (fluency); (2) males have a greater visual-spatial ability during adolescence and adulthood but not in childhood; and (3) males have a greater quantitative ability that is not apparent until early adolescence and is less marked than the differences observed in verbal and visual-spatial ability. The fact that both visual-spatial and verbal processes can be involved in the solution of some mathematical problems may account for the smaller differences observed between males and females on this subtest (Maccoby and Jacklin, 1974).

Racial differences

Different ethnic, racial, and national populations obtain different mean IQ scores on standard tests of intelligence. As noted at the beginning of this section, the relative contributions of heredity and environment are almost impossible to assess. On the average, however, it appears to be true that the highest mean IQ scores are obtained by mongoloid populations originating in Japan and China and caucasian populations originating in northern Europe.

A variety of theories has been developed to explain this phenomenon of IQ differences including the notion of **test bias**. Although, as just mentioned, global intelligence tests have been designed to equalize the relative contributions of each of the ability subsets to minimize sex differences, psychologists have been less successful in constructing **culture-fair tests** of intelligence, that is, those which can adequately measure mental ability separate from learned cognitive skills and independent of social or economic effects.

Influence of environment

Such environmental conditions as climate, nutrition, quality of available education, standard of living, and general cultural sophistication all appear to influence psychological development. However, three major social institutions are of particular importance to developing individuals because of their immediate and intimate impact on children and adolescents: family of origin, school, and peer group.

FAMILY OF ORIGIN

The first, smallest, and most important social unit to which a child belongs is the family of origin. The family serves three basic functions: (1) to ensure physical and economic survival, (2) to provide a social laboratory for psychological development, and (3) to produce autonomous persons who can separate physically and emotionally from the family of origin.

Although the family is composed of individuals, many of the tasks of the family are accomplished by subgroups of family members. These subgroups are functional units and therefore can also be termed subsystems. Three of these subgroups, or subsystems (Fig. 3), as described by Minuchin (1974) are of especial interest to us: (1) spouse, (2) parent, and (3) sibling.

The spouse subsystem originates at the time of marriage. Spouses provide certain physical and psychological supports for one another and negotiate the division of labor to maintain the household. At the time of birth of the first child, the

FAMILY SYSTEMS

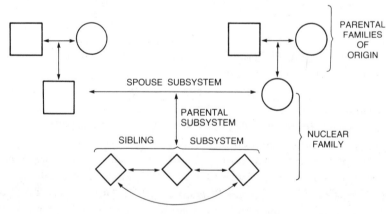

Fig. 3

parental subsystem is formed, and individual responsibilities that center around care for and socialization of the child ("executive" functions) are negotiated. With the birth of subsequent children, the sibling subsystem is formed, and certain negotiations are carried out by the children in defining their relationships and responsibilities to one another as peers within the hierarchy of the family. The hostile competition that commonly occurs among children in the same family during these negotiations has been termed **sibling rivalry.** Rivalrous feelings arise for many reasons, including a perceived loss of parental love upon the birth of a new sibling or envy of an older child's power and privileges. Patterns of sibling rivalry are influenced by particular birth orders and are modified by the sex of the siblings.

According to Minuchin, each of the various subsystems of a family is governed or bounded by a set of rules that defines who participates in the subsystem and how. Such a set of rules, or "boundaries," that simultaneously defines a spouse subsystem and a parental subsystem is clearly stated when a mother tells her daughter, "I want to talk with Dad alone now. Play in your room, and I'll be with you in 5 minutes." The degree of clarity and flexibility of these boundaries varies widely. Boundaries may range from diffuse (unclear) and freely permeable (too flexible) to rigid (too clear and inflexible). Lack of clarity and free permeability result in little or no distance between family members, no privacy, and no autonomy (the so-called **enmeshed family**). Strict rigidity results in poor or nonexistent communication across subsystems, thus handicapping the protective function of the family (the so-called **disengaged family**). A wide range of normal clarity and flexibility exists between the two extremes of enmeshment and disengagement.

Temporary leanings toward enmeshment or disengagement are normal occurrences in all families. For example, enmeshment between a mother and her newborn infant or disengagement of the midadolescent from the family is a common and expected developmental phenomenon. These temporary leanings may actually enhance the chances of success of the psychological tasks at hand. When, however, disengagement or enmeshment is the dominant or only mode of the family, serious dysfunction may occur. For example, if we postulate that diabetes mellitus is a form of psychosomatic illness, that is, an organic illness with a potentially large emotional component to control, the issue of communication across boundaries can be an important factor in how the child uses the illness in his family. The diabetic child in a disengaged family may have to resort to poor control and severe ketoacidosis to mobilize family support. On the other hand, a diabetic child in an enmeshed family overinvolved with the disease may remain in borderline control precisely to maintain a high degree of attention from the family (**secondary gain**).

The term "negotiation" has been used liberally in reference to families to underline the constant dynamic give-and-take that exists within and between subsystems. The introduction of new members, changes in employment status or other activities outside the home, and the development of new capabilities with maturation, among other factors, contribute to role changes and subsystem readjustments.

Some changes may occur only momentarily; others may be relatively permanent. For example, a mother involved in a game with her children may abide by their rules as a member of the play group but revert briefly to her executive role as a parent as is needed to maintain harmony among the siblings. As another example, a teenager may be given the responsibility of acting as a parent surrogate overseeing younger siblings while the parents are at work but revert to the sibling subsystem when the parents return.

The style of the family of origin, with regard to boundary clarity and flexibility and patterns of communication among members, provides the framework for the young adult who enters into a spouse subsystem in the next generation of the family. The ease or difficulty the individual experiences growing up in his family of origin will help to determine the characteristics of the new family. Frequently, second-generation families represent a melding of the two families of origin.

SCHOOL

School has two basic functions: education, or the teaching of facts or principles by a variety of methods including experience and rote memory, and **socialization,** or the process by which a society trains its children to behave like the adults of that society. Although both these functions could be served by the family alone, the opportunity to interact regularly with nonsibling peers and nonparent adults is facilitated in our culture by the school setting (Fig. 4). Indeed, one of the child's first regular and routine experiences outside the home is provided by attendance at school.

School represents a relatively structured transition for children from the supportive but circumscribed environment of the family to the world-at-large of young adulthood. This transition is theoretically accomplished through a series of small steps that gradually impose on the child increasing responsibility for himself. It should be kept in mind, however, that certain critical points in the school process may be overwhelming to some children and their families and result in such problems as **school refusal,** underachievement, and **truancy.**

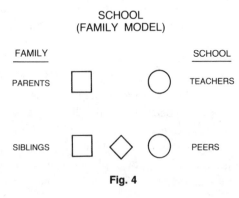

Fig. 4

For some children, school begins at 3. For all children, school is mandatory by age 5 or 6 years. For many children, the teacher, as the first adult outside the immediate family who plays a role in the youngster's life, takes on the characteristics of a parent surrogate or substitute. Such an analogy to the family is further strengthened by maintaining young children in a single classroom with only one or two teachers and a stable cadre of peers. This group of individuals remains together throughout most of the school day and develops a sense of cohesiveness and identity. "Special" teachers for areas such as art and music often take on the flavor of visiting relatives who provide a diversion or an extra dimension to everyday "family" life at school.

The most crucial aspects of this early period are the child's and family's ability to separate and feel secure that the environment of the school will be as nurturant as that of the home. We stress the mutuality of this separation process, since parental anxiety is at least as potent as child anxiety in making this transition into school a fearful or unsuccessful process.

Either late in elementary school or at the beginning of junior high school, the child loses the security of the single teacher–single classroom mode. For a variety of strictly educational reasons, such as differing abilities that cannot be accommodated within a single classroom or specialized teacher training or expertise, students learn how to negotiate throughout the school from classroom to classroom, how to relate to a variety of teacher personalities and techniques, and how to interact with a much larger peer population. However, most schools retain the concept of the "home" room (by whatever name) and the single teacher who compiles, monitors, and interprets an individual student's record. The teacher's position in this instance has moved from that of parent surrogate to that of advisor or even "friend," since, in many instances, the homeroom teacher may not have the student in any academic class.

The theoretical approach to how children and adolescents learn will be discussed in the section of this chapter on cognitive development. However, the educational process as it applies to the school system deserves attention separately.

Preschool and kindergarten appear to be primarily geared toward introducing the child to the context of school and the initiation of certain habits that are important to the educational process: promptness, fulfillment of assigned tasks, cooperation, and respect for others. The amount of purely academic work introduced at this level varies greatly. However, most authorities on "school readiness" (see, for example, Jordan and Massey, 1969) suggest that, prior to entering kindergarten, the 4- to 6-year-old child should have some concept of number rather than merely the ability to count; be able to discriminate shape, position, and form; know the basic colors; have enough hand-eye coordination to draw a straight line between two like objects; and have a certain level of receptive and expressive language.

Gross motor activity is not prized in the classroom; one of the first tasks of a child is to learn to control the impulse to be up and about. Since being busy, vigorous, and boisterous are hallmarks of the 4- and 5-year-old, the effort required to maintain decorum in the classroom may be considerable.

"Learning" plays a more prominent role in daily school activities starting in first grade. The beginning of homework and grades is variable, but in most educational systems, both have been introduced by the fourth grade. The tasks of school are now tangibly introduced into the home, and child, teacher, and parent have a somewhat objective yardstick by which to measure success or failure.

Achievement in the school setting is dependent on ability and motivation. Ability includes the intrinsic capabilities to perceive what is presented to the senses accurately, focus on a task and ignore distracting stimuli effectively, store learned material efficiently, and express oneself adequately.

Motivation is both innate and learned. The importance the child attaches to any goal and therefore the effort he will expend to attain the goal is affected by his temperament and the importance placed on the goal by others who are revered or feared.

For a variety of reasons, some of which are discussed in Part Two, some children or adolescents underachieve or fail to participate in school at all.

PEER GROUP

Peers provide each other with (1) information about appropriate behavior in a variety of situations, (2) opportunity to interact with age-mates as leaders or followers, (3) support during emotional crises, (4) a framework for developing individual value systems, and (5) a group identity as a forerunner of individual identity.

Peer group formation parallels children's abilities to form stable relationships but has its earliest precursor in the sibling subsystem of the family. Fascination with siblings, as demonstrated by laughing, cooing, and following, first appears in early infancy. The earliest peer-peer interactions occur at about the age of 12 months, when children who are placed near each other look at, approach, and explore one another during brief contacts usually lasting less than a minute (Durfee and Lee, 1973). Interactions progressively increase in duration and complexity, and by age 3 years most children have a characteristic way of relating to their peers. Some children tend toward negative social interactions characterized by dispute, protest, or assault; others are more positive or "pro-social" and exhibit cooperation, sharing, and affection (Bronson and Purkey, 1977). By about the age of 3 or 4 years, most children act independently in seeking friendships and engaging in social activities if other children are available for these interactions to occur.

In the earliest stages, before school begins, friendships are often defined by geographical location (the limits of the "block") or the adult friendships of the parents with other couples who bring children to play. During the early school years, the class is the main friendship group, although after-school geography may continue to influence how often classmates actually play together.

Once the original classroom becomes a part of a whole grade or even a mixture

PEER SYSTEMS

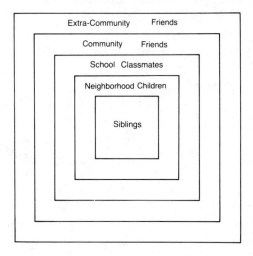

Fig. 5

of grades (with members of different classes coming together for various subjects), the pool for peer relationships broadens extensively. At the same time, children and adolescents develop a certain autonomy of mobility through the use of a bicycle or access to a car. Friendships now become defined by interest or ability, for example, by participation on a sports team or the school newspaper or attendance at most if not all of the same classes. The creation of such small friendship subgroups allows individuals to develop skills or to be leaders in settings outside, or in addition to, the strictly academic aspects of school.

Early friendship groups develop from the need for companionship during play activities. Relationships are relatively transient and invested with little emotionality. Young children show no evidence of conformity to group norms (Hartup, 1970).

In later childhood, friendships decrease in number but increase in intensity, and affiliation with a particular group demands strong allegiance. Peer subgroups develop characteristic identities. Membership in a group is defined by certain rules and regulations, and initiation ceremonies are common. Formal organizations such as scouts and 4-H also gain prominence at this time. Groups are typically homogeneous with regard to sex, ethnic and cultural background, and socioeconomic status, and all members purport to espouse certain values and standards.

During adolescence, the peer group supplants the family of origin as the most influential monitor of social behavior. Peer group–parental conflict often results in peer group supremacy in matters related to social activity and the development of value systems. In fact, an adolescent may deliberately choose membership in a peer group specifically because of its antithetical stance with regard to parental norms. Such parent-child conflict ultimately facilitates the development of individual identity and separation from the family.

Developmental theories

As indicated earlier, we have elected to focus on three major theories of human development to provide a broad theoretical base for examining certain behaviors that are observed in children and adolescents. Since no single theory is all-inclusive in accounting for human behavior, the presentation of several theories allows us a great degree of flexibility in interpreting behavior and in devising treatment strategies to help children and their families handle common stress situations effectively.

The first theory that we shall discuss is the **psychoanalytic theory** of development. The writings of Sigmund Freud (psychosexual development) and Erik Erikson (psychosocial development) will be presented. Psychoanalytic theory provides a conceptual framework for understanding the development of intrinsic personality structure and the development of the individual as a member of society who must encounter and resolve certain interpersonal conflicts as they relate to his functioning in the world. Psychoanalytic theory is an important tool for understanding a person's motivations for certain behaviors. The therapeutic component of this theory, psychoanalysis, on the other hand, is outside the purview of the pediatric practitioner.

The second approach to development, the **cognitive-intellectual theory,** is represented primarily by the work of Jean Piaget (cognitive development). We have also included the work of Lawrence Kohlberg (moral development) as an example of the application of the cognitive-intellectual theory to one aspect of human thinking. An understanding of how children and adolescents think about the world adds substantially to our ability to interpret behavior and, as importantly, to our ability to structure interventions so that they are adequately understood by our patients.

The third theory, **learning theory,** is a behavioristic approach to development based on **stimulus-response** (S-R) **psychology.** The early work of the social learning theorists attempted to translate Freudian psychology into S-R terms, although more recent writers have substantially changed this focus. To integrate learning theory within the developmental framework, we will emphasize the work of Robert Sears, one of the early social learning theorists.

Learning theory provides the practitioner with a rich source of intervention strategies and will form the basis for many of the techniques discussed in Part Two. At first glance, manipulation of behavior may appear to be a superficial approach to the management of stressful situations. However, it will become evident that truly effective management techniques based on a behavioral model actually involve a combination of approaches that takes into account the cognitive level of the child and is actually designed to help meet basic personality needs.

PSYCHOANALYTIC THEORY
Organization of personality

The total personality as described by Freud consists of three major systems: id, ego, and superego.

Id

Freud used the term **id** to designate the basic foundation of personality. The sole function of the id is to avoid pain (eliminate or reduce tension) and find satisfaction or pleasure. This **pleasure principle** is considered part of a universal tendency to maintain constancy in the midst of internal or external disturbances.

In its most primitive form, the id includes reflexive actions; for example, blinking at (gaining relief from) a bright (and therefore irritating) light. Since not all tension can be reduced by reflex action, frustration results. This frustration can lead to the development of an internal imaging of a tension-reducing object through a mechanism known as **primary process.** For example, the id of a hungry sleeper equates the subjective memory image or dream of food with the real object. The formation of such an image of a tension-reducing object is called **wish fulfillment.** In waking hours, as well, such mental representations help an individual satisfy id drives. Thus, the hungry awake person thinks of food.

According to Freud, the id represents the inaccessible part of the personality that cannot be modified by time or experience. Behaviors that are directed solely by the id are demanding, impulsive, nonrational, and self-centered. Interestingly, unrestrained id-motivated behavior, in seeking pleasure, may actually increase tension (pain) by eliciting punishment from the external world.

Ego

An intermediary system between the id and the external world was postulated by Freud and termed the **ego.** The ego is the executive function of the personality and is governed by the **reality principle,** an accurate perception of what exists outside the individual. The ego emerges as the child develops the distinction between self and nonself.

The aim of the ego is to obtain the maximum satisfaction of id drives that is possible in the real world confronted by the individual. This may mean postponement of gratification or acceptance of less than full gratification. The ego thus allows the individual to accommodate to or assert mastery over the external world by tolerating tension. That is, fullfillment of the pleasure principle is temporarily suspended in acknowledgment of reality.

The reality principle is served by **secondary process.** Whereas primary process consists of imagining or fantasizing a desired object, secondary process consists of discovering or producing a satisfying reality by a plan of action developed through thought and reason. Thus, the individual learns to function more intelligently and efficiently and master impulses and environment to ultimately attain greater satisfaction and pleasure.

Superego

Designated by Freud as the moral or judicial function of the personality, the **superego** represents the individual's striving for perfection, rather than either pleasure or reality, through assimilation and internalization of the traditional ideals, values, and moral standards of society as they are handed down from parents to children.

The superego is composed of the **ego-ideal,** the child's conceptions of what the parents consider to be morally good, and **conscience,** the child's conceptions of what the parents consider to be morally bad. These judgments represent another set of standards (like pleasure seeking and reality) to which the ego of the individual must adapt. Although very rigid initially, the superego softens with maturity in most persons.

Thought is synonymous with action to the superego (as it is to the id); therefore, the individual may experience guilt or satisfaction for merely thinking of doing something, even if the thought is never translated into action. Such feelings of guilt or satisfaction are hypothesized to represent superego-mediated psychological "punishments" or "rewards" of the individual.

According to Freud, these consequences may be physical as well as psychological. For example, although psychosomatic illnesses that have no underlying organic basis are considered by psychoanalytic theorists to be prime examples of pain or limitation of function resulting from superego displeasure, Freud theorized that *all* misfortunes, from an upset stomach to an injury, involve some degree of self-punishment. On the other hand, a physical reward mediated by the superego might be a vacation (without guilt) after a period of hard work.

There are no sharp boundaries between the id, the ego, and the superego. Drives, reality judgments, and ethical principles interact and blend with each other in all situations throughout life.

Instinctual drives

Freud conceptualized the human organism as a complicated energy system. His term for the form of energy that operates the three systems of personality and that performs such psychological work as perceiving, thinking, and remembering is **psychic energy.**

Freud further hypothesized that all of the energy for the work of the personality is derived from **instincts,** inborn conditions that impart direction to psychological processes. According to psychoanalytic theory, instinctual drives are divided into two groups: **ego-instincts,** like hunger, thirst, and escape from pain, which are concerned with self-preservation, and **libido,** or sex drive, which is concerned with species preservation. However, Freud used libido in a much broader context than merely as a synonym for sex drive. "The term libido can further be extended to mean a motivating life force which along with its primarily pleasurable and/or sexual nature also includes a drive to maturity" (Kenny and Clemmens, 1975, p. 121).

Each drive is considered to have a **source,** that is, some excitation (need or impulse) arising in some part of the body; the function of the subsequent behavior (**external aim**) is to reduce this excitation or achieve satisfaction (**internal aim**). Any external person or thing that must in some way participate for the individual to achieve gratification is known as the **object.**

Hunger can be considered an example of an instinctual drive. Stomach cramping (source) activates the hunger instinct and provides it with energy, or "energizes" it. This energy then gives goal direction to the psychological processes of perception (looking for food), memory (remembering where food was found on former occasions), and thought (planning a course of action to obtain food). The external aim (finding and eating food, the object) results in the elimination of hunger or satisfaction (internal aim). By repeated association, first mothers, and subsequently other food providers, become objects who are psychologically important and whom the developing person imbues with value (**cathexis**).

Defense mechanisms of the ego

According to Freud, the ego must deal with the anxiety aroused by threats and dangers to the individual. Three sources of anxiety are (1) instinctual anxiety (id), (2) objective anxiety (external threats from the world as perceived by the ego), and (3) anxiety of conscience (superego).

Table 2. Defense mechanisms of the ego

Defense	Definition
Primitive	
Repression	Memories, ideas, or perceptions kept unconscious
Displacement	Repressed impulses disguised to achieve satisfaction
Denial	World perceived as it is desired
Regression	Retreat to earlier developmental stage
Fixation	Developmental arrest
Immature	
Projection	Externalization of subjective feelings
Reaction formation	Concentration on opposite instinct
Mature	
Intellectualization	Concentration on nonaffective aspects of situation
Isolation (of affect)	Repression of feeling associated with idea, but not idea itself
Rationalization	Justification of unacceptable act by attributing creditable motive
Sublimation	Instinctual drive directed toward acceptable activity

Anxiety is ideally reduced by realistic problem solving. But it can also be reduced through use of **defense mechanisms,** which, by distorting reality, permit the individual to postpone satisfaction, find substitutions, or otherwise compromise among the impulses of the id, the threats of the external world, and the compulsions of the superego. Although indiscriminate use of or undue reliance upon defense mechanisms can impede personality development, occasional, discriminate, and well-circumscribed use of defenses can occur in the service of the ego as appropriate adaptations to temporarily overwhelming objective (realistic) anxiety.

A distinction has been drawn in psychoanalytic theory between defenses and controls. Whereas controls tame the expression of or modify a drive but do not block it, defenses distort consciousness and prevent the expression of a drive. Controls and defenses can influence both ego-instincts and libido. However, unlike ego-instinct drives, libido need not be gratified to ensure individual survival and therefore is subject to a wide variety of externally (socially) imposed constraints. This distinction in relative need for survival between these two classes of drives is the primary reason why elaborate defense strategies have been employed to deal with libido. In other words, society dictates that an individual control both appetite and sexual yearnings. Although society does not usually demand that an individual hide his hunger for food, it demands that he hide his hunger for sex.

The ability of the individual to employ various defenses is dependent upon maturation. That is, some defenses appear to be instinctual and are available to the very young child, whereas others become available only after further development including such events as the acquisition of the superego. A strict chronological presentation is impossible—indeed, both the order of appearance and relative "health" of various defenses differ according to different authors and their interpretations of how these defenses are used. Nevertheless, the selected defenses discussed next are presented in the following groupings: primitive (instinctual), immature, and mature (Table 2). Once a defense mechanism is developed, it can be employed by the individual regardless of his current developmental level.

Primitive defenses

Repression. *Primal* repression prevents an instinctual object-choice that has never been conscious (in the awareness) from becoming conscious. Repression *proper* forces threatening memories, ideas, or perceptions from awareness and sets up a barrier against reintroduction into awareness: anxiety-producing experiences are buried in the unconscious (the part of the personality represented by the id that is below the level of awareness). EXAMPLE: An individual may not see something in plain view that is anxiety provoking.

Displacement. In **displacement,** repressed impulses are disguised to achieve satisfaction. EXAMPLE: An individual who has no awareness of his anger toward his mother may express this hostility by acting out against other women in authority over him.

Denial. **Denial** is the perception of the world as one wants it to be rather than as it actually is: a distortion of a real situation. Denial may be achieved through act, by turning away and therefore not seeing; through word, by saying, with belief, that it is not so; or through fantasy, by day or night dreaming.

Regression. **Regression** is retreat to an earlier developmental stage in the face of anxiety or fear. EXAMPLE: An individual may display immature, dependent behavior in the face of illness (threat of bodily harm).

Fixation. **Fixation** is lack of progression to the next developmental phase. EXAMPLE: An individual may never progress beyond impulsive behavior.

Immature defenses

Projection. **Projection** attributes a dangerous drive (motivated by the id) or an undesirable characteristic (as defined by the superego) to the external world so that it becomes an objective anxiety and is therefore easier for the ego to master. EXAMPLE: "I hate her" becomes "She hates me."

Reaction formation. Since the instincts and their derivatives can be arranged in pairs of opposites (e.g., love vs. hate), the ego can repress an anxiety-producing instinct by concentrating on its opposite: unacceptable feelings are kept unconscious and are masked by the opposite, acceptable feelings (**reaction formation**). EXAMPLE: An individual who has hostility toward another person may be overly friendly to that person.

Mature defenses

Intellectualization. **Intellectualization** consists of focusing only on the nonaffective (non–feeling-related) aspects of a situation and thus attaining a purely cognitive understanding of a problem. EXAMPLE: A parent may react to the diagnosis of terminal illness in his child by unemotionally reading all the literature available on the disease and focusing totally on discussions of the statistical merits of different treatment regimens.

Isolation. Isolation is closely related to intellectualization. Although a variety of isolation mechanisms exists, a common example is **isolation of affect**: the repression (lack of awareness) of a feeling associated with an idea but not the idea itself. EXAMPLE: An individual may be insulted and understand that he has been insulted, but feel no conscious anger.

Rationalization. **Rationalization** is justification of an unacceptable act by changing its nature to make it more acceptable. EXAMPLE: A parent may severely beat a child in the name of discipline.

Sublimation. **Sublimation** transforms a primitive instinctual drive into an activity that is socially acceptable without marked loss of pleasure. EXAMPLE: An adolescent who is experiencing an increase in libidinal drives may spend time developing artistic representations of nude adults.

Table 3. Freud: psychosexual development

Life-span period	Erogenous zone	Stage	Source of libidinal pleasure	Conflict	Resolution
Infancy	Mouth	Oral	Touch; incorporation; biting	Weaning	Independence; emergence of ego
Toddlerhood	Anus	Anal	Expulsion; retention	Toilet training	Self-control
Preschool/ kindergarten	Genitalia	Phallic	Masturbation	Oedipus complex	Identification with same-sexed parent; emergence of superego
School age	—	Latency	—	—	—
Adolescence/ adulthood	Genitalia	Genital	Sexual stimulation	Incest taboo; frustration of genital impulses	Selection of heterosexual partner

Freud and psychosexual development (Table 3)
Sexual instinct

The **sexual instinct** as conceptualized by Freud includes drives for pleasurable activities that involve both genital and nongenital stimulation and manipulation of various body regions. A region of the body in which localized tensions arise that can be reduced through such manipulation is termed an **erogenous zone.** There are three primary erogenous zones and each is associated with a vital need: the mouth (eating), the anus (elimination), and the genitalia (reproduction). The action that the individual takes to reduce tension (derive pleasure) in an erogenous zone may or may not fill the vital need associated with that area (e.g., eating vs. thumb-sucking). Actions involving the erogenous zones bring the child into conflict with the parents. The resulting frustrations and anxieties lead to the development of a large number of adaptive mechanisms and defenses.

A sequential ordering of the prominence of each of the erogenous zones as a tension-producing body area gives rise to the psychosexual stages of development.

Oral zone (oral stage). The mouth is the first major source of tension and pleasure for the infant. In the **oral stage** pleasure is derived from the tactile stimulation of putting things into the mouth and biting. Tactile stimulation and the incorporation of objects yield oral erotic (sexual) pleasure, and biting yields oral aggressive pleasure. The mouth has at least five primary modes of functioning that, in analytic theory, are prototypes or models for certain later personality types: (1) taking in (acquisitiveness), (2) holding on (tenacity), (3) biting (destructiveness), (4) spitting out (rejection), and (5) closing (negativism). Whether any of these traits will actually become part of the mature personality is thought to depend upon the amount of frustration and anxiety surrounding the prototypic expression experienced by the individual. For example, it has been hypothesized that abrupt weaning may result in a strong tendency to hold onto things to avoid a repetition of the trauma of the weaning experience. As another example, oral aggressiveness by biting is considered prototypic for a variety of direct, displaced, or disguised aggressions: a child who bites with his teeth may become an adult who bites with verbal sarcasm, scorn, or cynicism or who chooses a career as a politician, lawyer, or editorialist.

The infant is dependent upon an external agent, usually his mother, for relief from oral stress and the fulfillment of oral pleasure. The mother can control the infant's conduct by giving food when he is good and withholding food when he is bad. Food is then equated with love and approval. Withholding food is equated with rejection and disapproval. The stage is thus set for the baby to become extremely anxious when the mother is rejecting or absent, since this signifies the loss of desirable oral supplies. If a great deal of anxiety develops in the infant over this threat to his oral pleasures, an overdependence upon the mother, as well as others, may develop. Instead of learning to satisfy his needs through personal effort, the infant develops a so-called oral-dependent character structure and expects others to provide things when he is good and withhold or take away things when he is bad.

If such dependence makes a person feel ashamed, a reaction formation may develop and cause the person to become overly independent in order to resist feelings of dependence on anyone.

Anal zone (anal stage). Tensions are thought to arise in the anal zone as a result of the accumulation of fecal material, which exerts pressure on the walls of the colon and the anal sphincter. Expulsion brings relief. Explosive elimination is considered by analytic theorists to be prototypical for emotional outbursts, temper tantrums, and rages.

Toilet training is usually the first crucial experience a child has with discipline and external authority. It represents a conflict between the instinctual drive for elimination and an external barrier, social authority.

Freud hypothesized that parental, especially maternal, methods of toilet training and attitudes toward such issues as cleanliness, control, and responsibility determine to a large measure the nature and extent of the influence toilet training will have upon personality development. A wide variety of mother-child interactions and their possible consequences have been described. For example, if the method of training is strict and punitive, the child may counter by soiling himself intentionally. When older, the child may react to authority figures by being messy, irresponsible, or disorderly. On the other hand, if a reaction formation against uncontrolled explosiveness develops, the child may become meticulously neat and fastidious.

According to psychoanalytic theory, retention, as well as expulsion, is a pleasurable sensation that the child may experience during the **anal stage.** Individuals who derive satisfaction from holding back feces and become fixated upon this form of erotic pleasure may develop interests in collecting, possessing, and retaining objects. Those who develop a reaction formation to retention, on the other hand, may feel impelled to give away possessions.

Sexual zone

PHALLIC STAGE. The period of development when the child is preoccupied with his genitalia as a body area of *self*-stimulation has been termed the **phallic stage.** According to Freud, both boys and girls experience a period of intense attachment to the parent of the opposite sex and hostility toward the parent of the same sex during this stage. This state of affairs has been designated the **Oedipus complex** after the mythological Greek character who killed his father and married his mother. The sex-specific rivalries that occur during this time have been termed the **Oedipal conflict** (males) and the **Electra conflict** (females).

OEDIPAL CONFLICT. Prior to the phallic stage, the boy loves his mother and identifies with his father; that is, he incorporates his father's qualities into his own personality. As sexual urges increase, however, the boy begins to crave exclusive sexual possession of his mother and becomes jealous and rivalrous of his father. However, the boy fears that, if he persists in his antagonism toward his father, he may be physically harmed through castration. As a result of this **castration anxiety,** the boy represses his incestuous desires for his mother and his hostility toward his father. After renouncing his desire for the exclusive love of his mother, the child may either identify with her as the lost object or intensify his identification with his father.

Typically, some identification exists with both parents, since Freud assumed that all people are constitutionally bisexual; that is, the tendencies of both sexes are inherited. The strengths of the child's identification with each parent will depend upon the relative strengths of his masculine and feminine tendencies and will ultimately give rise to the degree of masculinity and femininity he displays in later life. These identifications lead to the formation of the superego, which marks the resolution of the Oedipal conflict.

ELECTRA CONFLICT. Like the boy, the girl's first love object outside herself is her mother. However, she is less likely than is a boy to have an early identification with her father. When the girl becomes aware that she does not have a penis, she blames her mother. The strength of her love for her mother weakens; at the same time, she begins to prefer her father. Her love for her father, however, is mixed with **penis envy,** the feminine counterpart of castration anxiety. The conditions of penis envy and castration anxiety form the **castration complex.** However, whereas castration anxiety leads to the abandonment of the Oedipal conflict for the boy, penis envy is responsible for the introduction of the Electra conflict in the girl. The girl loves her father and is jealous of her mother.

As the girl realizes the futility of her position, she gradually abandons her pursuit of her father, and the process of identification begins. The girl is also bisexual, and the relative strength of her identifications with each of her parents is determined by the degree of her masculine and feminine predispositions. The formation of the superego is achieved in the waning phase of the Electra conflict.

PSYCHOSEXUAL LATENCY. Freud believed that both males and females undergo a period of **psychosexual latency** during which sexual impulses are repressed. Latency is considered to extend from the end of the period of the Oedipus complex to the reemergence of sexual impulses at adolescence.

GENITAL STAGE. According to psychoanalytic theory, sexual impulses reemerge at the time of adolescence and pubertal growth, marking the onset of the **genital stage.** Whereas pleasure seeking through oral, anal, and genital stimulation was considered the aim of the infantile forms of sexuality, puberty is thought to create another sexual aim: reproduction, through mature sexual attraction to a love object. According to Anna Freud, the balance between the ego and id becomes disturbed during adolescence, and internal conflict results. She lists the following three factors that influence this adolescent conflict (Muuss, 1975, p. 46).

1. The strength of the id impulse, which is determined by physiological and endocrinological processes during pubescence.
2. The ego's ability to cope with or yield to the instinctual forces. This in turn depends on the character training and superego development of the child during the latency period.
3. The effectiveness and nature of the defense mechanism at the disposal of the ego.

During early adolescence, there is thought to be rebellion against the infantile superego, which was adequate for the needs of the child but is not adequate for the adolescent or adult. A partial recrudescence of the Oedipus complex is created by this rebellion against the superego that, according to Freud, was formed at the point of resolution of the Oedipal or Electra conflict. The adolescent knows, however, that emotional closeness to the parent of the opposite sex is impossible because of the incest taboo. The adolescent has also learned from experiences during the phallic stage that real competition with the like-sexed parent is impossible. Eventually, both the boy and the girl seek independence from both parents. The boy completes his identification with his father and chooses a heterosexual partner like his mother. In similar fashion, the girl completes her identification with her mother and chooses a partner like her father. Full heterosexual maturity, or genital primacy, is attained when feelings directed toward a parent of the opposite sex are successfully transferred to a love object that is not taboo.

The genital stage is the longest phase of psychosexual development, lasting from adolescence to senility, when regression to the pregenital period is common. The genital stage does not displace the pregenital stages. Rather, the satisfaction of genital drives also satisfies pregenital impulses. In addition, the personality mechanisms and defense strategies of the pregenital stages become part of the individual's permanent character structure as manifested during the genital stage.

Erikson and psychosocial development

Erikson's work is solidly grounded on Freudian theory. However, whereas Freud addressed himself to the intrinsic development of the individual, Erikson has addressed himself to the development of the individual within the context of his social milieu.

As pointed out by Maier (1965), Eriksonian theory and Freudian theory differ in three major areas:

1. Erikson considers the ego, rather than the id, the major force for human development. That is, unconscious motivation (id) is considered an accepted fact, but the process of socialization (the nonlibidinal relationship of the ego to society; the steps by which a child becomes an adult) forms the basis of development. Thus, Eriksonian theory recasts Freud's developmental phases in nonsexual terms and becomes a theory of psycho*social* development.

2. Erikson replaces the classical child-mother-father triad with the historical-cultural-social reality of the family.
3. Erikson focuses optimistically on an individual's potential for successful resolution of developmental crises rather than pessimistically on the potential for psychological dysfunction.

Psychosocial development is an evolutional, stepwise process in which an individual, at each subsequent stage, is presented with the task of integrating himself into the structure of social institutions by confronting the opposing forces that influence his interactions with his environment. The individual's goal, at each critical period of development, is to establish a dynamic equilibrium among these forces with, ideally, greater prominence of the positive attribute, or ego quality. However, whatever equilibrium the person establishes produces a new set of forces as the basis for the next maturational phase, or "age."

The eight ages of man (Table 4)

Erikson's eight ages of man represent a reformulation and extension of Freud's five psychosexual stages. Although many similarities can be seen between the two theories as they relate to childhood and adolescence, the much broader context in which Erikson places the individual, as well as his more detailed treatment of adulthood, is readily apparent.

Erikson states two underlying assumptions in his construction of the psychosocial stages of development: "(1) that the human personality, in principle, develops according to steps pre-determined in the growing person's readiness to be driven toward, to be aware of, and to interact with, a widening social radius; and (2) that society, in principle, tends to be so constituted as to meet and invite this succession of potentialities for interaction and attempts to safeguard and to encourage the proper rate and the proper sequence of their unfolding" (Erikson, 1950, p. 270).

Thus, Erikson postulates a close relationship, which develops according to a sequential pattern, between physiological and psychological capabilities and environmental (social and cultural) demands. In addition, development is mutual. An individual cannot move beyond the readiness of his social context and vice versa.

Basic trust vs. basic mistrust. In earliest infancy, individuals experience a mutually satisfying relationship with the environment based on familiarity, regularity, and predictability. The development of trust requires a feeling of physical comfort. If this is present, an individual will extend trust to new experiences. If, however, the individual experiences physical discomfort or uncertainty, new experiences will be faced with apprehension or mistrust. Overcoming these feelings of discomfort forms the **basic trust vs. basic mistrust** phase.

Autonomy vs. shame and doubt. As children learn that personal behavior can be self-determined, they develop a sense of autonomy. Simultaneously, however, continued dependency in many areas of functioning is a realistic necessity and cre-

Table 4. Erikson: psychosocial development—eight ages of man*

Life-span period†	Psychosexual stage	"Age"	Description
Infancy	Oral	I. Basic trust vs. basic mistrust	"The general state of trust. . .implies not only that one has learned to rely on the sameness and continuity of the outer providers, but also that one may trust oneself . . ." (p. 248)
Toddlerhood	Anal	II. Autonomy vs. shame and doubt	"From a sense of self-control without loss of self-esteem comes a lasting sense of good will and pride. . ." (p. 254)
Preschool and kindergarten	Phallic	III. Initiative vs. guilt	". . . the child is. . .ready. . .to become bigger in the sense of sharing obligation and performance. . . (he moves) toward the possible and the tangible which permits the dreams of early childhood to be attached to the goals of an active adult life." (p. 258)
School age	Latency	IV. Industry vs. inferiority	". . .he now learns to win recognition by producing things." (p. 259)
Adolescence	Genital	V. Identity vs. role confusion	"The sense of ego identity, then, is the accrued confidence that the inner sameness and continuity prepared in the past are matched by the sameness and continuity of one's meaning for others, as evidenced in the tangible promise of a 'career.' " (pp. 261-262)
Young adulthood	Genital	VI. Intimacy vs. isolation	". . .the young adult, emerging from the search for and the insistence on identity, is eager and willing to fuse his identity with that of others. He is ready for intimacy. . ." (p. 263)
Middle age	Genital	VII. Generativity vs. stagnation	"Generativity, then, is primarily the concern in establishing and guiding the next generation. . ." (p. 267)
Old age	Genital	VIII. Ego integrity vs. despair	"Only in him who in some way has taken care of things and people and has adapted himself to the triumphs and disappointments adherent to being, the originator of others or the generator of products and ideas—only in him may gradually ripen the fruit of these seven stages." (p. 268)

*Based on data from Erikson, E. H. 1950. *Childhood and society.* New York: W. W. Norton & Co., Inc.
†Like the stages of psychosexual development, the psychosocial developmental stages are dependent upon the attainment of characteristics that are not easily quantifiable. The designated life-span periods identify the times of life when the concerns of a particular "age" are most prominent.

ates a sense of doubt in a given child about his ability to assert his full autonomy and ultimately exist as an independent unit. As another aspect of the **autonomy vs. shame and doubt** phase, feelings of shame about his previous much-enjoyed dependence arise as part of the child's instinctive revolt against authority.

Initiative vs. guilt. As children move rapidly forward in ever-widening social and spatial spheres, they are constantly challenged to new activity and purpose. Occasionally, what autonomy they have attained is frustrated by the autonomous activity of others that may not be in concert with their own. This conflict may impinge on the sense of trust that the child developed with his first caregivers. Mistrust may give rise to a sense of guilt for having gone too far in his strivings for initiative. Self-modulation begins in this phase of **initiative vs. guilt** with the development of a conscience that reflects parental and therefore sociocultural values.

Industry vs. inferiority. Mastery of tasks and a sense of doing well with and among peers are the most important accomplishments of the **industry vs. inferiority** phase. Children strive constantly to increase and improve their skills through use of tools and their knowledge of the world through systematic instruction. Children derive great pleasure in completing work through attention and diligence. Of danger to the child, however, is the sense of inferiority that may overcome him if he thinks that his products, and therefore he or his tools, are inadequate.

Identity vs. role confusion. During adolescence, the young person establishes his own identity. To Erikson, choosing an occupational identity is the primary task of the **identity vs. role confusion** phase of development.

The process of general identity formation begins with group identity. Often cruel in exclusion of peers, the "in" group attempts to clarify its group identity at the same time that its members are beginning to clarify individual identities. Erikson suggests that these cliques may serve as a defense against identity confusion.

Through the process of identity formation, the adolescent develops a separateness from the family of origin, although his ability to relate closely to others outside his family increases.

Intimacy vs. isolation. Once personal identity becomes established, the young adult is eager to fuse his identity with that of others: to develop intimacy, the capacity to commit oneself to partnership despite sacrifice and compromise. Erikson terms the antithesis of intimacy "distantiation": isolation from or destruction of those who are a danger to oneself or one's intimate relations.

"True genitality" develops during the **intimacy vs. isolation** phase. Erikson (1950, p. 266) writes:

In order to be of lasting social significance, the utopia of genitality should include:
1. mutuality of orgasm
2. with a loved partner
3. of the other sex
4. with whom one is able to share a mutual trust

5. with whom one is able and willing to regulate the cycles of:
    a. work
    b. procreation
    c. recreation
6. so as to secure to the offspring, too, all the stages of a satisfactory development.

Thus, having reached this stage, the individual is prepared to provide for himself, his loved ones, and society during adulthood.

Generativity vs. stagnation. The task of the second phase of adulthood, **generativity vs. stagnation,** is the provision of a social structure that will support and be conducive to the growth of the next generation. Generativity, less restrictive than procreativity, implies reaching out into the community to provide a force for stability or constructive change based on experience. Absorption in oneself drains time and energy away from communal efforts and can lead to personal and social stagnation.

Ego integrity vs. despair. In the final phase of life, **ego integrity vs. despair,** the individual surveys and appraises his existence. Ego integrity implies that this reflection is a positive one: the life led was a good one, and the choices made were right and proper. Such peace with oneself results in an appreciation of a higher order of being. Despair is the feeling that the life lived was inadequate or improper but that the time left is too short to start again.

COGNITIVE-INTELLECTUAL THEORY
Piaget and cognitive development

The work of Jean Piaget is almost exclusively centered on the development of **cognition,** the process of acquiring and using knowledge. As such, his research and writings focus less on the content of a child's thought than on its basic underlying organizational structure; that is, the reason for a thought rather than the thought itself. In addition, although Piaget states that emotions represent the motivational force behind intellectual activity, his work largely ignores emotion and concentrates instead on the structure of intellect. Last, Piaget's investigations have focused on individual optimal **competence** (what he *can* do) at a given developmental stage rather than **performance** (what he may actually or habitually do under ordinary circumstances).

According to Piaget, cognitive development occurs as a function of neurological maturation, an adequate social environment, experience, and constant internal cognitive reorganization. Heredity sets broad limits on intellectual functioning. In early infancy, primitive or innate reflexive activity determines most functioning. Thereafter, experience modifies or reorganizes these reflexes into purposeful mental and physical activities to the extent permitted by the individual's current level of physiological maturation.

Two major orienting principles form the framework for Piaget's theory of cognitive development: there is a tendency for all species to *organize* their activities, and there is a tendency for all species to *adapt*. **Organization** allows for a hierarchical ordering of activities; **adaptation** allows for dealing with the environment by using already available activities (**assimilation**) and by developing new activities in response to environmental demands (**accommodation**). In this context, definite stages of development can be identified depending upon the particular activities the child has available for use.

One of Piaget's basic tenets is that intellectual development proceeds in a stepwise, ordered manner in response to experience; however, the age at which a particular child achieves a certain level of cognitive ability is variable depending upon factors such as individual differences in the physical and social environment and physiological functioning. Specific age is thus less important than the orderly progression of learning. Transitional periods exist between developmental phases. During these periods children manifest some characteristics of the next stage. Selective teaching (the provision of particular experiences), if repeated and reinforced, can result in rapid acquisition of new intellectual skills or cognitive processes appropriate to this next stage.

Stages of cognitive development (Table 5)

Piaget has defined four periods of cognitive development: the sensorimotor, the preoperational, the concrete operational, and the formal operational.

Sensorimotor period. Extending from birth to approximately 2 years of age, the **sensorimotor period** is distinguished by the infant's use of his senses to gain information and the use of his increasing motor capabilities to seek out new experiences and modify his environment. The development of language marks the end of this developmental phase.

The sensorimotor period can be divided into six stages. A few descriptive characteristics of the child's abilities at each stage will help illustrate Piaget's concept of developmental sequencing during infancy:

Stage 1: Depends heavily upon reflex activity, although modification of reflex activity through experience can be seen (e.g., rooting behavior evolves into active searching for the nipple on sight).

Stage 2: Exhibits primitive anticipation (sucking at the sight of the bottle), curiosity, imitation, and **object concept** (a rudimentary understanding that an object has intrinsic permanence or an existence of its own but only as it relates to the child, as exemplified by the child's briefly watching the spot where an object has disappeared).

Stage 3: Makes more systematic and precise attempts to imitate familiar behavior (opening mouth, moving head from side to side in imitation of model).

Stage 4: Exhibits rudimentary thought and purposive action (removing an obstacle to a goal); attempts to imitate novel behavior; exhibits greater understanding of the existence and permanence of external, independent objects (looks for vanished object if series of displacements is not too complex).

Table 5. Piaget: cognitive development

Age (approximate years)	Stage	Distinguishing characteristics of cognitive function
0 to 2	Sensorimotor	*Preverbal* Reflexive activity leading to purposeful activity Development of object permanence, rudimentary thought
2 to 7	Preoperational	*Prelogical* Inability to deal with several aspects of a problem simultaneously Development of semiotic function (use of symbols, representational language)
7 to 12	Concrete operational	*Logical* Problem solving restricted to physically present or real objects and/or imagery Development of logical operations (e.g., classification, conservation, reversibility)
12+	Formal operational	*Abstract* Comprehension of purely abstract or symbolic content Development of advanced logical operations (e.g., complex analogy, induction, deduction, higher mathematics)

Stage 5 (climax of the sensorimotor period): Shows interest in producing novel behaviors, such as attempting to make new sounds or trying new methods to deal with an obstacle to a goal; imitates well.

Stage 6 (transition to symbolic thought): Begins to think about problems; can imitate an absent model from memory; uses words to designate ongoing events, immediate desires, or objects that are present; has a fully developed concept of **object permanence** (will look for a vanished object even if the series of displacements is complex; that is, the child understands that things exist independently of himself).

Preoperational period. Extending from about 2 to 7 years of age, the **preoperational period** is distinguished by several characteristics:

1. The appearance of *semiotic function*, "the ability to make something—a mental symbol, a word, or an object—stand for or represent something else which is not present" (Ginsburg and Opper, 1979, p. 70). The earliest mental symbols are formed through imitation—by looking at objects, handling them, and acting like them, thus incorporating information about them. Later, such graphic imitation becomes unnecessary because previously gathered information about the object has been internalized as a mental symbol. During this developmental stage, each child's mental symbol for an object or an event is personal and resembles that to which it refers or some particular experience the child associates with it.

2. The use of language in a representational way to designate absent objects or events. Initially, specific words are highly personalized and idiosyncratic and are not used in the same way adults use them. The child's words are **preconcepts;** that is, they are sometimes too general, such as designating all cars, trucks, buses, trains, etc., as "ride," or too specific, such as designating all types of boats, submarines, rafts, and floats as "sailboats." Nevertheless, the child is successful at imparting information and making his needs known to others, even those who have not shared in his experiences.

3. The appearance of initial reasoning. Reasoning is aided by memory of past events that imparts an intuitive quality (the ability to make guesses about future events) to the child's thinking. However, in new situations that are not adequately covered by past experiences the child lacks the ability to think logically. He may actually solve problems through intuition, but he cannot explain his reasoning in arriving at a particular solution. Reasoning in the preoperational period is also restricted by the use of **transduction,** or reasoning from a particular to a particular (i.e., seeing a relationship between two objects or events where none exists). For example, on a cloudy day a child might say, "The sun isn't out, so it isn't daytime."

Following are characteristics of thought processes in the preoperational child:

1. **Centration** (the inability to consider several aspects or dimensions of a situation simultaneously). Centration includes **syncretism** (a tendency to group

several apparently unrelated things or events together into a confused whole), **juxtaposition** (the failure to perceive the real connection among several things or events), and the failure to understand part-whole or ordinal relations.

2. **Irreversibility** (the lack of appreciation of successive changes or transformations).

3. **Egocentrism** (seeing the world only from his point of view, or believing that he is the origin of all actions in his world). The child's egocentrism is also manifested by **magical thinking** (the equation of thought and fantasy with action, that is, the feeling that his wish causes some external event).

Preoperational thought content is clearly influenced by **animism** (the belief that inanimate objects are alive as are people), **artificialism** (the belief that all things are made for a purpose), and **participation** (the belief that there is some continuing connection or interaction between human actions and natural processes).

Concrete operational period. Extending from approximately 7 to 12 years of age, the **concrete operational period** is distinguished by the development of logical thinking about *concrete* (physically present) problems. Some of Piaget's most widely known experiments were used to define this period of cognitive growth in which mastery of physical concepts is most prominent. The few examples that follow illustrate the child's capabilities or limitations and serve as guides to the amount and kind of information a child can successfully deal with during this stage of development.

During the concrete operational period, children learn to classify objects according to their particular characteristics. Thus, they can construct a hierarchical classification and comprehend inclusion. For example, if a concrete operational child is given a handful of pennies, nickels, and dimes, he is able to reason that the class of money includes and is larger than the separate denominations of coins. However, this ability to classify objects is restricted to real objects. The child's ability to classify imaginary objects is limited.

The child also learns to *conserve* the equivalence of continuous quantity, substance, weight, and volume. That is, he begins to understand that the amount, physical property, heaviness, and occupied space of a substance is not changed by physical movements or rearrangements.

Conservation of continuous quantity can be tested, for example, by presenting the child with two glasses, A and B, each filled with equal amounts of water (Fig. 6). Water from one glass, in this case B, is then poured, in turn, into glasses C and D and the set E. If the child asserts that the amount poured from glass B into the different glasses is always the same as that remaining in glass A, he is considered to understand conservation of continuous quantity. That is, the child recognizes that neither the act of pouring nor the size or shape of the container in any way changes the quantity of the liquid.

Similarly, children who have developed conservation of substance, weight, and

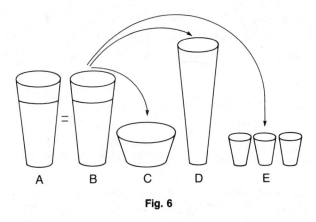

Fig. 6

volume are not misled by changes in shape or appearance to assume changes in equivalency. For example, when one of two identically heavy balls of clay is rolled into a sausage shape, the child who can conserve weight recognizes the continued equivalence of weight of the two pieces of clay regardless of appearance.

The ability to conserve implies that the child understands reciprocity, or compensation, and **reversibility,** transformation back to original form. In the clay ball/sausage experiment, for example, the child who can conserve recognizes that, as length increases, diameter decreases. He also recognizes that the sausage can be reformed into a ball which is identical to the ball that did not change shape and, therefore, identical to the manipulated ball.

The development of the ability to conserve follows a predictable pattern. Most children of age 4 or 5 years can understand equality; the child masters conservation of quantity and substance at age 6 or 7 years; conservation of weight at age 9 or 10 years; and conservation of volume at age 11 or 12 years (Ginsburg and Opper, 1979).

Formal operational period. Beginning in early adolescence and extending throughout adulthood, the **formal operational period** is distinguished by the use of abstract thought. Several characteristics of formal operational thinking are flexibility and effectiveness, complex reasoning, and the generation of hypotheses that take into account all possible combinations of eventualities.

A typical experimental situation devised by Piaget to test the emergence of logical thinking in the adolescent involves a problem in classical physics. When asked to determine the relative effects of length, weight, height, or force, alone or in combination, on the frequency of pendulum oscillation, the adolescent who exhibits formal operational thinking can design an efficient experiment, make accurate observations, and draw reasonable conclusions from empirical data. In addition, he can reason about a conclusion and derive new interpretations.

It has been found that not all adolescents, and perhaps not all adults as well, apply formal operational thinking to all aspects of reality. Rather, they tend to use formal operations in situations that are of particular personal interest or compatible with professional concerns. For example, adolescent females are more likely than are adolescent males to apply formal operations to interpersonal matters, and males are more likely than are females to apply formal operations to scientific matters (Elkind, 1975).

Tomlinson-Keasey (1972) has demonstrated that attainment of the highest level of formal operational thinking is actually rare at all age levels of adolescence. However, as Ginsburg and Opper point out, Piaget cautions that experimenters must provide "ecologically valid" tasks, those which are personally or culturally relevant, to adequately measure the cognitive ability of certain groups of individuals. That is, the traditional Piagetian tasks of classical physics, chemistry, and mathematics may be inappropriate in some settings. A dramatic example of how flexibility in experimental design may yield unexpected results was demonstrated in a study of Kalahari Bushmen by Tulkin and Konner (1973). In their experiment, a discussion of hunting was substituted for the pendulum test. In the course of the discussion, hypothesis formation and testing of the highest formal operational level were observed among the Bushmen.

The development of formal operations allows the adolescent to understand certain moral, political, and philosophical ideas and values for the first time (Brophy, 1977). Weiner and Elkind (1972, p. 171) write: "Adolescence is the era in which an individual becomes able to think abstractly and to deal with concepts like liberty and justice, to grasp metaphor and simile." Adolescents become preoccupied with social, religious, and political issues. Because they can conceive of all possible combinations and therefore all possible solutions to problems, they can also conceive the ideal, be it society, religion, or family. This new ability allows adolescents to see some of the contradictions and falsehoods embedded in their previously accepted beliefs.

Adolescents also understand the thought processes of others and wonder how other individuals see them and what these individuals really think about them. A belief that others may dwell on or constantly evaluate their appearance and behaviors constitutes the "egocentrism," or self-centeredness, of adolescence. Adolescent self-consciousness is a direct reflection of this egocentrism.

Elkind (1974) describes two components of adolescent egocentrism: the **imaginary audience** and the **personal fable.** The imaginary audience is a feature of early adolescence: "When a young person is feeling critical of himself, he anticipates that the audience—of which he is necessarily a part—will be critical too" (p. 91). The personal fable is described as follows: "a complex of beliefs in the uniqueness of his feelings and of his immortality. . ., a story which he tells himself and which is not true" (p. 93). The self-centeredness of early adolescence tends to decrease by 15 or 16 years of age, the point at which formal operational thinking becomes established; the adolescent can now distinguish between his own preoccupations and the thoughts of others and establish an intimate emotional relationship with others.

Kohlberg and the development of moral judgment (Table 6)

Research in the area of experimental honesty has generally failed to show a consistent increase in "resistance to temptation" in children between 4 and 14 years of age. Yet, it is apparent that the morality of adults is qualitatively different from that of the child (Kohlberg, 1969). To explain these differences, Kohlberg has attempted to apply cognitive-intellectual principles to the study of the development of moral judgment. Kohlberg's theory describes moral *thought processes* rather than *behavior*. Thus, his theory can help explain how and why a child arrives at a particular moral decision but does not provide a basis for altering the child's actual behavior.

According to Kohlberg's theory, thinking about moral issues proceeds through a fixed series of psychological stages that are dependent on and representative of an individual's general level of cognitive development. In addition, he suggests that there is a "cultural universality" to the sequence of stages, although the chronological ages at which certain stages appear are different in various cultures and may be dependent upon social experience as well as cognitive growth (Kohlberg, 1969).

Kohlberg has defined three levels of moral judgment that form the bases for six stages of moral development. In considering these stages, one must be aware of three points: (1) Controversy exists over whether stage 4 (conventional-authoritarian) and stages 5 and 6 (humanistic) actually represent alternative types of mature adult response rather than a hierarchical sequence. (2) Individuals who have attained certain levels of moral judgment reasoning have available to them and use lower levels of judgment on occasion. Kohlberg has termed this regression a "judgment of ease" rather than a "judgment of preference," since he assumes that an individual would, under all circumstances, prefer to use the highest level of moral reasoning available to him. (3) The motivation for a given behavior may not always be clear from the behavior itself. For example, it is not uncommon for the driver of a car to decelerate to the speed limit when a police car appears ahead on the road. Such behavior may represent a judgment of ease based on stage 1 (obedience-punishment) reasoning or higher order stage 4 ("law and order") reasoning.

Level I

At the **preconventional (premoral) level,** judgments or rightness or wrongness of an action reside in the action's external, physical consequences, the extent to which the action conforms exactly to established rules, and whether the action elicits punishment. Children whose logical reasoning is preoperational are cognitively limited to the preconventional level.

Table 6. Kohlberg: development of moral judgment

Age (approximate years)	Level	Basis of moral judgment	Developmental stage	Characteristics
0 to 1	I. Preconventional (premoral)	Consequences (including punishment), conformity to rules	1. Punishment-obedience	Egocentric, no moral concepts
1 to 2			2. Instrumental-relativistic	Satisfaction of own needs
2 to 6	II. Conventional (moral)	Good and right roles	3. "Good boy"–"nice girl"	Desire to please others
6 to 12			4. "Law and order"	Obligation to duty, respect for authority
12+	III. Postconventional (principled)	Principles; rights, values	5. Social-contract, legalistic	Relativism of personal values and opinions
			6. Universal-ethical-principled	Conscience dictates action in accord with self-chosen principles

Stage 1. No understanding of the social nature of moral conventions exists in the **punishment-obedience orientation.** Rules are perceived as absolutes. Motives or intentions are not considered.

Stage 2. In the **instrumental-relativistic orientation,** right behavior is that which satisfies an individual's own needs and occasionally the needs of others. The concepts of fairness, reciprocity, and sharing are used in this stage of moral reasoning but are entirely pragmatic ("I help you, you help me") and do not constitute a mature understanding of loyalty or gratitude.

Level II

At the **conventional (moral) level,** moral judgments reside in the performance of good or right roles, in the maintenance of conventional order, and in the fulfillment of the expectations of others with the anticipation of praise or censure by the social group with which the individual identifies. Unlike judgments based on the moral values inherent in level I, level II judgments consider the roles of significant others and respect their judgments regardless of the consequences of the behavior.

Stage 3. In the **"good boy"–"nice girl" orientation,** good behavior is that which pleases and helps others and which is approved by them.

Stage 4. In the **"law and order" orientation,** individuals focus on authority and fixed rules in their moral decisions. Right behavior consists of doing one's duty and showing respect for authority.

Level III

Moral judgments reside in individual personal conformity to principles that have validity in application apart from social authority and convention. This **postconventional (principled) level** of moral reasoning requires full formal operational thinking.

Stage 5. In the **social-contract, legalistic orientation,** right action is defined in terms of general individual rights and standards, and there is a clear awareness of the relativism of personal values and opinions. An emphasis is placed on procedural rules for reaching consensus, and laws are recognized as changeable through rational considerations of social utility.

Stage 6. In the **universal-ethical-principled orientation,** right behavior is defined as a decision of conscience in accord with self-chosen ethical principles. These broad moral principles are abstract (e.g., the golden rule) rather than concrete moral imperatives (e.g., the Ten Commandments). Universal principles of justice, reciprocity, equality of human rights, and respect for the dignity of human beings as individual persons are applied in moral decision making.

Moral dilemma example

Following is a moral dilemma and the kinds of judgments that might be made at each stage of moral development.

In Europe, a woman was near death from cancer. One drug might save her, a form of radium that a druggist in the same town had recently discovered. The druggist was charging $2,000, ten times what the drug cost him to make. The sick woman's husband, Heinz, went to everyone he knew to borrow the money, but he could only get together half of what it cost. He told the druggist that his wife was dying and asked him to sell it cheaper or let him pay later. But the druggist said, "No." The husband got desperate and broke into the man's store to steal the drug for his wife. Should the husband have done that? Why? (Kohlberg, 1969, p. 378)

Stage 1: Punishment-obedience
> PRO He should steal the drug because (a) he asked to pay for it first; (b) he is only stealing $200, not $2,000.
> CON He should not steal the drug because (a) he is using force; (b) he is doing damage; (c) he is stealing an expensive item.

Stage 2: Instrumental-relativistic
> PRO He is stealing not because he wants to, but because he wants his wife to live.
> CON The druggist is not wrong or bad, he is just making a profit, which is the reason for his business.

Stage 3: "Good boy"–"nice girl"
> PRO He is acting like a good husband who loves his wife.
> CON If he does not steal the drug and his wife dies, he cannot be blamed. He did everything he legally could.

Stage 4: "Law and order"
> PRO It is the husband's responsibility if he lets his wife die. He can pay the druggist later.
> CON It is natural for him to want to save his wife, but it is always wrong to steal, and he knows he is stealing.

Stage 5: Social-contract-legalistic
> PRO The law is unclear. Taking the drug may not be entirely right, but it can be justified.
> CON Although he cannot really be blamed for stealing, he is not justified in taking the law into his own hands. The ends do not justify the means.

Stage 6: Universal-ethical-principled
> PRO His choices are between stealing and letting his wife die. He must act on the principle of preserving and respecting life, which is a higher principle than the right of private property; therefore, stealing in this instance is morally right.
> CON He must consider other people who need the drug as much as his wife does; therefore, his action should reflect the value of all lives involved and not just that of his wife and his feelings for her. (Rest, 1968; cited in Kohlberg, 1969)

LEARNING (BEHAVIORAL) THEORY

Learning theory is based on stimulus-response (S-R) psychology, and the basic principles of learning theory are similar to those of strict S-R theory.

Basic principles of learning theory

1. Behavior is learned; however, innate, involuntary behaviors (reflexes) and genetic factors influence this learning.
2. All varieties of individual, combinations of, and patterns of behavior can be learned equally well provided no physical incompatibility exists among them.
3. Behavior is learned through **reinforcement**; such reinforcement may be external or internal and positive or negative.
4. Behavior can be **conditioned.**
5. Learned behavior results from many independent learning processes; therefore, behavior can be **shaped** through new learning.
6. Behavior can be learned through observation and **imitation.**

Conditioning

The two types of conditioning are classical and instrumental. **Classical conditioning** is the modification of a *reflexive* response previously associated in nature with one stimulus so that it can be evoked by another stimulus. Classical conditioning is exemplified by Pavlov's original experiments with the salivary response in the dog. A dog will salivate every time, including the first time, food is introduced into its mouth. Food is thus termed the **unconditioned stimulus,** and salivation, the **unconditioned response.** In his experiment, Pavlov paired another stimulus (a ringing bell) with the unconditioned stimulus by ringing the bell slightly before food was presented. After several experiences with the sequence of bell→food→salivation, the dog developed the sequence of bell→salivation even when no food was provided. The bell in this instance is the **conditioned stimulus** and the subsequent salivation, the **conditioned response.** (The character of the saliva in each situation was not chemically identical, although quite similar.)

In an experiment in classical conditioning, timing is important. Two stimuli that occur far apart in time will take longer to become associated and to elicit the same response. In addition, conditioning does not necessarily result from every pairing of two stimuli, although a wide range of possibilities is effective in eliciting such behavior.

In **instrumental conditioning,** a *nonreflexive* behavior is learned through reinforcement of correct responses. For example, an experimental situation can be devised in which a rat in a cage receives a pellet of food each time it depresses a lever. After the first press (which occurs by chance or random movement rather than as a response to a stimulus), the rat receives a pellet. The rat will then press the lever with increasing frequency to the point of satiation. The pellet of food is designated the "reinforcer."

In the preceding example, the rat's initial desired behavior occurred as a chance event because it is part of the rat's usual behavioral response. However, through instrumental conditioning, new actions that are not a part of the organism's behavioral repertoire can be taught through the process of shaping (reinforcing occasionally occurring behaviors to increase the probability that the next closer approximation to the desired behavior will occur). A classic example is described by Baldwin (1967, p. 328): "When Skinner wants to teach a pigeon to hit a pingpong ball through a pair of goal posts by pecking at it, he can't wait until the pigeon just happens to do so. He begins by reinforcing the pigeon whenever it is within a certain distance of the ball. The pigeon gradually learns to stay close to the ball. The experimenter now reinforces the pigeon only when he is close to the ball and looking in its direction, thus teaching the pigeon to keep his eye on the ball. In the next stage, the experimenter requires the pigeon to peck at the ball to receive a reinforcement. Finally, the pigeon must peck the ball in the right direction."

In both classical and instrumental conditioning, behaviors can be elicited by secondary or higher-order conditioning. For example, a flash of light could be paired with the bell in Pavlov's experiment. In time, the light (second-order stimulus) would elicit the salivation response. Similarly, after animals have been taught to use tokens for food in vending machines, they will perform other tasks for token rewards (second-order reinforcers).

There are several properties of conditioned behavior, including the following:

extinction "Undoing" a behavior by repeatedly failing to reinforce it.
inhibition Counteracting the expression of a behavior to avoid punishment.
partial reinforcement Inconsistent (random) reinforcement; the times to learn and to extinguish the behavior are *both* increased.
generalization Eliciting the same response with a variety of similar stimuli.
discrimination Limiting a response to one or a few specific stimuli by selective reinforcement.

In the foregoing discussion, we focused on learning that results from a direct effect on the performer. In fact, learning can also occur through observation and imitation. In **observational learning**, an individual watches other people, and his behaviors are modified by the rewards or punishments others receive. Imitative learning results from an individual being rewarded, either intrinsically or extrinsically, for copying the behavior of another (Miller and Dollard, 1941; Bandura, 1972). Imitation may also be facilitated or inhibited by observation of the rewards or punishments elicited by the model (Mowrer, 1960).

Characteristics of behavioral systems

Although learning and conditioning form the basic elements of the learning theory approach to behavior, in and of themselves they provide insufficient explanation for human behavior. Empirical data have demonstrated that other, more abstract concepts of behavior, a few of which are listed here, must be considered:

Stimulus response: All predictable behavior (response) is elicited.

Drive motivation: The organism's readiness to respond to a stimulus can influence the response.

Anticipatory goal response: Learned responses may occur too early and thus anticipate the situation in which the response is appropriate.

Habit: A response is learned, and the strength of the response is directly related to the number of times it has been reinforced.

Habit-family hierarchy: More than one sequence of behaviors may be elicited by a single stimulus and result in the identical reward. If one sequence has been selectively reinforced, it will be preferentially used; if all sequences have been equally rewarded, all will be used equally; if one sequence is prevented from occurring or is inhibited, the other alternatives are available.

Social learning theory

Of all the various subgroups that constitute the broad school of **behaviorism,** the early social learning theorists were most concerned with the issue of incorporating S-R principles into already existing developmental theories. Robert Sears, among others, was instrumental in incorporating psychoanalytic hypotheses into theories about behavior to the extent that these hypotheses could be explained or justified within the S-R cycle. More recent social learning theorists have been less concerned about reconciling S-R theory with other preexisting theories. However, to bridge the gap between the theories presented thus far and behaviorism, we will discuss the behavior system, dependency, and its relationship to development, as it was conceptualized by Sears.

In considering social learning theory, two points should be kept in mind. First, anthropology made a significant contribution to early social learning theory by identifying a number of common environmental factors that produce common learning processes in socialization. Interestingly, although these early theorists found that societies differ in the age, sequence, and manner in which various behaviors are socialized, the behaviors that require modification are fairly universal. That is, the behavior patterns of the child must be changed into those of the adult in all societies.

Second, an important aspect of the social learning theory approach is its attention to the dyadic nature of human behavior. That is, the social learning theorist sees the child in constant interaction with his environment and other individuals in that environment. A child's response to a stimulus becomes a stimulus itself for a response from another person, and so forth. Thus, the child's development of new and higher levels of functioning depends upon the ability of his environment to shape his behavior so that it conforms to the goal of the socialization process: the fulfillment of his developmental task to become an adult in his culture.

Table 7. Sears: a social learning theory of development

Life-span period	Phase	Description
Infancy	I. Rudimentary behavior: initial behavioral learning	Basic need requirements met within intimate parental environment Positive reinforcement is primary socializing agent
Toddlerhood/ preschool	II. Secondary motivational systems: family-centered learning	Socialization within larger family environment Negative reinforcement introduced as socializing agent
School age/ adulthood	III. Secondary motivational systems: extrafamilial learning	Social penetration into neighborhood and beyond Controls universally defined and strictly enforced

Development of dependency

According to Sears, the agents dictating social change for the child are, first, his parents, then his family, and, finally, his larger environment. Meeting basic physiological needs is the preoccupation of the infant, whereas secondary motivational drives (the desire to acquire such socially approved behavioral repertoires as, for example, self-feeding and -toileting) are the major forces behind later learning (Table 7).

The child is physiologically dependent on the mother from the moment of conception; he is physically dependent on her from the moment of birth. Psychological dependence on her (because of her central caregiving role) develops during early infancy, becomes strongest during middle to late infancy, and then diminishes but does not completely disappear throughout adolescence and adulthood.

Dependency is reliance on another for physical or psychological support. According to Sears, the earliest manifestation of dependency is innate, or reflexive, **attention-seeking behavior** (behavior that attracts the notice of the mother or some other caregiver). The mother then acts to meet the infant's physical or psychological needs as signaled by, for example, crying. Receiving this attention acts as a reinforcement to the infant for such behavior. After repeated experiences, the child begins to feel relief or comfort merely by the presence of the mother and discomfort by her absence.

In general, then, the following is hypothesized by Sears to be true about the child who is dependent: (1) attention is very influential over or strongly reinforcing of his behavior; (2) when he is reinforced by being given attention, he will learn new or other behaviors; and (3) he will be anxious when separated from his mother (source of reinforcement or comfort).

After about 8 months of age, this simplistic model is no longer adequate. Signs of maternal approval or disapproval rather than maternal presence per se begin to be associated with feelings of comfort or discomfort. The child gradually learns behaviors that bring approval (reinforcement). As a general class, these behaviors are socially conforming actions. Nonconforming behaviors are extinguished or inhibited as this first stage of the socialization process proceeds.

Three features of dependency deserve attention: (1) dependent behaviors are generalizable to people other than the mother, (2) the child will imitate behaviors that are modeled by any individual upon whom he is dependent, and (3) dependency must be unlearned almost as soon as it is learned, so that the child can become self-reliant or independent.

Helping the child to unlearn dependency can be accomplished by (1) ignoring inappropriate (dependency-maintaining) attention-seeking behaviors, (2) punishing such behaviors, or (3) teaching independent behaviors.

Persistent nonreinforcement, as the only teaching method, may be frustrating to the child, especially if he has become accustomed to reinforcement; that is, such frustration may lead to aggression and finally major outbursts that demand attention. The child thus learns to use violent behaviors for all attention needs.

Punishment can have two effects on the child's behavior. It can result in inhibition of the behavior or the creation of **dependency anxiety.** Dependency anxiety can lead to a fierce sense of independence manifested by a refusal to communicate with or behave affectionately toward the parents or other individuals.

Such apparent dependency anxiety has been found in aggressive adolescents (Bandura and Walters, 1959) where the child's conflicting feelings about his dependency and dependency anxiety have resulted in his learning *negative* attention-seeking behaviors. Although such behaviors are designed to elicit adult attention, the attention elicited is disapproving. Thus, the child satisfies his dependency through gaining attention, but he does not arouse his dependency anxiety because the attention that is given is negative, deprecating, or punitive. Such behavior may, of course, elicit fear of punishment; for some children, however, this may be preferable to a feeling of dependency (Baldwin, 1967).

The third method of helping the child unlearn dependence is to teach him independent behaviors, such as compliance with expectations, that now replace earlier behaviors. The child's identification with desirable models among adults or peers at home or in the community provides initial instruction through imitative or observational learning. Reinforcement, such as admiration or approval from peers, parents, or other adults, serves to perpetuate these socially acceptable behaviors.

According to social learning theory, the unlearning of dependency, by whatever method, creates a dependency drive in the adolescent. It is further hypothesized that the adolescent's conflict between dependency and dependency anxiety influences the strength of this drive. As noted before, drive designates the organism's readiness to respond to a stimulus. Thus, the stage is set for the adolescent to respond to this drive with the formation of an intimate, interpersonal relationship based on *mutual* dependency appropriate for his developmental stage.

Chapter 4

The relationship between physiological and psychological growth and development

Two basic premises are inherent in all of the theories of psychological growth and development that have been presented: innate, involuntary (reflexive) behavior is the foundation upon which all future behaviors are built, and psychological development is heavily dependent on physiological (especially neurological and sexual) maturation.

Only a small number of specific relationships between particular physiological characteristics and well-defined aspects of psychological development have been studied in any detail. However, several examples of the work that has been done will illustrate the relationships that are continually being discovered.

PHYSICAL DIMENSIONS AND SELF-ESTEEM

Several studies conclude that physical dimensions and size are related to an individual's ultimate psychological development. Clausen (1975) reported that both preadolescents and adolescents think that mesomorphs (muscular, stocky children) are seen as having leadership ability, athletic prowess, many friends, and aggressiveness. Endomorphs (fat children) and ectomorphs (thin children) are somewhat devalued.

Age at physical maturity also appears to affect people's perceptions of themselves and others. For example, Jones and Bayley (1950) reported that adult observers perceive early-maturing boys as more attractive and more relaxed than late-maturing boys. In another study, Clausen (1975) found that the self-esteem of an early maturer is often greater than that of a late maturer regardless of the person's true and ultimate capabilities. At least some of these perceptions are based on reality. Early-maturing males, in general, will be taller, heavier, and stronger than will late-maturing males. Thus, the boy who matures earlier, by virtue of his greater size and strength at a younger age, will usually be more successful in athletic programs, into which he will be accepted with alacrity. Given the importance our society attaches to physical prowess, the early maturer thus becomes the object of esteem and admiration from peers and elders alike.

On the other hand, Peskin (1967) hypothesized that early maturers had less time before pubertal growth to consolidate ego strength and would be more rigid and less exploratory in their attitudes. He found significant differences confined to the first few years after puberty, during which time the early maturer tended to respond to pubertal changes with inhibition and rigidity.

Although girls are not as interested as boys in being physically larger or stronger than their peers, early secondary sexual characteristic changes (breast development and menarche) may be highly valued and envied. On the other hand, early-maturing girls may intimidate male peers whose pubertal changes and growth will not occur until significantly later.

Regardless of their long-term consequences, it is apparent that during childhood and adolescence, physique and age at sexual maturation as well as cognitive skill and emotional expressiveness play very important roles in shaping the individual's early self-concept.

PHYSICAL SIZE, GROWTH PATTERN, AND INTELLIGENCE

Physically larger, especially taller, children score higher on tests of intelligence than do smaller children at all ages from 6 years onward. Part of the IQ-height correlation persists into adulthood (Tanner, 1978). Children who are physically advanced, on the average, score slightly higher on most tests of mental ability than do less physically advanced children of similar ages.

BIOLOGICAL POTENTIAL AND INTELLECTUAL CAPABILITY

Although both biological potential and environment appear to be critical to the ultimate expression of intelligence, twin studies have been used as a method to differentiate, if possible, the effects of these two factors (Erlenmeyer-Kimling and Jarvik, 1963; Wilson, 1972; Wilson and Harpring, 1972).

A foster child's performance on an IQ test has been found to more closely resemble that of his biological mother than that of his foster mother. Furthermore, Munsinger combined data from several studies of the intelligence of biological and adopted children and concluded that the correlation between the IQ scores of biological parents and their adopted children was higher than the correlation between the scores of adoptive parents and their adopted children despite long-term placement. Thus, the influence of biologic potential on the IQ of the adopted children was greater than the environmental influence provided in their adoptive homes (Munsinger, 1975a,b).

GENDER IDENTITY

The relationships between physiological and psychological growth and develop-ment are probably no better illustrated than in the development of **gender identity** (one's individuality as male, female, or ambivalent).

The ultimate expression of adult gender identity is preceded by a series of events. Sex is differentiated initially on the basis of chromosomal composition: 46 XX (female), 46 XY (male), or a chromosomal anomaly such as 45 X/46 XY (true hermaphrodite mosaic).

If the primordial gonad begins to differentiate as a testis, testosterone will be produced and will promote proliferation of the wolffian ducts to form male repro-ductive organs. If the individual differentiates as a female, it is inferred that a müllerian-inhibiting substance suppresses the development of the primitive müllerian ducts, which then become the uterus, fallopian tubes, and upper seg-ment of the vagina.

The morphology of the external genitalia of the newborn has an immediate psychological effect on the parents and family that persists for the remainder of the individual's life. Upon the birth of the infant and the determination of the child's sex, a set of cultural expectations immediately begins to influence all communica-tions to and about the child, including the choice of the child's name, the kinds of external reinforcers that are employed (blue vs. pink clothes; toys provided as the child matures), and even the subtle differences in parental voice inflection and handling of the infant that occur with differences in the sex of the infant and of the particular parent.

As the child matures, the behaviors of others, as well as his image of his body in comparison to that of others, serve as cues about how to internalize his concept of himself as a sexual being. Money and Ehrhardt (1972) hypothesize that for a young boy, for example, behaviors that are specific for the female gender role as determined by his culture are available to him but are not used. Instead, behaviors that are masculine are incorporated into his behavioral repertoire. In learning theory terms, "appropriate" sex role behaviors are reinforced, and "inappropriate" behaviors inhibited. Juvenile gender identity gradually emerges during childhood; adult gender identity is probably firmly set by the time of puberty.

As young people mature, their somatic and pubertal changes directly affect their psychological growth and development. Cultural tradition, however, prescribes how they will express their newly acquired adult sexuality.

In the United States, sexual behavior during adolescence varies according to the adolescent's age. Many early adolescents may express their undifferentiated sexuality through masturbation (self-stimulation of the genitalia often to orgasm) and/or homosexual behavior. These modalities of sexual expression appear to be less threatening to the insecure, early adolescent than are the intimate behaviors of heterosexual expression.

Once heterosexual behavior begins, it follows a common but not invariable pattern. Usually boy-girl encounters begin in early adolescence with group or crowd dating—several girls and boys together with minimal pairing off. At a later stage, pairing off of partners occurs, initially in the social context of "double dating." Although such behaviors as holding hands, kissing, petting, and coitus can occur at any time during the development of relationships, coitus is usually confined to the late-adolescent or individual dating stage.

It is estimated that by 19 years of age, approximately 55% of unmarried women and 60% to 70% of unmarried men have experienced coitus at least once. It is also important to emphasize that nearly 45% to 50% of unmarried adolescent females have *not* experienced coitus (Zelnik, Kim, and Kantner, 1979).

Homosexuality, long regarded as an indicator of dysfunctional gender identity formation, has received an increasing amount of attention during the past several years. In cultures other than our own, homosexual behavior has for centuries been accepted as a normal sexual outlet and a sign of masculinity. The extent to which such a view will become prevalent in this country is as yet unknown.

Thus, males and females are reared differently, according to their particular phenotype. They develop a sense of their own gender identity through environmental reinforcement of certain kinds of behavior that meet the expectations of their particular culture with regard to the expression of their male and female sex roles. However, certain physiological and psychological capabilities must be present in the individual before full expression of sexuality can be achieved.

Chapter 5

Strategies for providing clinical care

As in all clinical practice, the diagnosis and management of biosocial problems consist of (1) data gathering, (2) interpretation of data, (3) diagnosis, (4) intervention (including referral), and (5) evaluation of treatment.

DATA GATHERING

The data gathering process for biosocial problems requires many of the same skills already at the disposal of the practitioner, including interviewing and physical examination. Some familiar laboratory studies and some less familiar psychological tests performed by specially trained professionals may also be required.

Interview

The interview is the most critical component of the diagnostic process and deserves careful attention.

The "set" for the interview is often negotiated during the parents' or patient's call to the office to make an appointment. For example, the issue of how soon after a problem has been identified an appointment can be arranged determines urgency; the question of which family members should attend the visit determines who is or feels involved.

Interviews are ideally done in a private setting in which the practitioner and the patient and/or parents can talk without fear of being overheard. If available, a room without an examination table is ideal.

The parents

Parents should be interviewed together so that both parents' points of view are represented and so that one parent will not bear the entire burden of reconstructing the history. If one or both parents are employed, a compromise in mutually available meeting times may have to be arranged.

The parents of a preschool or young school-age child should always be interviewed, since they are, appropriately, the major source of information about the child's perceived problem and the individuals who can provide the most inclusive history. The parents should be seen separately from the child for at least part of the interview. This privacy accomplishes two things: it allows the parents to talk without distraction, and it allows the parents to discuss sensitive issues that the child may not fully understand or that he may misinterpret.

Whether the parents of an older school-age child or adolescent are interviewed separately from the patient or even at all depends upon the wishes of the patient and the judgment of the practitioner. Several factors influence this decision. For example, if marital issues are thought to play a major role in the child's dysfunction, or if the parents are in obvious disagreement about management of the problem, a private interview is appropriate.

The child

All child and adolescent patients should be interviewed alone for at least part of the visit. Such a maneuver provides important information regarding the child's or adolescent's (1) willingness or ability to separate from the parents and vice versa, (2) ability to form an independent relationship with the practitioner, (3) major concerns that may be substantially different from those presented by the parents, and (4) thoughts about causes of the problem and possible solutions that, again, may differ from those offered by the parents.

The preschool and young school-age child should be allowed and perhaps encouraged to bring a **transitional object** (e.g., a toy from home) into the private session to increase his sense of security in an unfamiliar setting. Toys in the office, a chalkboard, or even a small supply of paper and pencils for free drawing can be used to help the child begin talking. Indirect questions about the presenting problem usually result in much more information than direct questions. Children are apt to offer more information when the problem is discussed in terms of a doll, an animal, or "some children" rather than in terms of themselves.

The older school-age child, although better able to communicate information verbally, may appear more wary and actually less communicative. This behavior is a hallmark of the child between 10 and 12 years of age who is in a transitional phase of psychological development and may find it difficult to relate to adults. Asking a child, in advance, to bring artwork or other handiwork from home or school can provide a nonthreatening focus for the beginning of the interview.

The interview with the adolescent is a major element of the data gathering process. The structure of the interview will reflect the adolescent's developmental stage. A good interview, according to a skilled adolescent psychiatrist at our institution, sounds much like an everyday conversation.

The early adolescent, who thinks in concrete operational terms, will respond better to questions aimed at specific content matter than to open-ended questions. The interviewer should begin the session with topics that are particularly familiar to the patient, such as friends, school, or other activities, and then move gradually to the presenting problem.

Late adolescents, who use formal operational thinking, are somewhat easier to interview. They have the capacity to handle open-ended questions, have insight, and can think into the future. They are often able to express their own feelings as well as consider the feelings of otl.ers.

The midadolescent may have the thought process characteristics of either the early or the late adolescent, depending upon his developmental age. However, the midadolescent may also be struggling with issues of independence and thus find it difficult to talk openly with an authority figure, the practitioner.

Order of the interview

Whether the school-age child or adolescent should be seen before or after the parents is a frequently asked question. Some people choose to announce the child's name in the waiting room and take as a starting point for the interview whatever family member or group comes forward. It is our suggestion that the practitioner develop a personally comfortable style, since there are advantages and disadvantages to all systems. For example, seeing the child or adolescent first gives him a sense of importance; however, many children fear that the information they give will then be relayed to the parents in their private session. Seeing the parents first often makes the child feel that he has been branded and has the impossible task of undoing his parents' complaints; however, he may also be relieved by knowing that what he has shared will not be immediately transmitted to the parents, since they have already had their time alone.

Felice and Friedman (1978) have suggested certain guidelines for interviewing adolescents. Actually, most of these guidelines are applicable to younger children and parents as well, including creating an appropriately warm and empathetic atmosphere, maintaining confidentiality, obtaining complete information that includes perceptions and feelings pertinent to the problem, and summarizing the interview so that the patient and the practitioner are in accord about the content of the session. Particularly careful and serious attention should be paid to the adolescent who may be mistrustful of the adult practitioner. Full, honest communication often requires two or more interviews.

Regardless of the particular format the practitioner chooses, a summary session, with patient and parents together, should be held toward the end of the appointment time. This session can also be used to make decisions regarding the next step in information gathering or intervention.

Content of the interview

Although the information that should be obtained during the course of the initial interview(s) may vary somewhat depending upon the complaint as well as the age of the child, a basic format for the content of the interview is outlined on the next two pages.

Nuclear family
   Ages of parents and siblings
   Marital history, including previous marriages, separations, divorces
   Educational background
   Employment status
   Religious and social affiliations
   Major medical and/or psychiatric problems
   Relationships to child
Extended family
   Ages and health of grandparents, aunts, uncles, etc.
   Presence in the home
   Relationships to child
Others living in household
   Ages and health status
   Relationships to nuclear family and child
Child's health history
   Illnesses (including allergies)
   Accidents
   Surgery
   Hospitalization
   Patient/family response to these problems
Child's developmental history
   Milestones
   Perceptions of adequacy of growth and development
Child's behavioral history
   As infant
   As toddler
   As preschooler
   As schoolchild
   As adolescent
School history
   Nursery/preschool
   Age entered kindergarten/separation problems
   Present school, grade, and teacher
   Attendance
   Academic performance
Peers
   Ages
   Frequency of contact with child
   Favorite activities together
   Apparent relationships to child
Patterns of discipline
   Who disciplines
   Methods
   Effectiveness
   Degree of parental agreement
Expectations for child's future
   Father

Mother
Child
Detailed account of problem
  Definition
  Onset
  Frequency
  Precipitating factors
  Effect on child, family
  Coping methods of patient, parents
  Coincident family problems
  Professional advice sought and results

Several aspects of this suggested history outline need to be highlighted. In the scheme presented, family composition and traditional medical concerns are discussed at the beginning of the interview, since these are comfortable topics in the usual practitioner/patient/family relationship. The primary complaint is reserved for discussion until the end of the interview for two reasons: the interviewer has an opportunity to see how the parents or child handle less emotionally charged matters and to get a feeling for the family and how it functions. If not obtained early, this information may never be gathered because of preoccupation with the presenting complaint. Indeed, some families will actively try to interject discussion of the chief complaint throughout the entire interview and will need help to focus on these others issues. In a family already well known to the practitioner, some or all of this information may have been obtained earlier and need not be gathered again.

In the discussion of the problem, it is important that both the mother and the father be encouraged to give their perceptions individually. The practitioner should pay close attention to discrepancies in the history or obvious disagreement between the parents about the seriousness of the problem or its management. The child's or adolescent's perceptions should also be obtained if at all possible.

Confidentiality

This issue is of importance to all members of the family. Since the child or adolescent is the patient, the practitioner must make it clear to him that no information will be given to others unless the practitioner and patient have discussed the issue of sharing and reach some agreement. Two stipulations should be made to this agreement with regard to the information to be given to the parents: the practitioner will share information about significant illness, and the practitioner will share information if the patient or others are in danger. Otherwise, the child or adolescent can be reassured that what he says is confidential.

It is also important to let the parents know that what is discussed between them and the practitioner will not be discussed with the patient unless it has been previously agreed that this information can be shared.

INTERPRETATION OF DATA

The interpretation of data is the step in which pathogenesis is considered and requires knowledge of physiological and psychological development. We contend that no single theory adequately explains all aspects of human development: a combination of explanations, which takes into account physiological, psychosexual, psychosocial, and cognitive and moral reasoning status, forms a reasonable basis from which to interpret behavior. In some situations, the relative contribution of a particular aspect of development may overshadow all others. In most situations, all aspects of development play some part.

The extent to which the interpretation of behavior is shared with the patient and/or his family varies. Actually, full disclosure is usually not necessary. Although writing specifically about the Oedipus complex, Selma Fraiberg, in *The Magic Years*, states what we believe is a reasonable dictum: "There are millions of parents today who have never heard of the Oedipus Complex and who wouldn't recognize it if they saw it in their children, and most of these parents are successfully rearing their children without this information" (1959, p. 204).

On the other hand, a full and detailed interpretation of the child's behavior that considers all aspects of the developmental process impacting on the child and the family must be kept in mind by the practitioner. By doing so, the practitioner can choose an intervention strategy with a high likelihood of success or systematically investigate reasons why a strategy has been unsuccessful.

DIAGNOSIS

The diagnosis is the summarization: a concise description of or conclusion about the problem based on signs and symptoms and their possible causes. Diagnostic categorization forces the practitioner to make a clinical judgment regarding the severity of the problem and to arrive at a decision about treatment, including possible referral. As with most maladies, the diagnosis is the information shared with the patient and family. How much the dynamics of the diagnosis need to be discussed will depend upon the patient and the family. In keeping with our preceding comment, too detailed an explanation may actually be detrimental to the coping style of the family.

INTERVENTION

First and foremost, we would like to underline our belief that therapy does not have to be spelled with a capital T. Since psychoanalysis is outside the skill realm of the pediatric practitioner and the cognitive-intellectual theory lends itself to understanding cognitive processes but does not provide a therapeutic strategy, we have chosen to emphasize counseling based on relationship and behavior modification as the prime treatment modalities useful for pediatric practice. We will also discuss referral as the pediatric practitioner's tool in dealing with individuals or situations that he does not wish to treat.

Types of treatment strategies

Biosocial therapy is often based on a particular kind of relationship between the practitioner and the patient, the practitioner and the family, or the patient and/or family and other social organizations. In this context, friendship can be therapeutic because a friend bestows a feeling of self-worth on the individual whom he befriends; direction can be therapeutic because it gives focus to an otherwise disorganized situation; limit setting can be therapeutic because it defines acceptable and unacceptable behavior for individuals who have not learned to make this distinction adequately; supportive listening can be therapeutic because it allows an individual to verbalize feelings and arrive at a self-determined plan of action; and the mobilization of other resources (e.g., Big Brother–Big Sister programs, scouting, and religious organizations) can be therapeutic because they help to meet otherwise unfulfilled needs.

The relationship strategy takes time, concern, and some expertise in choosing the correct modality for the particular situation. Its impact should never be underestimated. The clinician who uses it wisely often prevents the patient's behaviorally or developmentally based symptoms from progressing toward fixed dysfunction— the goal of treatment.

Behavior modification therapy is a specific treatment modality that requires some understanding of S-R psychology. Behavior modification is based on the premise that, since a certain behavior is learned because it or its result brings gratification to the individual, it can also be altered by changing the gratification attained or by offering a greater incentive for another behavior.

The development of a successful behavior modification program requires substantial preplanning and good communication about specific expectations. Thus, one must pay close attention to the following questions:

1. What is the behavior of concern?
2. Is the final desired result to alter behavior, extinguish an old behavior, or initiate a new behavior? ("Alter" implies that the behavior pattern needs to be shaped and thus approximations to the desired behavior will be rewarded. "Extinguish" implies that a particular behavior pattern needs to be stopped entirely and thus the behavior of concern will either never be reinforced or will be negatively reinforced. "Initiate" implies that a new behavior needs to be learned and thus the behavior will always be positively reinforced whenever it appears.)
3. What type and schedule of reinforcement is suitable for a particular child? (For example, small rewards given frequently result in faster change initially in all age groups; delayed gratification is suitable later in the program, particularly with more mature children.)

Having answered these questions, the practitioner can devise a program in cooperation with the parents and the child.

The practitioner must provide support to the parents or other caregivers who are responsible for carrying out the behavior modification program. Although this is true throughout the program, it is particularly true at the beginning, when the child may test limits even more than usual, and at times of relapse, which occur most predictably during stress or when an incentive is losing its appeal and a substitution should be considered.

Some parents refuse to participate in a reward-based program because of their belief that their children should do "what is right" merely on that basis. Our experience has been that, if tangible rewards are coupled with positive verbal reinforcement and an increase in parental attention to the desired behavior, a reward system is usually not necessary after several weeks or a few months. Instead, children begin to work toward goals such as spending time with their parents in enjoyable activities. This change in the desired reward incentive reinforces the parent as well as the child. Such mutual reinforcement marks the beginning of the end of the therapist's involvement.

Referral is also a treatment modality, since it sets the stage for further intervention. A great deal of practitioner finesse is required to negotiate referral well. Some of the many reasons for selecting referral in a particular situation are the type of problem, its severity, past experiences with a family or patient that have been unrewarding or frustrating, or a personal relationship such that the practitioner does not think he can assume an effective counseling role with the family.

The practitioner should identify particular colleagues or facilities within the community with whom he is comfortable communicating and whose expertise he respects. A letter of referral or, better, a telephone call, should precede the patient to the consultant's office to expedite evaluation and intervention.

A good referral is one in which all involved—the patient, family, practitioner, and consultant—have communicated:

1. The child and parents should know why they are being referred and agree to the referral (usually this explanation includes reference to the need for consultation from someone with expertise in a particular area to facilitate treatment, and occasionally the severity of the problem also needs to be stressed to ensure compliance).

2. The practitioner should support the referral and withdraw from direct care of the biosocial problem without relinquishing his responsibility for medical care. (Referral can be perceived by the family as a rejection by the practitioner; therefore, the assurance that the practitioner remains a vital resource for the child's medical needs must be given. However, unless the distinction is clearly drawn between the areas of involvement of the consultant and the practitioner, the patient and family can play them against each other and impede treatment.)

3. The consultant should be fully aware of the reasons for the referral and have expressed a willingness to help the patient and family.

The practitioner must recognize that the consultant will negotiate certain stipulations about treatment with the family that will include confidentiality. The amount of information the consultant shares with the practitioner during the course of the child's or family's therapy will depend upon the consultant's discretion. Co-operative relationships between professionals over time will, however, help to increase feelings of mutual trust and respect for each other's competence.

Guidelines for the formation of intervention "contracts"

Both counseling and behavior modification programs are appropriate interventions with children, adolescents, parents, or entire families. However, open-ended counseling sessions or too-broadly defined behavior modification programs can lose their focus and lead to frsutration for the patient, family, and practitioner. Thus, we have found it helpful for the practitioner to enter into a *contract* with the patient and/or family for a predetermined number of sessions (such as three or four) during which one or a few specific goals will be reached.

The practitioner should have definite objectives for each session so that time will not be wasted. The amount of time spent in each session is variable and depends both on the business to be done and the individuals attending. Altthough parents and older adolescents can focus their attention for 45 to 60 minutes, a younger child or adolescent may be able to do so for only 15 to 30 minutes. The quality of the session, not the quantity of time, is important.

Crisis counseling

In addition to regularly scheduled, office-based strategies, the practitioner may be asked to provide crisis counseling. Usually, crisis counseling is limited to one or two contacts. Frequently, such counseling is performed by telephone. Pediatric practitioners are adept at using the telephone for interventions in physical illness and can do so as well in acute biosocial situations. Often the patient or family merely needs reassurance or confirmation that their own commonsense plan is reasonable and should be carried out. On the other hand, whether the patient or family needs to be seen in the office or at a hospital emergency room or to be referred directly to a mental health professional should also be determined during the course of the call, and appropriate plans made immediately.

Inpatient hospitalization

It is becoming increasingly common for the practitioner to hospitalize children on pediatric and adolescent medical units for the diagnosis and initial management of biosocial problems. If a question exists as to whether the youngster's problem is an emotional or a physical one, an inhospital admission can be particularly helpful. In addition, hospitalization often mobilizes the family as well as the health care providers to clarify the exact nature of the problem and to begin to develop liaisons with psychologists and/or psychiatrists who may either help to arrange a psychiatric hospitalization or provide ongoing outpatient care, if necessary. We have used hospitalization generously for children with behavioral problems, children and adolescents with psychosomatic illnesses, and adolescents who have made suicidal gestures or who are depressed. Nurturing, caring staffs of pediatric and adolescent inpatient units who are attuned to the developmental needs of children can often help otherwise physically and mentally healthy young people negotiate crisis situations successfully.

EVALUATION OF TREATMENT

At the end of the proposed intervention, progress is *evaluated*. Whereas the success of the intervention must be determined immediately in crisis counseling, the office or hospital "contract" lends itself to a more leisurely evaluation at the end of the predetermined number of sessions or days in the hospital. The options are the same in all situations: to continue (based on partial resolution with the expectation of further improvement), to stop (based on substantial or complete resolution of the problem), or to refer (based on little or no progress in what was thought to be a remediable situation).

Termination

Termination can be more difficult to negotiate than is the initiation of treatment. Sometimes the practitioner will be ready to terminate before the patient and vice versa. Parents are usually fairly open about their beliefs that their particular business has been accomplished and that they wish to terminate. The practitioner, however, must be satisfied that such an appraisal is true and does not represent instead a fear of actually dealing with their problems. If the latter is the case, a referral is appropriate, although the parents may not comply.

Children, particularly adolescents, on the other hand, sometimes are unable to make straightforward statements that they think that their problems have been sufficiently resolved. Noncompliance either in carrying out specific recommended behavior or in attendance can be a useful guide that separation is at hand. However, such noncompliance should be distinguished from general noncompliance or the negativistic behavior of an unwilling patient who may require the help of a more experienced therapist.

Limitations

Some patients and families have life circumstances that are so disorganized or disrupted that definitive treatment of the situational crisis (a return to normal functioning) is impossible even in the most skilled hands. We are usually able, however, to help almost every patient or family function better to some extent in some areas of concern to them.

If a family does not recognize a particular behavior or symptom as a problem, the likelihood that the family members will seek or follow through on treatment is low unless we can convince them of the seriousness of a specific situation. If the child is in danger, either physically or emotionally, the practitioner has a moral obligation to press the family into accepting treatment, either directly or by referral. On the other hand, child advocacy in pediatric practice, in its broadest sense, demands that, although we do our best to point out our concerns as professionals, we must also learn to accept less than perfect, but *adequate*, patient and family functioning as a social reality. Imposing our personal standards, indiscriminately, on others can be as detrimental to our child patients as is ignoring their cries for help.

PART TWO

CLINICAL APPLICATIONS

This section is designed to provide a framework for the application of developmental theory to clinical practice. The 21 case vignettes that we have selected for presentation focus on contemporary biosocial problems for which practitioners are commonly asked to provide care. These problems occur as a result of situational or reality-based stress in three major areas of child or adolescent functioning: family life, school, and health.

Family problems that may adversely affect the child's development are moves by the family, divorce, death of a family member, and role or job changes of the parents. School problems will be considered in the context of the most frequently mentioned concerns of attendance, achievement, and behavior. Illness, or the absence of health, is a situational stress, since it can have negative effects on the person who is ill and on the family who provides emotional and financial support for its ill member. The impacts of acute, chronic, and fatal illnesses will be examined. Our overall emphasis will be on helping to avoid or minimize the potentially adverse effects of situational stresses on the development of an otherwise normal child or adolescent and his family.

Included in the discussion for each developmental age are an overview of the normal physiological and psychological growth and development characteristics of that stage, illustrative case vignettes with discussions of the specific situational stresses confronting the child and his family, and suggestions for providing strategic clinical care through the integration of theory and practice.

Chapter 6 • The child from 3 to 5 years (nursery/preschool age)

Physiological growth and development

MALES AND FEMALES: Relative decrease in the physical growth rate
   characteristic of infancy. Rapidly developing gross motor skills;
   rudimentary fine motor skills.

Psychological growth and development

FREUD	Transitional phase: anal stage →phallic stage
ERIKSON	Transitional phase: autonomy vs. shame and doubt→initiative vs. guilt
PIAGET	Preoperational period
KOHLBERG	Preconventional level
SEARS	Family-centered learning

Chapter 6

The child from 3 to 5 years (nursery/preschool age)

FAMILY: Death

CONCEPTS DISCUSSED: *Death of a grandparent*
Child's concept of death
Teaching about death
Night fears

   Jennifer was a 4-year-old nursery school student whose mother called the practitioner for a parent counseling appointment because of Jennifer's "preoccupation with death."

Data gathering

   Past history. Jennifer had enjoyed good health all her life. Her growth and development had been entirely normal.

   Family history. Jennifer was the older child of a 30-year-old lawyer and a 27-year-old homemaker and had a 2-year-old brother. The entire family was in excellent health and enjoyed active outdoor living.

   School. At age 3, immediately after achieving bowel and bladder control, Jennifer had been enrolled in a nursery school, which she attended three mornings a week. She was currently in her second year at the school.

   Peers. Jennifer was well liked by her schoolmates and played regularly with two of them who lived nearby. She was quite verbal and seemed to be a natural leader among her friends.

   Office visit. Both of Jennifer's parents attended the session with the practitioner and reported that Jennifer seemed obsessed with concerns about dying. When asked about any experiences their daughter had had with death, they related that 4 months previously Jennifer's paternal grandmother had died unexpectedly after a short illness. Although Jennifer had rarely seen her grandmother, who lived several hundred miles away, the family had visited her in the hospital 3 days before she died. Jennifer had been told that her grandmother was very sick. The purpose of their visit was explained to her as a way to "make Grandma feel better." Jennifer's first comment to the grandmother was, "Please feel better, Grandma." She was very concerned when they left the hospital about whether, indeed, they had made her grandmother better.

When her grandmother died, Jennifer seemed unaffected, although very solicitous at times toward her obviously grieving parents. Jennifer and her brother remained with family friends for 4 days while their parents attended the funeral out of town.

During the next 3 months, Jennifer repeatedly asked why her grandmother had died, since Jennifer had tried to make her feel better. Any mention of death, dying, or being sick provoked both specific questions about her grandmother's death and general questions about being dead. Her parents answered her questions in terms of their religious belief of "going to heaven to be with God." They also tried to reassure their daughter that her grandmother had liked Jennifer's visit to the hospital and had been very happy to see her.

Jennifer began to ask if she, her parents, particularly her father, or her brother would ever die. She became tearful and clinging when her parents told her that everyone and everything that is alive will die sometime, but usually not until they are very old. The parents reported spending much time with Jennifer holding her, trying to reassure her about their expectation of a long life together.

The parents also told the practitioner that the nursery schoolteacher had called them about Jennifer's uncontrolled weeping when the class pet hamster had died approximately 2 months after Jennifer's grandmother's death. The teacher remarked that, of all the children in the class, Jennifer had seemed the most perplexed when the dead hamster was replaced with another hamster the next day. Jennifer had then asked the teacher several times if she would get a new grandmother soon.

Both parents thought that they had tried to answer Jennifer's questions with sensitivity and openness but that her continual questions were an irritation to both of them. Her father was particularly affected and sometimes became tearful when Jennifer talked about his mother. Approximately 6 weeks prior to their visit to the practitioner, both parents had told Jennifer that they did not want to discuss death and dying any more, that they had explained it to her as much as they could, and that talking about her grandmother's death made her father sad.

Approximately a month before the parents' visit to the practitioner, Jennifer demanded a night-light and began going into her parents' bedroom once or twice each night "for no reason."

Discussion

The development of the concept of death is a gradual process that is influenced by a wide variety of factors, including the child's cultural and familial environment, cognitive abilities, and past experiences with death.

Although children less than 4 years of age have a very limited concept of death, even the infant can probably sense the anxiety and sorrow felt by parents or other important caregivers who have suffered a loss.

Children younger than 4 consider death a reversible process. Between 5 and 9 years of age, children first develop a fascination with death, which they sometimes think of as a personified being. This fascination gradually gives way to a matter-of-fact interest in the details of death and dead things. By the age of 9 or 10 years, most children understand the logical and biological essentials of death, including its irreversibility. Teenagers appreciate the meaning of death but often do not accept the reality of personal death.

Teaching about death at all age levels is becoming increasingly common. Such instruction can be approached in two ways: formally, through didactic lectures or discussions, or informally, by capitalizing on the many instances of death a child encounters in nature.

Both methods have advantages and disadvantages. The didactic approach allows the instructor, whether teacher or parent, to exert some control over the kind of information that is provided to the child and to handle the topic of death as an intellectual exercise. On the other hand, preschoolers or elementary schoolchildren may not be receptive to such discussions unless they are introduced through a ploy that captures the children's interest, such as a discussion of a story in which the characters provide the experiential background.

Instances of death in nature can provide somewhat less contrived approaches to the subject; however, they run the risk of provoking a strong emotional outburst, especially if the death involves a cherished object such as a pet. However, since pets provide important relationships for children, grieving about and mourning a lost pet allows the child to experience loss, feel sadness, and learn about the irreversibility of death.

• • •

Jennifer, at 4 years, was a normally active, growing, and developing young girl who enjoyed excellent health. Like all members of her nuclear family, she participated in active outdoor living that emphasized health and vigor. She was well liked by her peers and appeared emotionally stable.

Jennifer had gained autonomy over her bodily functions and was beginning to learn to take initiative in her daily activities. We know little about her psychosexual development, although she had probably entered the phallic stage as evidenced by her preferential concerns about her father and his welfare. In addition, the loss of her father's mother may have elicited both overt and subtle ministrations from Jennifer's mother, and Jennifer's solicitous behavior may have reflected imitation of (identification with) her mother.

Cognitively, Jennifer was functioning at the preoperational stage of thinking.

Her perceptions of the world were colored by her inability to think logically, ego-centrism, magical thinking, and animism, artificialism, and participation, among other factors. Although she was extremely verbal in asking questions and demand-ing explanations, the repetitious quality of her inquiries indicated her inability to fully comprehend the answers she was given.

Children, by age 2½ years, are just beginning to grasp the vocabulary of death, using first the word "die" and shortly afterward "live." At 3 years, children expect a worm crushed between strong but uncoordinated fingers to inch along the ground again. They are amazed and incredulous to hear that parents do not have the power to make dead birds fly and make the same request over and over again with other birds, butterflies, and insects.

To a child of 4, death is reversible: being dead at one moment in time does not preclude being alive at another, later time, and "forever" is a day, an hour, or perhaps just a few minutes.

Death in nature surrounds the child and often is inflicted by him, not out of perversity or to fulfill any sadistic impulse, but because he does not know his own strength and because death has no real meaning. Yesterday's crushed worm is for-gotten by tomorrow. The child and his parents neither feel nor display grief, al-though occasionally the child may be asked to be more careful. Unlike maiming a creature, killing the creature is not accompanied by admonitions of "don't hurt." The creature can no longer feel, the deed is done, and the family passes on to another activity.

The death of a person or animal that was loved is often accompanied by little or no personal emotion, especially if it is the child's first experience with death. Most 4-year-olds appear to have the confident expectation that the person or animal will return, much like they have learned to expect—in developing their sense of trust in the predictability of their world—that Mommy or Daddy can go away but will always come back.

Although death may be accompanied by attendance at, or even performance of, an elaborate burial ceremony, the child has a sense that, whereas this is a novel experience for him, others have experienced this before and soon the buried per-son or animal will be back, acting as usual. Even the sight of a cold, lifeless body has no meaning, since this could easily be sleep or "playing dead," a common game among preschoolers and young schoolchildren.

The grief of those around him has an impact on the child, although he may show his distress in unexpected ways. For varying amounts of time, usually mea-sured at most in hours and more often in minutes, the child may shed personal tears or use a subdued voice in imitation of the adults around him. Just as com-monly, however, he may not appear to react at all, the clearest statement the child can make that he does not understand. Regardless of his initial reaction, the child, who has a short attention span, soon returns to his normal daily activities. Disruptions in his routine necessitated by parental unavailability, for example, often result in more disruptive behavior than the event of death. Although his parents or others may view this as selfishness, in reality it is the self-centeredness of egocentrism: a need to meet his own demands on his own time.

Jennifer's interest in death reflected normal behavior for children of this age. The fact that her family had experienced a loss may have made them somewhat more aware of her interest than they might have been otherwise. In addition, however, they had some legitimate concerns that were specific to her experience with her grandmother.

First, Jennifer had visited her grandmother to "make her feel better." Although her parents used this expression to indicate a psychological feeling of well-being, Jennifer interpreted their remark to indicate a physiological well-being. The repeated questions she asked about this particular point indicated that she believed that she had not done her job well, had failed, and was in some way responsible for this event that made her parents sad.

In the context of the "good boy"–"nice girl" orientation of the conventional level of moral reasoning, Jennifer may have been confused. She had been a "nice girl" and had done what her parents had requested, but her efforts had seemed to fail: her grandmother had died, and the event had brought her parents sorrow. Although this is a relatively precocious moral reasoning stage for someone of Jennifer's chronological age, it appears to have been a motivating force for this young girl in this instance.

Second, Jennifer began to get a sense that dying was an unwished-for event that had happened to her father's mother. This naturally led to her concerns about her own immediate family. The desire for security and continuation of the happiness in her life seemed threatened, and she asked for multiple reassurances that loss through death would not befall her. The explanation that everyone dies but usually when they are old may be true, but cannot be completely comforting, since Jennifer has no real concept of number or time.

Third, the death of the classroom hamster could have been used more effectively to give all the children an opportunity to experience a loss through death. Watching a child mourn a pet when replacement seems so simple can be extremely difficult for parents or teachers. However, it is important for children to use this experience to learn how to talk about death and to tolerate loss. A discussion of what to do with the animal's dead body, a burial service, and even disinterment at some future time by the children who want to know what decomposition is are all appropriate. Although a child's interest in death and dead things often appears to border on the morbid, in actuality it represents a straightforward desire to understand what is beyond his comprehension.

Fourth, Jennifer's desire for a night-light and her nightly visits to her parents' room represent the need for reassurance and help in mastering her fears of evil creatures, or personifications of death, who may do her harm. Fear of the dark is common among preschoolers and young schoolchildren, regardless of their experiences with actual death, and may persist for several years.

Defense mechanisms/coping styles/adaptive behaviors

Jennifer was a verbal child who was able to voice her concerns and receive support and explanations from her parents. The fact that she did not fully understand the explanations is probably less important than the fact that her parents displayed physically comforting behaviors, patience, and a willingness to talk together and answer questions as well as they could. The irritation that the parents, especially the father, began to feel after several months of continued questioning is a common parental response. However, instead of merely limiting the amount of time that they would spend on the subject, they made discussions of death taboo. When Jennifer no longer had this verbal outlet, her anxiety and misperceptions about death resulted in some behavioral changes.

For many preschoolchildren, death is equated with sleep (Nagy, 1948). A dark bedroom at night becomes an inviting place for visits from goblins or monsters who may "make them dead." A night-light provides an external defense against such fears.

Jennifer's nightly visits to her parents' room represented her need to make certain that they were safe and alive and to be reassured about her own safety.

Intervention

The practitioner should reassure the parents that Jennifer's interest in death represented a common and completely normal developmental stage. The parents should be encouraged to continue their open discussion about death, but for their own emotional comfort they should limit the amount of time they spend discussing the subject and ask Jennifer to explain as clearly as she can what her specific questions are at a given moment. Answers that are too long or peripheral to the point in which the child is interested are almost never satisfying. Some children and parents can benefit from reading books about death written especially for them (see Suggested Readings).

Jennifer's questions about her grandmother may well recur for several more years. These questions may emerge either unexpectedly or at times when Jennifer is confronted with reminders of her grandmother or other experiences with death.

Although visits to her parents' bedroom should be discouraged through the use of a positive reinforcement program that rewards her for staying in her room, the need for this symptom will also be decreased by further discussion of her concerns about death. The request for a night-light is extremely common among children this age and is actually a good safety precaution in families with young children who toilet alone at night.

Indications for referral

If a child's anxiety about death interferes with his or his parents' daily functioning, the practitioner should consider referral to a mental health specialist. Marked behavioral changes can occur following a death in the family, but these are often related to changes in routine; the absence of the parents, who are out of town; or the emotional unavailability of the parent(s) because of deep mourning. Although the child may be the identified patient, care should be exercised in evaluating the entire family, since the child's behavioral changes may be a reflection of pathological grieving in another family member.

SCHOOL: School phobia

CONCEPTS DISCUSSED: *The special, or "vulnerable" child*
Maternal role change
Working mothers
Mother-child separation anxiety

Robbie was a $3^{8}/_{12}$-year-old boy who had been enrolled in a nursery school for a week when his mother called the practitioner for advice about her son's refusal to go to school.

Data gathering

Past history. Robbie had been the product of an uneventful 36-week pregnancy, labor, and delivery. He had had mild respiratory difficulty requiring oxygen therapy and remained in the hospital for 6 days after birth.

His health since that time had been entirely normal except for a broken arm at age $2^{1}/_{2}$ years when he fell from a treehouse in the backyard while under his mother's supervision.

Although Robbie's motor development had been excellent, his language development had been mildly delayed. At age 2 years, he continued to indicate his wants by whining, gesturing, and, occasionally, single words. It became apparent that his family tended to anticipate his needs, thus decreasing the need for him to use language. The mother had responded well to some suggestions from the practitioner and her nurse clinician, and by $2^{1}/_{2}$ years of age Robbie was consistently using phrases and short sentences. However, he still tended to use behavior rather than words to express himself when upset.

Robbie was daytime toilet trained by age $3^{1}/_{2}$ but continued to wear diapers during the night.

Family history. Robbie was the fourth child and only son of a 38-year-old father who worked as a telephone repairman and a 35-year-old mother who had just begun working as an aide in a local nursing home. Robbie had three sisters, ages 14, 13, and 11 years, all of whom had entered kindergarten uneventfully between 5 and 6 years of age and were average students.

The family's health history was unremarkable except for two miscarriages that his mother had had 5 and 4 years prior to Robbie's conception. According to the practitioner's records, the pregnancy with Robbie was unexpected but not unwanted. Robbie's mother worked as a supermarket cashier until she was 7 months pregnant. At the time of Robbie's birth, his mother had a bilateral tubal ligation. The parents were delighted to have a son.

Robbie was described by the parents during routine well-child care visits to be delightful, outgoing, charming, extremely bright, and very athletic. A slightly different perspective was offered by Robbie's 11-year-old sister, who called her brother "spoiled rotten" and a "monster."

Present history. Robbie was enrolled in the morning nursery school program so that his mother could work part-time. Robbie's mother was not happy about her return to work before her son entered kindergarten, but reported that financial pressures on the family made it absolutely necessary for her to do so. She had hoped that her mother, who lived next door, would baby-sit, especially since she had been the only other adult to stay with Robbie when his parents occasionally went out for an evening. However, the grandmother had recently developed cataracts, and the nursery school arrangement was the only alternative available to the family.

The mother reported that on the first day of school Robbie had screamed and refused to let go of her hand at the classroom door. She took him home. For the remainder of the week his behavior had been the same. Despite the teacher's assurances that Robbie would settle down after his mother left, she was unable to leave him. She admitted feeling very guilty about leaving her son with strangers at such a young age but also expressed some concern about losing her job if she missed work the following week. The mother was extremely concerned about and perplexed by her son's behavior. She said several times, "I never had this trouble with my daughters." She also expressed a concern about an increase in Robbie's tantrum behavior at meals and at bedtime since she had tried to leave him at school.

Discussion

Overt fear of separating from parents (particularly the mother) upon entrance into nursery school or kindergarten is extremely common, particularly in the first-born or last-born child in a given family. Usually, this separation anxiety is shared by the mother. The child's fear of the unknown is an early demonstration of the anxiety that all individuals. including adults, feel in unfamiliar situations or when undertaking new projects. The mother's fears are actually similar. Her anxiety, however, centers on her entrance into a new period of her life, either as a school-child's mother or as a woman with no children at home and the consequent loss of her familiar maternal role.

Sympathetic but firm handling by the teacher and reassurance from the practitioner usually result in a resolution of the problem within a few days.

•   •   •

Robbie, at age $3^8/_{12}$, was an active, healthy child who had grown and developed well despite some early neonatal problems. His language delay was apparently more situational than intrinsic, and he showed marked improvement when his and his family's behavior was modified.

Robbie's family constellation is of particular interest in attempting to explain the episodes at school. As the youngest child by several years, probably the last child his mother would bear, the only son, and a child who had had a mild yet anxiety-provoking illness in infancy, he was a special, or "vulnerable," child to his parents and one who they believed deserved close and constant attention (Green and Solnit, 1964).

The fact that Robbie had sustained an injury while in his mother's presence would tend to make her even more vigilant. Her fear of leaving her son with strangers probably reflected her many concerns about their ability to provide adequate supervision, just as she had been unable to do so, and her mixed feelings at the prospect that they might perform this task better than she had. In addition, Robbie's mother was strongly invested in him and was probably somewhat threatened by the possibility that he might develop a significant relationship with someone else. As a final point, the entrance of her "baby" into school marked the end of a life stage for her that she thought was coming earlier than she really wanted.

The boy, on the other hand, was accustomed to his mother's constant presence and unwilling to give it up. He probably sensed her ambivalence about his entrance into school and responded to her negative feelings by displaying fear of separation.

Robbie's fear of the unknown may have been more extreme than that seen in many children his age because of his almost total lack of experience with adults other than his parents and grandmother. A successful integration of a child into group life appears to depend on transfer of interest from the parents (Oedipal stage) to the community (latency) (A. Freud, 1965). In social learning theory terms, the child needs to move from a totally family-centered orientation to one that includes extrafamilial motivational systems as well. In Robbie's case, this transition had probably not yet taken place.

Defense mechanisms/coping styles/adaptive behaviors

Robbie could sense his mother's ambivalence about sending him to school and reacted to her concerns and fears by being afraid to separate from her. His innate fear of the unknown led to refusal to attend school. Because he frequently used behavior rather than language to express himself, he reverted to tantrums. After observing her child's unhappiness and perceiving herself as the cause of his distress, his mother reacted by withdrawing her demand that he attend school. Multiple daily episodes of tantrum behavior were thus reinforced or rewarded by a return home. Having attained his objective, Robbie began using these behaviors in other phases of family living as well.

Intervention

As in all forms of **school phobia,** the first object of treatment is to get the child to attend school regularly. The prognosis for early school phobia is excellent, and the symptom is usually resolved after a few days of consistent separation. It is not unusual, however, for school phobia to recur transiently in subsequent grades in elementary school or upon entrance into a new school. Many children with the more severe form of school phobia found during adolescence have a history of early school phobia or separation difficulties in other settings.

Management usually focuses on supporting the mother, with the help of the father, if necessary, to leave her child regardless of his emotional state. Allowing her to vent her concerns about the potential inadequacy of surrogate caregivers and then offering reassurances about specific areas of misgiving are also helpful. It is appropriate to suggest that the mother and teacher meet together. The mother can then give the teacher information about the way she handles the child at home and also learn about the rules of the school and how children tend to adapt quickly to their new routine. If the mother believes that the teacher is allying with her rather than displacing her, the mother will feel more comfortable. Very rarely, it may be necessary for the practitioner to be present at such a meeting as a mediator or facilitator.

Follow-up with the mother by telephone after the child's first day in school can help to reinforce her behavior and give her support to continue the separation process.

Indications for referral

Referral for treatment of early school phobia as a single symptom is, for all practical purposes, never necessary. If, however, the mother expresses concern about her difficulties with separating in general or her anxiety over a changed maternal role, she might benefit from some counseling that focuses on her as a person. If the child's behavior upon entering school is a symptom of major behavioral problems, particularly those stemming from poor limit setting, parent counseling that focuses on discipline as a method of instruction or guidance, rather than punishment, may be helpful.

ILLNESS: Surgery

CONCEPTS DISCUSSED: *Hospitalization*
Preparation for surgery (parents and child)
Castration anxiety

Jason was a $4^{10}/_{12}$-year-old boy who was admitted to the hospital the afternoon before he was scheduled for surgical repair of an inguinal hernia.

Data gathering

Past history. Jason had been in good health all his life and had developed normally. The hernia had been discovered by his father while bathing Jason a month before.

Family history. Jason was the middle child and only son of a 31-year-old father who worked as a bus driver and a 29-year-old mother who worked as a homemaker. Jason's 7- and 2-year-old sisters were both well.

Prehospital course. Jason had been examined by his physician and the consulting surgeon within 2 weeks of the discovery of his hernia. Jason and his parents had been given several explanations of the defect and the proposed surgery. Prior to his admission, Jason and his parents were invited to a prehospitalization party in the pediatric unit for children from 3 to 10 years of age so that they could become familiar with the ward setting and hospital equipment. They were unable to attend because of a conflict in the father's work schedule and the mother's unwillingness to take Jason by herself.

Hospital course. Upon admission, Jason and his parents were introduced to the nurse who would be his nursing care coordinator during his hospitalization. Jason and his parents seemed somewhat apprehensive; it soon became clear that they had almost no experience with hospitals and were unsure about how the surgical procedure would be performed. Although reluctant to say so at first, the father finally admitted his concern that his son would be sterile after surgery, a question he had been unable to ask either of the physicians who had examined Jason.

The nurse invited the parents to join Jason and her while she explained hospital routine and the surgical procedure to their son. Jason was given a male doll wearing hospital pajamas.

NURSE: Jason, this doll is named Randy, and he's wearing special hospital pajamas. All the children who are going to stay here all night wear pajamas just like these.

I'm going to show you some of the things that we use here in the hospital. Here's a blood pressure cuff, a thermometer, and a stethoscope. Your mom or dad has probably taken your temperature at home, and I'm sure your doctor has listened to your heart, so I bet you know all about some of these already. Let's listen to Randy's heart. *(Demonstration.)*

Tomorrow morning, we're going to give you an injection, or shot, to help you relax. This is a syringe and needle made for Randy. Let's give him a shot to help him relax and sleep before his operation.

JASON: *(Slowly takes the syringe and after several attempts manages to fill it with water.)*

NURSE: Very good, Jason. Now you tell Randy that he can say "ouch" as loud as he wants, but he needs to stay very still. I'll hold his leg to help him not move, and I'll say ouch as you give him the shot.

JASON: *(Gives the injection carefully and slowly, looking to his parents for reassurance.)*

NURSE: That's right. Do you have any questions, Jason?

JASON: *(Shakes his head "no.")*

NURSE: Now that Randy is all relaxed, let's put this special mask over his face to help him breathe. You might want to put one on, too, just to see how it feels.

JASON: *(Puts mask on willingly and seems to begin enjoying himself.)*

NURSE: The doctor is going to do a special operation on you, Jason, to fix your hernia. A hernia is a loose muscle. No one knows exactly why some children have loose muscles. Sometimes children wonder if they did something wrong to make the muscle loose. You may have wondered the same thing. But nothing you or anyone else did made your muscle loose.

I bet you have lots of muscles in your body. Can you show me one?

JASON: *(Flexes his biceps.)*

NURSE: Very good! Now, your loose muscle is in your groin—that's between your tummy and your leg. Let's look at Randy's groin. I want to show you that Randy's penis is near his groin. Sometimes, boys worry that the doctor might hurt their penis. But this is a special operation where that won't happen. Put a crayon mark on Randy where his groin is and where the doctor will be doing the operation.

JASON: *(Performs this task easily.)*

NURSE: When the doctor does the operation, he makes a small opening called an incision in your skin, and underneath is the loose muscle. He takes some thread like the thread your mother uses at home to sew buttons and sews the muscle to make it tighter and stronger. Then he sews up the hole in your skin or puts pieces of tape over it. Would you like to put some tape on Randy?

JASON: Oh, yes, please.

NURSE: When the operation is all over, Jason, and you feel all rested, you can go home and show your sisters where you had *your* operation, if you want to.

Now, Jason, I'm going to leave Randy with you while I do some other work. I'll be back in about 15 minutes, and, if you or your mom or dad have any questions, I'll answer them. I'll also tell you more about your room and all the things in it.

Discussion

Even minor, elective surgical procedures can provoke a great deal of anxiety in parents and children alike. Parents who are unfamiliar with hospital routine and who have received explanations that they did not adequately understand often arrive at the hospital with either no clear perception whatsoever or a variety of fantasies about what a particular procedure entails. Specific, concrete information, especially if reinforced visually, can allay anxiety and help the child and parents cope more effectively with the hospital experience.

Children who think that they *do not* have an adequate understanding of why they are in the hospital, what procedure will be performed, or what behavior is expected of them can have terrifying experiences during either the induction or reentry phases of anesthesia. These can result in long-term behavioral changes (Levy, 1945; Eckenhoff, 1953; Jackson et al., 1953). To minimize such psychological trauma, most pediatric surgeons stress the need for careful and well-timed explanations that begin at least a few days before surgery is scheduled (Mellish, 1969).

• • •

Jason was a basically healthy child who had an asymptomatic condition requiring hospitalization and surgery. The fact that he was subjectively well and had a noticeable but not prominent groin asymmetry renders explanations that include "making him feel better" inapplicable. Thus, he may require slightly more technical detail about the reasons for hospitalization than might a child who is symptomatic.

Jason was in the preoperational stage of thinking as defined by Piaget. He could not draw logical conclusions or inferences, and his ability to understand new situations was limited by the similarity that his past experiences bore to his present situation. For a child who has never been sick and who has never experienced hospitalization, explanations must be basic and should also be focused on objects that he can touch or otherwise experience through his senses.

Because of his egocentrism and magical thinking, Jason may think that he was in some way responsible for his hernia, which to him may represent a "punishment" for some real or imagined disobedience. Although he may not be able or willing to express this thought, it should be presented as a thought common among children, and he should be offered reassurance.

Although a herniorrhaphy does not involve the genitalia, it involves the general genital region. A boy Jason's age may well have some castration anxiety. Again, direct questioning by an unfamiliar person may not elicit such concerns. Thus, mentioning this worry as one that many boys have, then offering reassurance, is a good approach to this sensitive topic. In Jason's case, actual castration might actually be a concern to him as it was to his father. However, in a broader sense, fear of bodily harm or intrusion, regardless of the specific site, is a common theme among children Jason's age, who are just beginning to develop a sense of their bodies as one measure of who they are. They are also beginning to develop a sense of privacy and may find it particularly difficult to discuss their bodily concerns.

Last, talking with Jason about going home and showing his incision to his sisters is a way of reassuring him that his stay in the hospital is limited and that he will eventually return to his normal routine.

Defense mechanisms/coping styles/adaptive behaviors

Regression, refusal to participate in medical procedures or activities of daily living (eating, toileting, bathing), withdrawal, or acting-out behaviors are all available to children as ways of coping with hospitalization. Prior knowledge of coming events, doll play, and role rehearsal with explanations of expected behavior are vehicles available to the child for overcoming anxiety, establishing trust, and co-operating effectively.

Intervention

The pediatrically oriented nurse who admitted Jason excellently prepared him for the experiences he would have in the hospital. When all members of the team (physician, surgeon, anesthesiologist, and nurse) are aware of the type and extent of the explanations each offers, reinforcement in the same or similar language becomes possible and adds to the child's understanding of hospitalization and surgical procedure. Many pediatric nursing services maintain a handbook of age-appropriate explanations about common surgical procedures. Physician familiarity with these guidelines can help ensure accuracy and similarity of the explanations from different professionals.

The nurse's sensitivity to the parents' unfamiliarity with hospital routine and the planned surgery led her to include them in her explanations to the child. Such a tactic ensures that all family members have received the same information. Leaving the boy alone with the doll in his parents' presence allowed the family to discuss particular points and formulate questions that did not arise during the explanation.

Last, the nurse did not give all of the instructions and information to the patient and family at one time. Instead, she chose to focus first on the surgical procedure and to reserve information about the child's room (e.g., use of the toilet or bedpan, eating, and bathing) for some time afterward. The exact order in which information is given is probably not as important as trying to make use of the setting or any spontaneous questions to lead naturally into a discussion of a particular point. In this instance, the child's and parents' anxiety, which led to feelings that they had no understanding of the surgical procedure, made this a reasonable place to begin. Once the child knows why he is in the hospital, explanations about what he can and cannot do while there will make more sense.

Indications for referral

Children who have had particularly long, complicated, or serious hospitalizations in the past may be extremely fearful of readmission. In most instances, informal visits to the hospital during periods of health serve to lessen the child's anxiety and help him to establish friendship relationships with ward personnel, especially among nursing and activities staffs. In rare cases, referral to a mental health specialist is indicated if the child's anxiety prevents such informal visits prior to hospitalization or leads to incapacitating fears in other areas of medical care.

Chapter 7 · The child from 5 to 7 years (early school age)

Physiological growth and development

MALES AND FEMALES: Relatively quiescent stage of slow, progressive physical growth. Gross motor skills acquired much more readily than fine motor skills.

Psychological growth and development

FREUD   Transitional phase: phallic stage → latency

ERIKSON   Transitional phase: initiative vs. guilt → industry vs. inferiority

PIAGET   Transitional phase: preoperational period → concrete operational period

KOHLBERG   Transitional phase: preconventional level → conventional level

SEARS   Transitional phase: family-centered → extrafamilial learning

Chapter 7

The child from 5 to 7 years (early school age)

FAMILY: Divorce

CONCEPTS DISCUSSED: *Enuresis*
Working mother
Remarriage
Effects of father absence
Bibliotherapy

Kevin was a 5½-year-old kindergarten student whose mother called the practitioner regarding her son's 4-month history of intermittent enuresis.

Data gathering

Past history. Kevin had enjoyed excellent health throughout his life. His growth and development had been entirely normal. He had been fully toilet trained at 2½ years of age and had had no "accidents" since his third birthday until the onset of his present symptoms.

Family history. Kevin was the only child of a 24-year-old father who was an insurance agent and a 24-year-old mother who worked as a store clerk.

Kevin's parents had been high school sweethearts. After graduation from high school, his father entered the local community college. During the fall of that year, Kevin's mother, who was a senior in high school, became pregnant, and the respective families insisted on an immediate marriage. Kevin's father left school for a semester to work. When Kevin was 2 months old, his mother began working part-time, and his father returned to school and worked weekends, evenings, and during the summers. The couple cared for Kevin between them, but also received some baby-sitting assistance from their families. When Kevin was 3 years old, he was enrolled in a day-care center, and his mother began working full-time.

According to Kevin's mother, the couple argued constantly. When Kevin was almost 4, his father completed college and immediately moved out of the home into a nearby apartment. A year later, the couple was formally divorced.

During the period of separation and divorce, Kevin spent one 3-day weekend a month with his father. Because Kevin's mother and father would not speak to each other, Kevin opened the door for his father when he came to pick him up and was dropped off in front of the house where he and his mother lived when he was returned home.

The divorce proceeding was bitter. A month after the divorce was final, Kevin's father remarried. His new wife had a 4-year-old son. Kevin had met the woman and her son on two occasions prior to the marriage when they were introduced as "Daddy's friends." They all seemed to get along well together during these two meetings.

On the day of his father's remarriage, 5 months prior to his visit to the practitioner, Kevin, who had appeared excited about the event, refused to go to the wedding "because Mommy's not going."

Kevin's father moved his new family into a two-bedroom house in the suburbs, and Kevin resumed his monthly visits. He slept in a bunk bed in his "brother's" room. For 2 or 3 days prior to visits with his father, Kevin was active, boisterous, and talked incessantly about his coming weekend and all the activities (especially sports-related events) his father had planned for him. His mother had a great deal of difficulty controlling Kevin and reported many episodes of spanking, dismissal to his room, and withholding of privileges.

For several days after his visits, Kevin would be withdrawn and would refuse to talk about his weekend with his father. He often crept into his mother's bed after wetting his own. After this period, Kevin would become "himself" again: outgoing, affectionate toward his mother, and helpful around the house. However, he often questioned his mother about why she had to work and told her that he liked his father better than her because they "did" lots of things together. In addition, he asked what he had done to make Daddy leave and when his mother and his father would get married again. The mother found these questions and comments irritating and frustrating and usually refused to discuss them.

Discussion

Divorce is becoming an increasingly common occurence in our society. In 1976, there were 2,133,000 marriages and 1,077,000 divorces, resulting in a divorce rate that was approximately 50% of the marriage rate. More than 60% of all divorces involved one or more children (Hetherington, Cox, and Cox, 1978). In addition, divorce is twice as common in the teenage population as in the older population (National Center for Health Statistics, 1974).

Most divorces are preceded by a period of overt or covert hostility within the family. In some situations, divorce may actually be a constructive solution to destructive family functioning. However, the transitional or "family restructuring phase" following divorce can be extremely stressful: family members must assume new roles, discord and turmoil are prominent, and the time and energy for mutual support are often lacking.

All children of divorce consider themselves or their actions pivotal factors in the breakup of their parents' marriage regardless of whether their presence or activities contributed directly to the disintegration of the nuclear family. The wish for the reunion of the biological parents is very strong and often persists into adolescence.

The long-term effects of father absence on a male child have been investigated. The characteristics of the father-son relationship before separation, the age of the child at the time of separation, the duration of the absence, the availability of father surrogates, and the behavior of the mother, among other factors, seem to influence a boy's personality development (Biller, 1970).

Father-absent boys appear to be more feminine, that is, more dependent and less aggressive, than father-present boys, especially if the child was younger than 4 years of age at the time of separation (Hetherington, 1966). However, neither direct sex-role preferences (favorite games or toys) nor teachers' ratings of sex-role adoption appear to be significantly affected (Biller, 1968).

Father absence appears to be positively correlated with aggressive acting-out or antisocial behavior, perhaps as a reaction formation or an overcompensation for the more feminine type of passive behaviors that boys have learned from their mothers (Biller, 1970).

Cognitively, boys from father-absent homes tend to have a feminine score pattern on intelligence tests, which reflects a global-conceptual rather than an analytical-conceptual style of thinking (Carlsmith, 1964).

The effects of fatherless homes on the subsequent development of girls appear to be somewhat more varied and less predictable than those described for boys (Kestenbaum and Stone, 1976). However, the emotional adjustment of such girls to mature heterosexual relationships may depend on the degree to which their Oedipus complex was resolved.

Fathers who maintain contact with their children appear to have an impact on their children's development that is proportional to their involvement. However, even highly involved noncustodial fathers exert less influence on their children than do custodial mothers (Hetherington, Cox, and Cox, 1978).

• • •

Kevin, at age 5½ years, was in a period of relatively slow, but constant, physical growth. However, his activity level was high, and his need for exploration of his environment and interaction with his peers great. His gross motor coordination was becoming increasingly good and was reinforced by active games. A beginning interest in organized sports, despite a poor understanding of the rules of the game, was appropriate to his developmental age.

Cognitively, Kevin was in the preoperational, or prelogical, stage of thinking as defined by Piaget. Although he was able to use instrumental language fairly well as a means of describing objects or his experiences, his ability to discuss his emotions or feelings was limited. In addition, his thought processes were influenced by egocentrism and magical thinking, two particularly important factors in his understanding—or lack of understanding—of his parents' divorce. For example, his egocentrism made him think that he or his behavior was in some way central to and therefore responsible for the divorce of his parents. He could not understand that the divorce was the result of their (adult) problem and not his. This poor understanding was evident from his repeated questions to his mother about what he had done to make his father leave: that is, his father's absence must be "punishment" for Kevin's disobedience.

Magical thinking, the equation of thought and fantasy with action, can be a particularly potent factor in the child's thinking about the event of divorce when the father of a boy in the Oedipal stage of development leaves the family. For example, according to Freudian theory, Kevin, at about age 4, would be competitive with his father for the affection and attention of his mother. It is not unusual for a son at this age to say to his mother, "I wish you and I could stay together at home forever. Daddy could stay at his office." Indeed, if Daddy "stays at his office" by moving out of the home, the child, because of his magical thinking, feels a great sense of responsibility for causing the separation.

Boys at this age, however, also have affection for their fathers and admire and emulate them. Thus, children are attached to both parents. When the crisis of divorce arises, children often feel that they are placed in a position of having to choose between their parents. Indeed, if the child is placed with one parent, even if by court order and not his stated wish, he may think this represents a personal desertion of the other parent. Children may be quick to indicate why they like one parent more than the other under certain circumstances or for a particular (usually material) reason, just as Kevin told his mother that he liked his father better because they "did" things; however, their love and need for each of their parents is very strong.

Defense mechanisms/coping styles/adaptive behaviors

Kevin's ability to express his emotions and concerns verbally was limited. Thus, in attempting to deal with what in reality was beyond his comprehension, his behavior changed.

Interestingly, during his parents' separation Kevin displayed few, if any, signs of distress. It can be hypothesized that the family routine may not have been changed substantially at that time, since his father was probably relatively unavailable while he was in college and working part-time as well. Indeed, family turmoil may have occurred less often during that year, particularly if Kevin's mother anticipated that the divorce would not become final.

During the divorce proceeding, which was acrimonious, Kevin's mother's negative feelings about her husband were heightened. The father's early remarriage probably contributed to a sustained level of bitterness during the succeeding few months.

Kevin's response to his father's wedding represented a common reaction. The boy probably thought that his biological parents were going to be reunited. He probably also thought that any discussion of families living together referred to him, his mother, and his father. Although it is apparent from his questions during later months that he did not really understand what marriage meant, it is certain that his fantasy (the reunion of his biological nuclear family) was not being fulfilled.

Kevin's behavior around the time of his visits to his father and his new family demonstrates the boy's ambivalence about the situation. Before visits, he was active, boisterous, and boastful to his mother about the plans he and his father had made. Part of Kevin's behavior can be explained as a rejection of his mother at the same time he thought that she was rejecting him by sending him away. This negative attention-seeking behavior could be interpreted as a reaction to his anxiety about his heightened feelings of dependency on his mother.

We have no information about Kevin's visits to his father, but it would not be unusual for him to make many comparisons between the two homes and between his relationship and that of his "brother" to his father. He might also talk incessantly about his mother as a way of maintaining contact with her, or he might not talk about her at all, for fear of being rejected by his father.

When Kevin returned home, he tried to compensate for his perception that he had betrayed his mother by having fun with his father. To feel more comfortable in displaying his dependency on his mother, it was necessary for him to regress in his behavior; thus, he became enuretic.

Intervention

Management should focus on at least two areas: helping Kevin to understand why his parents became divorced and what that means in terms of his past, current, and future relationship with each of them and helping him to modulate his behavior, which, at present, is his only method of self-expression.

Kevin's mother needs support and direction to present the realities of the divorce to her son as objectively as possible. Some parents choose to discuss strategies beforehand with a physician, nurse practitioner, or social worker and then present the information privately to their child later. Other parents prefer to have the initial discussion with their child in the presence of a professional who can help with the explanation and provide cues for further discussion.

Explanations need to be short and focused on the questions or areas of concern to a given child. Some children, however, seem unable to form questions. Gentle probings that begin with "Some children think . . ." or "Some children worry about . . ." can often provide leads about topics needing explanation. For example, "Some children think that it's their fault their parents got divorced. I don't know if you've thought about it, but I know that your daddy's going away had nothing to do with you." Putting the concern into words and then providing reassurance regardless of whether the child acknowledges the concern as his own can be very helpful.

The child can also be helped to form coping strategies by reading or having read to him books about children who have experienced divorce. Talking about the storybook children's feelings and how they handled them and then helping the child to verbalize his emotions is termed "bibliotherapy." For many families, such an approach through a third person, the storybook character, provides an excellent vehicle for discussion of their own feelings. In addition, some children of divorce often feel embarrassed or singled out by their situation and less worthy than their peers who have an intact family. It is important for them to know that other children have divorced parents and that it is a subject which can be discussed openly.

Behavioral problems often disappear as the child becomes less anxious. Positive reinforcement for acceptable behavior can hasten these changes. Kevin's enuresis was a manifestation of his dependency on his mother. Reassurance about her love for him, as well as a positive reward system for nights that he remained dry and in his bed, would be appropriate.

If possible, both biological parents should be seen by the practitioner so that their explanations and approaches to the child will be similar and therefore reinforcing. It may not be possible to see the couple together for months or even years after the divorce because of their unresolved feelings about each other. However, some agreement about consistency of approach and mutual compromise should be reached even if it is mediated only through the professional.

Indications for referral

Family disruption and turmoil following divorce are anxiety provoking for the child and may influence the child's abilities to function in a variety of settings, including those at school and with his peers. If concern exists that true emotional disturbance rather than response to external situational stresses is contributing significantly to the child's aberrant behavior, referral to a mental health professional is warranted. Concurrent parent counseling or individual therapy, at least for the custodial parent, may also be beneficial.

SCHOOL: School readiness

CONCEPTS DISCUSSED: *Social maturity*
Cognitive readiness
Male and female differences in school readiness

Tony was a 5½-year-old boy whose mother called the practitioner in late September for advice about continuing her son in kindergarten.

Data gathering

Past history. Tony's general health was excellent, and his preschool physical examination had been completely normal. He had grown consistently along the twenty-fifth percentile for height and weight since birth. He had walked at 9 months and was always active and adept at gross motor activities. He was reliably toilet trained by 4 years of age.

Family history. Tony was the second child of a 33-year-old carpenter, who worked for his father, and a 30-year-old homemaker. Tony's 7$\frac{1}{2}$-year-old sister was in the second grade where she was doing well. Whereas Tony was physically active and seldom sat still long enough to listen to bedtime stories, draw, or even watch television, his sister was quiet and had always preferred sedentary activities like playing with dolls and coloring. She had learned to read a few words before entering kindergarten.

School. Tony's mother had enrolled him in kindergarten the previous May. During the registration procedure, one of the school personnel noticed that Tony's birthday fell precisely on the cutoff date for admission and approached his mother about whether she believed that her son was ready for school. Tony's mother had been advised to seek counsel from her physician about Tony's school readiness, but had elected not to do so primarily because her daughter had done well despite being young for her class.

Tony had gone willingly to school. However, from the first day, he had appeared unhappy. He mentioned that all of the children were bigger than he was and picked on him. He also told his mother that they knew about more things than he did and that some of the children could tell time and tie their shoelaces. He had attempted both of these activities, but had not been successful.

Tony had had two episodes of enuresis, followed by uncontrolled crying at school. He had been very aggressive, loud, and strong-willed at home both of the afternoons after wetting his pants.

Tony's mother had spoken with the kindergarten teacher the evening before her call to the practitioner. The teacher had expressed her feeling that Tony was significantly less mature than the other children in class and would benefit from waiting another year before entering school. Tony's mother was not receptive to the idea of removing her son from school and again mentioned that her daughter had been young for her class but was doing well.

Peers. Tony played with several neighborhood friends, all of whom were a year or more younger than he was. He had always been very active and somewhat aggressive in his play and generally got his way. His play after school had become significantly more aggressive since school began, and Tony's mother had received daily telephone calls from her neighbors about Tony's fighting with other children.

Discussion

The timing of entrance into school can have a significant impact on the child's entire educational career and his perception of himself as a worthwhile, contributing member of society.

One of the aims of education is to continue and help complete the socialization process, which begins in the home. Organized education is the tool that our society uses to civilize (transmit knowledge, beliefs, customs, and skills to) its young members.

To benefit from formal education, the student must already have achieved a certain level of skill in interpersonal relationships and have assimilated or be ready to assimilate certain factual knowledge. In addition, he must have the capability to master new forms of expression and communication through a learning process that requires attention, as well as the fine motor and perceptual skills that will allow him to participate successfully in the classroom, thus deriving a sense of achievement from his activities.

If a child enters school before he is cognitively and socially prepared, he may experience consistent failure leading to insecurity and unhappiness. Such feelings make him intolerant of frustration and may eventually lead to apathy or total withdrawal from school.

Parents are often unaware of their child's particular strengths and weaknesses. They may perceive their child's early school failure as the fault of the system rather than as a reflection of the child's need for greater maturity before assuming the student role.

• • •

Tony was an active boy whose early mastery of gross motor tasks gave him little time to master sedentary activities that demand sustained attention and fine motor coordination. Tony's relatively late toilet training could be an indication of some delay in learning to anticipate needs or to follow routine. Tony's differential development in these several areas serves as a good demonstration of the variable rates at which a given child develops certain skills.

Tony's behavior is in marked contrast to that of his sister, who was described as a quiet child who demonstrated excellent abilities in tasks that require fine motor coordination and concentration. The differences between these two siblings could reflect a number of factors, including sex and birth order.

Gender differences in rate of development are well known. Tony's mother assumed her son would adjust well to kindergarten because her daughter had done so. However, the earlier maturation of girls in almost all spheres of physiological and psychological development has become a widely accepted fact.

Ordinal position within the family can influence development, although the effect is unpredictable. For example, some authorities hypothesize that the older child is likely to be more verbal (and thus more successful in the classroom) because of greater language stimulation from adult company. Nonfirstborn children are often thought to be more physically active because of the desire to compete with, and the need to protect themselves from, the older sibling. These are not clear-cut findings. For example, it can be argued that higher birth order can either delay language acquisition because of the anticipation of needs or "talking for" by the older child or stimulate language acquisition through imitation.

To complicate matters, Tony was at the stage of developing his initiative and overcoming his sense of guilt when his attempts to try new experiences or devise plans of action conflicted with the actions and plans of others. Because this was a relatively new stage for him, his actions could be easily influenced or suppressed by the more experienced children in his classroom. The leadership role that Tony had earned in his neighborhood was seriously challenged in his school setting. Constant put-downs could ultimately result in loss of self-esteem and an unwillingness to take the initiative in any new circumstance.

Defense mechanisms/coping styles/adaptive behaviors

Tony was faced with several stresses in the classroom. The first was socialization with children whom he perceived as much larger and stronger than he: an unusual situation for Tony, who generally played with younger children. In addition, Tony perceived himself as cognitively less able than his classmates.

Tony tried to cope with the stresses. First, he asserted himself physically. When this behavior failed to achieve his desired goal, he regressed and became enuretic and tearful in the classroom.

To reassure himself about his physical strength and leadership position, Tony became more aggressive with his younger playmates. He also tried to undo his embarrassment about his enuresis by asserting his will at home in the safety of a familiar environment.

If families approach a health care professional for advice in anticipation of school registration, they can be directed to several extremely helpful parent-oriented screening tests for school readiness. As an example, the *School Readiness Survey* (Jordan and Massey, 1969) is often used by school and medical personnel to advise parents about the suitability of school enrollment for children between 4 and 6 years of age. Ideally, such a screening test should be administered several months before school begins. If a child appears to be completely unprepared for the classroom, enrollment should be delayed. If a child tests in the borderline category, these results can be used to help parents focus their informal daily living teaching on certain areas.

Since Tony had already been enrolled, the practitioner should suggest that the mother request an evaluation by the school psychologist as soon as possible. Removal of the child from the kindergarten setting is probably less traumatic than having the child repeat a grade later in his school career. Just as important, however, is the need for a prompt decision early in the year so that the child's painful memories of entrance to school and his behavioral disruptions at home will not have permanent negative consequences.

An educational evaluation will be helpful to the parents by defining specific areas of cognitive weakness. In addition, the formality of testing followed by an interpretive conference will add some objectivity to what was becoming an emotionally laden situation between the teacher and the mother.

Indications for referral

Most children can be prepared for successful entrance into kindergarten through home training and instruction. Placement in a nursery or preschool, however, may be appropriate for children whose home environment is emotionally or educationally impoverished or who have little or no access to peers.

The need for parent education in the principles of child development should be assessed in all families. Referral to a parent training program, in conjunction with or separate from a school enrollment for the child, should be made as indicated.

ILLNESS: Sudden accidental death

CONCEPTS DISCUSSED: *Grief and mourning*
Bereavement counseling
Effects of sibling death
The "replacement" child
Immigration and social isolation
Effective communication across language barriers

Theresa, a $6^{1}/_{2}$-year-old first grader, was struck by a car while riding her new bicycle in front of her house in the presence of her mother and sister. Despite attempts to resuscitate her by her mother and father and ambulance personnel, Theresa was pronounced dead at the scene of the accident. The driver of the car was not charged.

Data gathering

Past history. Theresa had been completely well and had developed normally.

Family history. Theresa had been the older daughter of a 45-year-old grocery store operator and a 28-year-old homemaker. Theresa's mother was 6 months pregnant at the time of the accident. Theresa's sister was 3 years old.

Both parents were immigrants to America. Theresa's father had come to the United States with his family when he was 15 years old. After almost 20 years in this country, he had been able to purchase the grocery store that he currently operated. When he was 36 years old, his engagement to his wife had been arranged, and she had immigrated to America to be married. Whereas Theresa's father spoke English quite well, her mother spoke only broken English and used her native language at home and within the neighborhood.

The father maintained close contact with members of his extended family who lived nearby. He was active in a number of ethnic and religious organizations. His wife, on the other hand, had not seen any of her family since her immigration. She was relatively close to her husband's family, but obviously missed the support of her parents and siblings. She had few personal friends. Although religiously devout, she was not active in church affairs and tended to concentrate all her time and energy on caring for her husband and children.

School. Theresa had attended a parochial school where she was considered an extremely polite and talented student.

Peers. Although Theresa had lived in a neighborhood with many children, including a large number of cousins, she had had a close, almost maternal relationship with her younger sister. They often played together in preference to playing with others.

Discussion

Approximately half of all deaths of children between 1 and 14 years of age are the result of injuries. In 1976, it was estimated that accidents claimed the lives of about 12,000 children (Woolsey, Thornton, and Friedman, 1978). The sudden accidental death of a child often denies the family access to many of the hospital- or chronic care facility–based support systems that have been developed to help families cope with child death. Support for such families thus comes almost entirely from the community or from professionals who are actively sought by the family at the suggestion or direction of the community.

The role of the practitioner in instances of sudden death can take many forms, among which are (1) "the initiator," who actively offers and provides anticipatory bereavement counseling; (2) "the consultant," who provides bereavement counseling after the family has developed and identified symptoms or concerns in another member; and (3) "the casual participant," who provides bereavement counseling in conjunction with treatment of nonrelated illness or health maintenance in other family members.

The type of intervention provided by a particular practitioner will depend upon his prior knowledge of and interactions with the family, including his understanding of other support systems available to them, his expectations about future contact (the presence or absence of family members who will remain in his care), and his comfort in discussing the issues of grief and mourning.

• • •

Theresa's family presents some unique, although not uncommon, problems when considering what kinds of suggestions or interventions might be appropriate in helping them to cope with the death of their older daughter.

The father. As a self-made man approaching middle age, Theresa's father had a history of being a hard worker who upheld many of the traditions of his particular foreign upbringing. He was the dominant family member in community affairs and had assimilated well into his new environment. He expected his wife to assume the majority, if not all, of the child care and housekeeping responsibilities. There is a sense that he was continuing his drive for greater financial security and probably took great pride in his own accomplishments and those of his family, especially his children.

His social and religious affiliations may provide him with an adequate support system. On the other hand, he may become embittered and possibly renounce his religion, in particular (Hemenway, 1978).

The mother. Theresa's mother is faced with a number of situational circumstances that may impact negatively on her ability to cope with her daughter's death. The language barrier may make it difficult for her to adequately communicate with and understand community authorities who will be involved in reporting and investigating Theresa's death. The fact that she has few, if any, supports of her own, except as derived from her husband's family, puts her in a vulnerable position for blame and recrimination, since she was supervising her daughter at the time of the accident. Such unilateral parental responsibility can lead to overwhelming guilt. In addition, her pregnancy has changed her usual hormonal balance and may affect her coping abilities. Last, if she experiences a severe grief reaction (including anorexia and insomnia), it may adversely affect her unborn child.

Because of her probable guilt, her possible feelings of emotional isolation from her husband and his family, and the unavailability of a counterbalancing support system from her own family, Theresa's mother may become overprotective toward and smothering of her younger daughter.

The younger sister. At 3 years of age, Theresa's sister was old enough to have some perception of the accident and will certainly be able to feel, if not understand, the family's bereavement. Since she is approaching the age when children develop night terrors, it would not be unusual for her to have difficulty sleeping. In addition, she may develop an intense need for closeness and protection at a time when her parents may be least able to provide her with such attention. This need may be particularly strong for this child, since her older sister had been one of her closest companions. Her mother's possible overprotectiveness and the child's memory of the accident may make her phobic about playing outdoors, crossing the street, or riding a tricycle or bicycle. It will probably heighten her awareness about death for the rest of her life (L. A. Szybist, 1978).

Since, at age 3, Theresa's sister has no real concept of death, only a rudimentary concept of time and a short attention span, her overall reaction to her sister's death may alternate between blasé acceptance and apparent unconcern and repeated questions about the accident and the whereabouts of her sister and demands that Theresa return home to play with her.

The unborn child. Parents who are intensely grieving the loss of a child often have an overwhelming desire to replace the dead child with an infant. This replacement baby may bear the same or a very similar name and will often be expected to fulfill the dreams that the parents had for their dead child (C. Szybist, 1976). Although many of the potential hazards must be considered, Theresa's unborn sibling, at 6 months gestation, might be in a somewhat less vulnerable position in this family. Attachment to the unborn child probably began as soon as the parents discovered the pregnancy. The fetus may have been given an affectionate name as soon as quickening was felt. Because Theresa had probably related to the unborn child and made plans for the baby with her parents, their identification of the infant with Theresa may be less pronounced than it would be in a family in which pregnancy is planned after the death to substitute an infant for the lost child.

Intervention

Whatever role the practitioner elects to play in helping this family cope with Theresa's death, he must assess the particular problems likely to be faced by each member. The father's recrimination, the mother's guilt and isolation, the sister's frightening experience and cognitive inability to understand death, and the potential for the infant to be perceived as a replacement child all need attention. As in all families who have lost a child, regardless of setting or duration of illness or injury, the extended family, religious support systems, friendship groups, and community sympathy contribute to the resolution of grief. The physician, because of professional experience and expertise, can provide a great deal of support and consultation to the entire family by interpreting their feelings, clarifying points of view, helping the family to explain death to other children, and giving reassurance about the somatic and psychological symptoms of grief.

Outreach contact with suddenly bereaved families has been recommended within 2 to 3 days and again within 2 to 3 months and near holidays and anniversaries, at least during the first year after the death (Woolsey, Thornton, and Friedman, 1978).

Indications for referral

Grief is a highly individualized process manifested by a variety of physical and emotional responses including insomnia, anorexia, and auditory and visual hallucination about the dead person. At times, the feelings and bodily sensations experienced in mourning can lead bereaved individuals to express the fear that they are "going crazy." However, although the term "pathological grief" is used frequently, it is, as yet, a poorly defined entity. We actually know very little about normal grieving; widely varying and culture-specific rituals and expectations for the bereaved, which can exert such profound effects on the mourning process, must be considered in any assessment of the relative health of individual or family functioning after a death.

One of the only invariable indications for referral to a mental health specialist is a request by a bereaved individual for such a referral. However, the suggestion that counseling might be of benefit should be considered in situations in which a significant disruption in daily living activities continues, without any signs of improvement, for a period of time in excess of 2 to 3 months. Significant, disruptive holiday and anniversary reactions are common for at least 1 to 2 years and in some people persist for a lifetime. Although such periods of intense feeling through memory may be uncomfortable for others to observe, they are not necessarily pathological if, at other times, the bereaved individual functions adequately.

Physiological growth and development

MALES: Relatively quiescent stage of growth and development. Fine motor skill increases.

FEMALES: Late in this stage, may begin to experience growth and habitus changes consistent with the onset of puberty. Fine motor skill increases.

Psychological growth and development

FREUD   Latency

ERIKSON   Industry vs. inferiority

PIAGET   Concrete operational period

KOHLBERG   Conventional level

SEARS   Extrafamilial learning

Chapter 8

The child from 7 to 10 years (latency)

FAMILY: The blended family

CONCEPTS DISCUSSED: *Somatization*
Depression
Family move
School adjustment
"Honeymoon" phase of new relationships
The child as a spouse replacement

Judy was an 8-year-old third-grade girl whose mother called the practitioner because of her daughter's 6-month history of recurrent headaches.

Data gathering

Past history. Judy had enjoyed good health all her life. Her development had been normal.

Family history. Judy was an only child. Her father, who had been an air force pilot, was killed in a flight training accident at age 30 when Judy was 2 months old. Judy's mother was currently 35 years old and had worked as a secretary in a manufacturing firm. Almost a year prior to Judy's visit to the practitioner, her mother had married her employer, a 44-year-old widower who had a 13-year-old daughter and 10-year-old twin sons. Judy and her mother had moved into her stepfather's house in an affluent suburb immediately after the marriage.

School. Judy has always been an average to above average student in her former school. Since entering her current school, her grades had been poor. Although her attendance had been very good, for the 2 days before her mother's call, Judy has stayed home because of her headaches.

Peers. Although well liked and popular among the children in her former urban neighborhood, Judy had been unable to form any friendships in her new setting. She was unwilling to invite classmates to play at her new home after school and, after a couple of apparently unhappy experiences, never accepted invitations to play elsewhere.

Office visit. The practitioner, who had known Judy all her life, asked to see her in his office alone. Judy seemed much more quiet and uneasy than usual, although she had generally never been a very verbal or outgoing child. Nevertheless, Judy was willing to answer questions about her headaches. She described these as frontal and occurring at a variety of times during the day including bedtime, but never during the night when she was asleep.

After examining Judy carefully and testing her vision, the practitioner reassured her that "nothing serious" was wrong. Judy seemed unrelieved and almost tearful at the news but said nothing. The practitioner asked her to wait in the waiting room while he talked with her mother.

PRACTITIONER: Tell me how things are going for you in general.

MOTHER: Just marvelously. My husband is wonderful to me and to Judy. He's very kind and considerate, and I just couldn't ask for a better husband for myself or a better father for Judy.

PRACTITIONER: And your stepchildren?

MOTHER: They're very nice. Their mother died about 6 years ago and they've been cared for by at least 3 different housekeepers since that time. I think they're delighted to have a new mother. We had a long time to get to know one another before the marriage, and they've made me feel like a member of the family from the very beginning.

PRACTITIONER: And Judy?

MOTHER: You know that Judy and I have always been close. For a long time all we had was each other. I had so much love to give to her. She was my confidante and sounding board when I had decisions to make, even though she probably didn't understand half of what I was saying or going through.

I remember having so many misgivings when I went to work when she was in nursery school. I used to feel so guilty that whenever I'd get a day off, I'd plan something very special just for the two of us. You used to tell me not to try to be the perfect mother, but that's easier said than done.

When I started working for my husband, we hit it off immediately. He and I understood each other. But whenever we dated, Judy hated being left behind, so we did a lot of things that included all of the children. I really thought Judy liked him and his children, but now I just don't know.

PRACTITIONER: What exactly is going on?

MOTHER: I mentioned the headaches to your secretary when I called, but I think they're a reaction rather than the main problem.

Judy didn't want to leave our old apartment. She cried so when she said goodbye to her friends, even though I'd told her lots of times that she could visit our old neighborhood anytime. She did very well in her previous school. At her new school she's barely passing. But the thing that bothers me most is her unwillingness to really join the family.

PRACTITIONER: How does she show you that she hasn't joined?

MOTHER: For almost 6 months, she's spent most of her time in her room after school and on weekends complaining of headaches. At first, we all reacted by hovering over her and changing our plans to be with her. Usually I'd spend time alone with her in her room to comfort her. But now it's been going on so long. I know that my husband is perplexed by Judy's behavior and that my stepchildren are beginning to ignore her.

PRACTITIONER: And you?

MOTHER: I'm getting irritated because I'm in the middle. I feel as if I'm betraying Judy if I side with the rest of the family against her, and yet I also think that she could be a lot more considerate of us.

PRACTITIONER: Does she talk to you about her feelings?

MOTHER: I wish she would so that we could get the whole thing out in the open. But she tells me she doesn't know what's bothering her, and I certainly don't know what the problem is. She's an extremely lucky girl to have such a wonderful new family. I can't seem to be able to get that point across to her.

PRACTITIONER: Judy isn't the kind of girl who talks very much about her feelings, at least to me. But let's ask her to come back in and see if she can help us out.

JUDY: *(Enters examining room with tearstained face.)*

MOTHER: What's the matter, Honey?

JUDY: *(Silence.)*

PRACTITIONER: You know, Judy, when I told you that there's nothing seriously wrong with you, you began to cry. You've been crying since then, I bet. I was mistaken. There really is something quite wrong that's causing your headaches. You and I and your mother have a lot to talk about. Let's sit down together.

Discussion

The blending of families requires the simultaneous adjustment of three major subsystems: (1) a new spouse subsystem must develop, (2) the sibling subsystem must reorganize into a new peer group with a different hierarchy, and (3) the two separate parental subsystems must fuse to encompass all of the siblings.

In addition to these family system changes, all members of the **blended family** must adapt to a new social milieu and a changed status within the community.

Change implies loss. For some members of a newly blended family, change may signify the loss or perceived loss of important intrafamily and extrafamily relationships and supports. In healthy blended families, new relationships provide compensatory support systems. However, not all members of newly blended families adjust to the new situation at the same rate. Conflict often arises during the initial period of disequilibrium.

•   •   •

Judy was a healthy and normally developed child of midlatency age, usually an emotionally quiescent phase of psychological development. Cognitively, Judy was at the concrete operational stage as described by Piaget. Thus, her thinking processes were generally limited to an understanding of the principles of tangible, physical reality.

One of the most important tasks Judy had was the development of a sense of particular individual talent, or a perception of herself as a productive, industrious member of society. Peer group relationships, although lacking the extreme intensity of preadolescence, were an important part of Judy's life and formed the yardstick by which she measured herself.

Two factors were of particular importance to Judy's concept of herself. The first was her mutually close and dependent relationship with her mother; the second, her strong attachment to and reliance upon her friends.

Judy's mother's bereavement in early adulthood led her to focus much of her energy and emotional commitment on her daughter as a replacement for her dead husband. The mother was able to express her ambivalence and feelings of guilt when she relinquished part of her daughter's care to others when Judy entered nursery school. This ambivalence and guilt resulted in the mother's seeking an even closer relationship when they were together. When Judy's mother was able to seriously consider and participate in a peer relationship with her future husband, thereby necessarily restricting her time with Judy, Judy reacted by demanding that she be fully included in her mother's activities.

Children often believe that the total amount of love a parent has is limited. Because they equate attention with love, to them, less attention necessarily means less love. Therefore, Judy could not help but be jealous of her stepfather. Because they received attention from her mother, her stepsiblings were objects of jealousy as well.

Judy's previous world included a number of friends with whom she seemed quite close. At the time of her mother's marriage, Judy perceived herself as losing not only her mother's love, but also the support of her social group. Her new home was in an entirely different and apparently socioeconomically higher setting. Part of her reluctance to make friends may be a reflection of her fear that she was inferior to her classmates and neighbors. Certainly, her past experiences, opportunities, and material possessions may have given some realistic basis to her assumption that "different" was synonymous with "not as good."

The school to which she transferred probably had higher educational standards and a student body of generally greater achievement than her former school. Thus, her poor school performance could be the result of both her depression and isolation and the stricter academic expectations of her new class.

Interestingly, early in her mother's marriage Judy appeared to have adjusted adequately. Such a "honeymoon" phase is not unusual. Novelty and unfamiliarity with the tolerated limits of behavior often result in "good" behavior because of fears of rejection. Once the irreversibility of personal commitment to a relationship becomes apparent, however, frequency of acting out or other unacceptable behaviors increases. In other words, a child usually must feel comfortable in a setting before feeling free enough to express negative feelings.

Defense mechanisms/coping styles/adaptive behaviors

Because Judy tended to be a nonverbal child, **somatization** provided her with a way to (1) increase her contact with her mother, thus helping her to feel reinstated as the primary person in her mother's life; (2) avoid confrontation with the family members toward whom she felt jealousy and anger; and (3) excuse herself from having contact with peers who she was afraid might reject her. Judy's headaches had progressed to the point where they were beginning to interfere with her attendance at school, probably heralding the onset of school phobia and perhaps indicating a deepening of her depression.

Intervention

Reassuring the family that the headaches are not a sign of organic illness is best accomplished by a careful history and physical examination including visual acuity testing. This reassurance, however, must be coupled with an interpretation of the pain as real and as a symptom of significant tension.

Treatment is twofold and involves an immediate return to school and the identification and reduction of tension-producing situations for *all* family members, including the symptomatic child.

In Judy's case, her mother had probably tried to be extremely fair in the time and attention she gave to all members of the family. Of necessity, this would radically reduce her availability to her daughter. Parents generally feel obligated to have no "favorites" among their children. In reality, different children have different needs. As examples, some children require more attention, some can assume responsibility and therefore earn particular privileges earlier, and some need more help in mastering certain skills. In other words, some children need more parenting than do others. Mothers and fathers who recognize and respect these differences among their children are actually more effective and better satisfied parents.

Judy's mother should be helped to understand that, although she had been ready to move out of the mutually dependent relationship she had formed with her daughter, Judy was not necessarily ready to do so. Thus, the mother should be encouraged to effect a more gradual separation while at the same time providing Judy with more support to make new friendships and develop a closer relationship with her stepfather and stepsiblings. To do this, the mother, in essence, must "give in" to her daughter's demands for more attention by spending short but predictable times alone with her. However, by keeping the goal of ultimate separation clearly in mind, this regression will be short term.

In addition, Judy's mother should be encouraged to take more of the initiative in inviting both old and new school friends to the family home. By having contact with her former friends and having her worth to them reaffirmed, Judy may gain more confidence in establishing new friendships.

Last, Judy's classroom placement may or may not be appropriate. The mother should be encouraged to ask for consultation from the school psychologist.

Follow-up with the practitioner, either personally or by telephone, should be scheduled at least biweekly for about 2 months and thereafter as necessary for supportive counseling.

Indications for referral

If Judy does not return to school immediately; if her depression, as manifested by somatization, does not begin to resolve within a 1- to 2-month period; or if she expresses suicidal ideation, a formal mental health referral should be made. If she continues to be unable to make friends, or if her feelings of personal worthlessness persist, peer group therapy should be considered.

SCHOOL: Poor achievement

CONCEPTS DISCUSSED: *Learning disability*
Hyperactivity
"Soft" neurological signs
The parent as "teacher"

Ted was a 9-year-old fourth-grade boy whose mother received a call in November from the school nurse that Ted was spending increasing amounts of time walking around the room or staring out the window in arithmetic class. Since his parents had been concerned from the beginning of the school year that Ted was "staring off into space" during mealtime, his mother took the advice of the school nurse and contacted the practitioner for an appointment to evaluate Ted for "seizures" or "hyperactivity."

Data gathering

Past history. Ted had been the product of a 38-week gestation with a birth weight of 3062 g (6 pounds 12 ounces). He had done well as a newborn and went home with his mother at 3 days of age. He had no unusual medical or developmental problems as a preschoolchild.

When he was 7 years old, Ted sustained a mild concussion when he fell off his bicycle. He did not lose consciousness, had no neurological impairment, and returned to school after a day of rest and observation at home.

Family history. Ted was the oldest of three children of a 32-year-old father who managed a local fast-food establishment and a 30-year-old mother who worked part-time in her husband's business. Ted had an 8-year-old sister and a 6-year-old brother. Although both parents had graduated from high school, Ted's father had had difficulty in reading throughout school. Ted's siblings were doing at least average work in school. A maternal uncle had petit mal epilepsy during childhood. There was no other family history of seizure disorders, diabetes mellitus, or other neurological or metabolic disease.

School. Ted was enrolled in a nursery school for a year and entered kindergarten uneventfully at age $5\frac{1}{2}$ years. Both Ted's behavior and grades were average to above average until he was in the third grade, when he began to have some difficulty in arithmetic class. Ted received extra help in arithmetic two afternoons a week from mid-April until the end of the school year. He passed the subject with a "poor" for the year. This was in contrast to his grades of "satisfactory" to "good" in reading and social studies. The teacher reported neither exceptional activity nor staring episodes to Ted's parents, the school nurse, or in his final evaluation of the boy. Ted had entered a regular fourth grade class 2 months before his visit to the practitioner. He did not receive supplementary arithmetic instruction during or after school.

Peers. Ted had several male friends in his neighborhood with whom he liked to play after school. He seemed to be full of energy and enjoyed active sports, which he played well. His parents did not think that he was overly active as compared with his peers. However, they reported that he seemed to be aggressive in his play, always wanted to have his own way, and always wanted to be "right." He had difficulty accepting his team losing even in informal backyard games. A few former friends had begun to refuse to play with him during the preceding fall because of his "poor sport" attitude.

First office visit. Ted was examined by his practitioner who confirmed the history by calling the school nurse and also by talking with Ted's parents. Although the boy's inattention at school was primarily confined to arithmetic class, he occasionally had staring episodes in other classes. In addition, the parents again reported similar behavior at home.

A major area of conflict between the boy and his parents around arithmetic homework became apparent. The parents reported that Ted seemed overwhelmed by his homework problem sheets, which often contained 20 to 25 problems on a single piece of paper. The parents related that Ted was able to do the problems when they were presented to him singly on 3×5 cards. His work pace was very slow, however, and arithmetic alone took an hour and a half of "constant battle" after dinner, since Ted was constantly up and around rather than concentrating on his work. The parents had mentioned their success with the 3×5 card approach to his teacher, but she had indicated that such special treatment was impossible in her classroom of 30 students.

Review of systems underlined that Ted had no recent history of accidents, headaches, eye changes, or vomiting. Ted said that he liked school but not arithmetic class, where he felt "dumb" because he could not do his work on time or answer the teacher's questions in class and felt mocked by the other children.

Physical examination revealed a healthy, prepubertal boy. His visual acuity and visual field examination were normal, as was the remainder of his neurological examination, including a search for "soft" neurological signs such as mixed laterality in hand, foot, and eye preference; poor sense of direction in space; and gross and fine motor incoordination. Ted was right-handed.

Laboratory studies included normal hemoglobin, serum glucose, and serum electrolyte levels. Skull x-ray films and an electroencephalogram obtained during the week following Ted's physical examination were also normal.

Second office visit. After receiving the laboratory reports, the practitioner informed Ted and his parents of the results. He then recommended that Ted be seen by the school psychologist for psychometric testing.

School evaluation. Educational testing revealed that Ted was functioning at the midsecond-grade level in arithmetic. He had very poor attack skills in mathematics and had never properly learned simple rote memory multiplication tables. In addition, he was so unsure of his skills that he was less able to perform arithmetic tasks that were presented in large groups as a timed exercise than he was when these same tasks were presented individually and with no time limit.

The psychologist recommended that Ted be placed in a special education arithmetic class for remediation. In addition, he asked Ted's parents to supervise a 15-minute period of skill training in mathematics Monday through Thursday evenings each week for 2 months. Ted was given no other arithmetic homework.

Follow-up. By the end of the school year, 5 months after special placement, Ted had increased his arithmetic skills by 9 months. His teacher arranged for him to progress to the fifth grade, but to continue his special education in arithmetic the following year. The number of staring episodes observed by teachers and reported by the school nurse to the practitioner had diminished substantially during the spring but had not completely disappeared. Ted was noted to be more attentive and relaxed at home.

Discussion

Staring episodes may present a difficult diagnostic problem. For example, the onset of petit mal epilepsy characteristically occurs between 4 and 8 years of age. Absence spells, which may last from 15 to 30 seconds and occur several to hundreds of times a day, are not usually associated with postictal confusion and therefore may be difficult to distinguish from voluntary inattention. Psychomotor or temporal lobe seizures may also appear as staring episodes. However, these are typically associated with automatisms, some degree of postictal confusion, headache, and drowsiness.

The prevalence of learning disabilities, formerly termed "minimal brain dysfunction," in the school population has been variously reported but probably occurs in about 5% to 20% of all children. The initial evaluation of such children usually takes place at a median age of 9 years (E.D. Thomas et al., 1973). Although associated with a wide variety of so-called soft neurological signs that can be elicited on careful neurological examination, the diagnosis of learning disability requires the combined expertise of medical and nonmedical professionals.

It is important to distinguish among mental retardation, true hyperactivity, and a learning disability. It is especially important to stress to the family the excellent potential for academic progress that can be obtained through early detection of a disability and sustained attention to remediation.

•   •   •

Ted was a prepubertal boy who had not yet begun the extremely active somatic and sexual growth and development characteristic of adolescence. According to Eriksonian theory, Ted was firmly entrenched in the task of developing a sense of industry and overcoming his sense of inferiority. Given that school is a prominent facet of his life and can be a major source of either satisfaction or dissatisfaction, achievement in schoolwork is critical to him as he develops his sense of self-esteem. Positive feedback from his peers, teachers, and parents is an important influence on how he sees himself. Considering himself unintelligent, even in one class, can have far-reaching implications for his entire educational career.

Ted's aggressive approach to sports, at which he was successful, may have represented his attempt to compensate for his deficiencies in the classroom. Although his friends appear to have been relatively tolerant of his behavior, the withdrawal of some boys from his usual play group may mark the beginning of some social isolation from his peers.

The responsibility Ted's parents felt to supplement their son's classroom time by acting as teacher-surrogates at home is time honored. However, when a child is learning disabled, such activity can result in severe parent-child conflicts, especially if the parents do not have the skills to alter the learning environment to meet their child's particular needs.

Thus, even a well-circumscribed and only moderately incapacitating learning disability such as Ted's can lead to disruption in all spheres of a child's functioning: at school, confusion between the teacher and child; in the playground, alienation from friends; and at home, parent-child conflicts. The final result can be an individual who dislikes and/or resents compulsory education, who may not complete school, and who develops a poor image of himself and his capabilities.

Ted is concrete operational in his thinking. As such, he is tied to the here and now and able to deal only with immediate crises or threats. The long-range effects of his way of coping with stress are unknown to him and beyond his comprehension.

Defense mechanisms/coping styles/adaptive behaviors

In the classroom Ted used avoidance to escape the realities of the difficulties he was experiencing in arithmetic. Unfortunately, the more inattentive he was, the more difficulty he had learning. Thus, his coping behavior could be considered maladaptive. On the other hand, by increasing the gap between himself and his peers in arithmetic achievement and by confining his staring activity primarily to that class, he was able to focus professional attention on his particular needs. In a larger classroom with a heterogeneous student group or in the face of disinterested parents, Ted's behavior might well have resulted in outright school failure.

Intervention

Given this child's positive family history for a seizure disorder and the history of occasional staring episodes in a wide variety of settings, it is reasonable to include both organic and emotional etiologies in the differential diagnosis of his behavior.

Although "hyperactivity" is often mentioned as a cause of school problems, true hyperactivity is probably fairly uncommon. As Kinsbourne (1973) mentions, a child might be hyperactive (fidgety and restless) in the classroom for at least three reasons: (1) he may not be intelligent enough to understand what the teacher is saying, or the teacher may not be saying anything understandable; (2) he may be anxious or preoccupied with emotional concerns that interfere with concentration; these anxieties may be specific to a particular setting or more global preoccupations; or (3) he may be truly hyperactive—organically or constitutionally driven to constant high levels of activity. Children in the first group are helped by psychometric testing and placement in a more appropriate classroom setting. Children in the second group are helped by a change in setting or by counseling. Children in the third group are often helped either by a carefully planned and executed behavioral modification program and/or through the use of medication.

From his history of high but not abnormal activity levels and his selectively poor concentration in arithmetic class, Ted's problem of restlessness in the classroom does not represent true hyperactivity. Rather, this behavior appears to be a combination of a poor grasp of the fundamentals of arithmetic and anxiety and perhaps even depression over his chronic failure in the class.

Having ruled out a seizure disorder, metabolic disease, or true hyperactivity, any of which might respond to drug therapy, the practitioner should refer the family to school personnel for further evaluation and treatment.

Remediation programs that specifically address themselves to well-defined areas of disability have the greatest chance of success. Cooperation between home and school can be based only on a clear understanding of reasonable expectation in each setting and a high level of communication among parents, teacher, and child. Parents may need to be taught new skills in homework supervision that stress short periods of intensive work and positive reinforcement. Sometimes, however, parent-child conflicts over homework can only be resolved by encouraging the parents to relinquish their teacher-surrogate roles completely for a period of time.

Classroom teachers may also need to learn flexibility in their approach to children with particular needs. A special education teacher can either provide a student with direct one-to-one or small-group instruction or devise simple, efficient, alternative instructional methods for the regular teacher to use in the larger classroom.

Indications for referral

Continued concerns about poor self-concept (perhaps manifested by withdrawal, acting-out behaviors, self-depreciation, or lack of motivation) may warrant individual counseling. Continued aggressive play, especially if coupled with the loss of more friends, may benefit from either individual counseling or peer group therapy.

ILLNESS: Chronic illness

CONCEPTS DISCUSSED: *The medically sophisticated parent*
Information and compliance
"Hidden" disability

Danny, an 8½-year-old third grader, was admitted to the hospital as a newly diagnosed diabetic in moderate ketoacidosis.

Data gathering

Past history. Danny had grown and developed normally.

Family history. Danny was the second child and only son of a 39-year-old obstetrician and a 36-year-old homemaker. Danny's three sisters were 10, 6, and 2 years old and in good health.

School. Danny had attended a cooperative nursery school for 2 years and had entered kindergarten uneventfully at age 5½. His attendance and grades were excellent.

Peers. Danny was very active in Cub Scouts and had a number of neighborhood friends with whom he played regularly. His favorite sport was soccer, and he played in a community junior soccer league.

Present illness. A week before his admission, Danny had an episode of enuresis. This had been very disconcerting to him and his family, but his parents had decided not to make an issue of the "accident." The morning of Danny's admission, the school nurse called the boy's home to report that Danny was frequently requesting bathroom and water fountain privileges. That evening Danny told his father that he had been getting up once or twice each night to urinate. Danny's father tested his son's urine, which was 4+ for glucose and moderate for ketones. He called the practitioner, who arranged to have Danny hospitalized immediately.

Hospital visit. Late the following afternoon the practitioner visited Danny, who was doing well. The father asked if he and his wife could talk privately with the practitioner.

PRACTITIONER: Danny's doing extremely well. I hope we can get him regulated and home in a few days.

FATHER: I shouldn't have passed over his bed-wetting last week.

PRACTITIONER: I think anyone would have done the same thing.

FATHER: He was so embarrassed that I don't think he's really slept all week because he was afraid to do it again.

PRACTITIONER: Danny's a boy who likes to please you.

FATHER: Oh, I know. I feel so bad for him. There were so many things I wanted him to do in life that now he'll never have a chance to do.

PRACTITIONER: Such as?

FATHER: Well, I guess he'll have to give up soccer and Cub Scouts. He'll be very disappointed about Cub Scouts. He and I have already signed up for a father and son weekend in a couple of months, and now we can't go.

PRACTITIONER: Hold on. Are you and I talking about the same Danny? If he doesn't *want* to play soccer or be in Cub Scouts, that's one thing. But his diabetes isn't going to stop him.

FATHER: But, diabetes . . .

PRACTITIONER: I think I've just figured out what you're thinking. Your work with diabetic women who have difficult pregnancies has colored your view of your son's illness. Most of the diabetics that you've seen recently have been in trouble. But they're a small proportion of all the diabetics in the world, and pregnancy is only a short period in their lives. We need to reeducate you.

MOTHER: I can't tell you how relieved I am to hear you say all this.

PRACTITIONER: You mean you had this bleak picture, too?

MOTHER: Well, I've been getting my information from my husband, and he's really been devastated. Everybody seems to think that just because I'm a doctor's wife, I know all about diabetes. But I was a kindergarten teacher before our oldest daughter was born, and I really don't know anything about diabetes at all, except the horror stories about patients that my husband has told me.

PRACTITIONER: We routinely have a nurse specialist in diabetes and a dietician talk with parents when their children are admitted. We also have some literature specifically for children as well as some for parents. Did anyone tell you about all this?

MOTHER: No.

PRACTITIONER: I'll get you some pamphlets right now so you can read them tonight. Tomorrow I'll have the nurse and dietician come by at some time that's convenient for both of you. They prefer to talk to both parents together if possible.

MOTHER: I'd appreciate it very much. I've felt excluded from all of the discussions the staff has been having with my husband about sugar and ketones and units of insulin.

PRACTITIONER: That reminds me that you're going to need some instruction in giving insulin. *(To father.)* When was the last time you actually gave insulin subcutaneously to anyone?

FATHER: *(Laughing)* Would you believe never?

PRACTITIONER: Absolutely! Let's make sure that all three of you get a chance before you go home. We'll talk some other time about who'll give the shots regularly. Part of that decision is Danny's. I'll meet you in Danny's room in 10 minutes so I can get you started on some books. Your son's probably feeling very confused and left out, too.

Discussion

A positive correlation between the availability of information and the overall quality of total patient care, particularly in areas that demand patient participation or compliance, has been repeatedly demonstrated (Williams et al., 1967; Francis, Korsch, and Morris, 1969; Tagliacozzo and Kenju, 1970). It has also been noted that physicians sometimes overestimate a patient's understanding (Charney, 1972) and that emotional factors often interfere with the family members' ability to comprehend information that is presented (Steinhauer, Mushin, and Rae-Grant, 1974).

With medically sophisticated parents, a tendency may exist to overestimate their knowledge of particular disease processes or prognoses. This is particularly a problem if the child has an illness that the parent rarely encounters in his specialty area. Parents tend to contribute to this poor communication system by appearing well informed to avoid embarrassment. The parent may also demand highly technical information, which is usually freely given, but which he may or may not be able to put into the proper perspective because of the emotionalism usually associated with caring for a close family member.

The lay spouse of a medically sophisticated parent is particularly vulnerable in this situation. The spouse relies heavily on the physician, nurse, or technician parent for information. However, because of the miscommunications or misinterpretations just mentioned, this information may be inaccurate or incomplete.

• • •

Danny, at $8\frac{1}{2}$ years, was a normally growing and developing boy whose interests were appropriate to children during the period of psychosexual latency. For example, he was learning the skills of team play. His interest in task mastery made membership in an organization like the Cub Scouts in which he could earn merit badges very attractive. In addition, his identification with his father and his desire to participate in gender-specific activities were revealed by his enjoyment of father-son programs.

Cognitively, Danny was in the stage of concrete operations as described by Piaget. His knowledge and understanding of the world was restricted to his past experiences and to physical reality. His sense of time included a concept of years, but he probably considered anyone in adolescence or beyond old. His ability to plan for the future was limited.

Danny's family played a large role in his life and in his desire to please ("good boy"—"nice girl" stage of moral reasoning). He was generally compliant and of even disposition. His peers and his relationship to them were also important primarily as a gauge for measuring his abilities. The need to be like them in every detail was only beginning to emerge and would not become a dominant force in determining his behavior for at least another 3 to 4 years.

Defense mechanisms/coping styles/adaptive behaviors

Although we know little from the vignette about Danny's reaction to his illness, his physician's impression that he was confused and anxious about his illness is probably correct because he lacked specific concrete information about his hospitalization. Once he has enough information so that he can understand and comfortably explain his illness in simple terms, his anxiety should decrease significantly. At his age, he should enjoy keeping limited records about his daily urine testing and can comprehend to some extent the need to increase or decrease his insulin based on his urinary glucose and ketone levels. His compliance in the many other areas of his life should carry over into his attention to the details of his illness.

Because diabetes is a "hidden" disease, Danny has a choice about whether he will reveal his illness to anyone. His willingness to share information will depend heavily upon how diabetes is presented to him. If he perceives diabetes as a liability, he will hide it from friends and eventually deny his illness and the restrictions it imposes on his activities and diet. If the disease is presented positively, he will probably feel freer to talk about it. Frequently, such children will actually boast about having diabetes. Later, as the novelty wears off, the disease no longer remains a topic of particular interest or discussion and is merely accepted by peers.

Intervention

The practitioner's management was excellent. Patient and family education are ongoing elements of the care of children who have any chronic illness and must be geared to each person's specific needs.

One other consideration, however, should be mentioned. In caring for the child of a medically sophisticated parent, the physician in charge should help the parents clearly understand that he is the child's physician and will be responsible for medical care. One method of determining when it is appropriate to consult him is to request that he be called whenever the lay parent has a question about management. This frees the medically sophisticated parent from the responsibility of inappropriate decision making and may be a great relief.

Indications for referral

Psychosocial problems encountered by a child with a chronic physical disorder have been suggested to lead to more serious social disability than the direct effects of the physical illness (Mattsson, 1972). In particular, fluctuating control of juvenile-onset diabetes frequently appears to be related to emotional factors (Swift and Seidman, 1964; Tietz and Vidmar, 1972).

Although concerns about compliance and the ability to cope with the restrictions of an illness have often been mentioned with regard to adolescents, approximately 50% of diabetic children of latency age have also been shown to have moderate to severe adjustment problems. For example, 24-hour urinary glucose excretion was two to three times greater in poorly adjusted compared with well-adjusted patients. Interestingly, parental self-esteem seemed to correlate most closely with the child's adjustment (Grey, Genel, and Tamborlane, 1980).Thus, diabetes can be thought of as a "psychosomatic" illness, where the term is used to designate a physiological disease, the course of which can be strongly influenced by emotion.

"Brittle" diabetes in children and adolescents results from the influence of psychological factors until proven otherwise. Thus, repeated hospitalizations for ketoacidosis or hypoglycemia deserve an indepth assessment of child and family functioning and referral for treatment as indicated (Greydanus and Hofmann, 1979a,b).

Physiological growth and development

MALES: Onset of growth spurt.

FEMALES: Maximum velocity of height spurt. Will soon experience menarche. "Tall girl"–"short boy" phase.

Psychological growth and development

FREUD	Transitional phase: latency → genital stage
ERIKSON	Transitional phase: industry vs. inferiority → identity vs. role confusion
PIAGET	Late concrete operational period
KOHLBERG	Conventional level
SEARS	Extrafamilial learning

Chapter 9

The child from 10 to 12 years (preadolescence)

FAMILY: Change in parental role

CONCEPTS DISCUSSED: *Previously married parents*
Early adolescent irritability
Marital discord and child behavior

Carole was an $11\frac{1}{2}$-year-old sixth-grade student whose mother called the practitioner in January because Carole had been very irritable and crying frequently for 4 months.

Data gathering

Past history. Carole's past health had been excellent. Her development had been completely normal. She was premenarchal.

Family history. Carole was the older of two daughters of a 38-year-old father who was a sixth-grade teacher in Carole's elementary school and a 40-year-old mother who worked as a homemaker. This was the second marriage for both parents. Carole's father's first marriage, which had been childless, had ended 14 years before. Carole's mother had been married at age 18 and divorced 2 years later. Resulting from that union was a 21-year-old married daughter who lived in another state.

Carole's younger sister was 10. The girls had always got along fairly well together, although during the past year Carole had become less tolerant of her "little" sister. They frequently quarreled over borrowing each other's clothes or other possessions. Carole also wanted more privacy when she had friends at their home and did not want her sister to accompany her when she went to other girls' homes.

School. Carole had always maintained excellent attendance and average to above average grades in elementary school. During the late summer, just before entering the sixth grade, Carole learned that her father would be acting principal because of the sudden departure of the regular school principal to another district. Carole's father had then applied for the principal's job, but learned in October that it was unlikely he would be hired on a permanent basis. In a heated argument with the school board, he had threatened to leave the school district entirely if he did not become principal. A couple of weeks prior to the mother's call, an individual from another community was hired as principal, and Carole's father returned to teaching, taking over Carole's class. Carole immediately asked to be assigned to the other sixth grade in her school.

Peers. Carole had several girlfriends in her neighborhood with whom she frequently played after school. They enjoyed visiting each other's houses and sleeping overnight. Usually, they spent their time listening to records, reading teen magazines, and talking about clothes, hairstyles, and boys.

Office visit. The practitioner saw Carole alone first.

PRACTITIONER: Your parents are concerned about your crying spells. Do you have any idea about what's going on?

CAROLE: Everybody irritates me, my sister especially. She always wants to go everywhere and do everything I do. She's such a baby. I don't want her around when I'm with my friends.

PRACTITIONER: You said that everybody irritates you. Does that include your mom and dad?

CAROLE: Oh, yes. My dad really wanted to be principal, and all the kids know that. My mother told me that he said we might move away if he didn't become principal, and I really don't want to move. I don't want to leave my friends. Next year I'm going to be in junior high, and I'm scared about that. It's a big school, and I'd hate to make it worse by moving and having to go to a new school where I didn't even know anybody. That would be terrible.

PRACTITIONER: How is school this year?

CAROLE: It *was* okay, even though dad was the principal, until he started teaching my class. I asked to be put in the other class right away. He told me that he had no choice and wasn't sure I'd want to leave my friends, and that's why he hadn't arranged to transfer me. But at least he could have asked me. Having my father was just too awful, and all the kids made comments about it. I had to transfer, and now I've lost all my friends right in the middle of the year.

PRACTITIONER: Don't you know anyone in your new class?

CAROLE: Oh, sure. Some of the kids were in my fifth-grade class, but it's different. It's not the same.

Following this interview, the practitioner examined Carole. She was of average height and weight and clearly undergoing her growth spurt. She was noted to have Tanner stage II-III breast development, with the left breast slightly larger than the right breast. Her neurological examination was normal.

The practitioner reassured Carole about her development, including her breast asymmetry, and told her that her menarche would probably occur within the next several months.

He then asked to see her parents alone.

Interview with Carole's parents

PRACTITIONER: First, let me tell you that Carole is growing well. She is of normal height and weight for her age, and she's beginning to show some secondary sexual changes. She should be menstruating soon. She . . .

FATHER: Doctor, what does her growth have to do with the problem we're here for? What about her crying and irritability? Carole is becoming impossible. When she starts getting touchy, I would like to take her over my knee, but my wife won't let me.

MOTHER: Carole's not the only one who's touchy, Doctor. My husband is impossible, too. I can't even talk to him about minor problems without his flying off the handle.

FATHER: I'm not convinced you're any better.

PRACTITIONER: It seems that everyone is feeling a great deal of tension in your family. Let me answer your question about the possible relationship between Carole's growth and development and her crying jags. As youngsters enter adolescence, they experience a surge of hormones that may make them more irritable at particular times. Parents of girls are usually more aware of their child's irritability than are parents of boys. This irritability is sort of like that experienced by some older women during their menstrual periods. So you see, there may be a relationship between Carole's growth and her behavior. But, in addition to these physical factors, Carole and both of you seem to be more tense than I've ever seen you before.

FATHER: I've been under a terrible strain since I didn't get the principal's job at school. I really thought I had it, but then I heard that they were going to look outside the system. When I heard that, I told them that either I got the job or I'd leave. I really had no intention of leaving when I said it, but I thought they'd respond to that threat. Now I feel that I must leave. Have you seen the local newspaper's coverage, Doctor? I'm in a bind because I really don't want to leave, and my wife and children love it here. We've been here ever since we got married. I've got tenure. Starting again when you're almost 40 is pretty hard.

MOTHER: My husband really needed to move up. We're heavily in debt, and I've been thinking about going back to work. But my husband just won't have it. He keeps telling me that his first marriage didn't last because his wife worked, and he won't go through that again. As a matter of fact, I made a promise not to work when we got married, but now I think that I was pretty unrealistic. The difference in pay between being a teacher and being a principal is just what we need. It would have solved at least some of our problems, but now we don't even have that.

PRACTITIONER: You make it sound like there are other things beside money that have been bothering you two.

MOTHER: We've been having problems with our marriage for several years. Money is part of it. My wanting to get out of the house once the girls started going to school is part of it. My husband's ambitions that just never seem to materialize are part of it, too. We seem to argue all the time. We've talked about separating, but neither of us really wants that either.

PRACTITIONER: How do your children understand all of this?

FATHER: Carole has heard us argue, and she gets involved by trying to stop the arguments. I'm convinced she has crying spells and tantrums just to get our attention. Then we focus on her and seem to vent a lot of our anger toward each other on her. Ever since October it's become much worse. But you can understand something intellectually and not be able to do anything about it emotionally. And the topics she brings up when she's in one of her moods always reflect what *she* wants, what *she* needs. It's maddening.

PRACTITIONER: Perhaps you could give me an example.

FATHER: This business about changing her class to the other sixth grade. I thought long and hard about what to do, and she immediately gets her back up.

PRACTITIONER: Did you discuss the options with Carole?

FATHER: . . . I must have.

MOTHER: I don't think so.

FATHER: I really can't remember. There have been so many things to discuss with so many people. I haven't been in a friendly, rational discussion with anybody for months.

PRACTITIONER: I think Carole's behavior represents the effects of both the increasing irritability often associated with her stage of development and the tension and uncertainty she feels at home. You two are really preoccupied with some important decisions about careers and family. I think it's difficult for you to find the kind of time and energy Carole seems to need right now. She's frightened about possibly having to move and losing her friends, and I think she's also worried about her family and what's happening to all of you. How do you feel about my asking my nurse practitioner to see Carole weekly for a while? They've known each other for a long time and seem to get along very well.

MOTHER: I'd really like that. I know I'm not giving Carole the kind of attention I should, but I seem to be exhausted all the time worrying about what's happening to us.

PRACTITIONER: Which brings me to the two of you as a couple. What you have told me today concerns me. To be perfectly blunt, I think you could profit from some marital counseling.

FATHER: We've talked about it once or twice in our saner moments. We've both been through broken marriages before and really don't want to go through it again. What I need right now is someone to help *me* decide about my job and what I'm going to do about my threat to quit.

PRACTITIONER: I suggest you lay it all out on the table for a counselor to help you decide how you're going to reach a decision. You may need to have some time alone. Perhaps each of you needs to discuss some issues alone. I don't have the expertise to answer that question for you, but I can recommend someone for you to call to help you out.

Follow-up. Carole was seen weekly for a month and then biweekly until early July when the family moved to a nearby city where her father got a job as a sixth-grade teacher. Carole was helped by the nurse practitioner to focus on the positive aspects of the move. In addition, the family was encouraged to include the girls in their planning. For example, Carole and her sister accompanied their parents on several trips to select their new home. Carole wrote to her best friend faithfully for almost a year after her move and visited her overnight just before school started and during Christmas vacation.

Carole's mother began working part-time after school began. The family remained intact.

Discussion

The potential for change in parental role, particularly when job related, can lend uncertainty to family life and may be reflected in a child's behavior. Coping with uncertainty may be more difficult than coping with what has happened or what is definitely going to happen. Preadolescents may be unable to adequately express their feelings verbally and thus may resort to acting-out or withdrawn behavior.

•   •   •

Carole's physical growth was normal for her age. Her breast development was proceeding well despite some asymmetry, a common finding during this stage of development. Some of her irritability might have been related to fluctuation in estrogen and progesterone levels, also common among girls of this age.

Carole had friends, mostly girls, with whom she enjoyed typical peer activities: talking about topics of mutual interest, listening to records, looking at teen magazines, and visiting each other's homes. Peer group attachments are becoming increasingly important to a child of this age. At times parents may begin to sense a strengthening of the peer pull away from the family.

Carole was beginning to develop her sense of physical identity as a woman. However, she associated closely with like-sexed friends, and their interest in boys was mostly observational as she and her friends talked and read about them. During dances and other social activities within this age group, the dichotomy of sexes is readily apparent: the boys are usually found huddled in one corner and the girls in another, watching but not quite daring to touch.

Carole was very aware of what was going on in her environment. However, she was also egocentric and oriented toward the present. She lacked insight into the way her father and her sister, in particular, felt. She could not relate her own feelings of tension to their stresses and feelings of tension as well. Thus, she was still thinking in concrete operational terms and had yet to move into formal operational thinking.

Defense mechanisms/coping styles/adaptive behaviors

Carole's most effective way of expressing her distress was through her irritability and crying spells. These behaviors served initially as a means of directing her parents' attention away from their own problems and represented the only way that Carole believed she could help maintain the integrity of the family. Isolated crying spells, although effective at first in bringing temporary relief to her family, became increasingly ineffective. Having no other coping mechanism available at this point, Carole escalated these behaviors. The final result was that they served to mobilize real help for her and her family.

Intervention

Carole was clearly caught in a situational circumstance that could be helped by supportive counseling. Female health professionals are often particularly effective in providing short-term support and counseling to preadolescent girls, who need nonthreatening, nonjudgmental adult women with whom to identify and communicate effectively.

Indications for referral

The practitioner's primary role with the parents in this case was to acknowledge their marital problems as real and provide support to them in seeking professional intervention. Formal mental health treatment for the child should be considered if anxiety or tension reaches the level of interfering with such activities as school performance or peer interaction or if the child expresses suicidal ideation.

SCHOOL: School failure and substance abuse

CONCEPTS DISCUSSED: *Substance (alcohol) abuse*
Depression
Acting-out behavior
The "ideal family" fantasy

Greg, an $11\frac{1}{2}$-year-old sixth grader, was examined by his practitioner in the local emergency room at the request of the school principal. Greg had been found lying on the ground in the schoolyard when he had failed to return to his classroom after lunch recess.

Data gathering

Past history. Greg had grown and developed normally.

Family history. Greg was the youngest child of a 47-year-old stockbroker and a 45-year-old homemaker. Both parents were very active socially and seldom home evenings or weekends. They entertained frequently at their large suburban home or their country club. Greg's older brother and sister were 19 and 21 years of age respectively, and both attended college out of town.

School. Greg had been a very good student and had maintained excellent attendance through the fourth grade. In fifth grade, his grades had fallen slightly: toward the end of the school year the teacher had observed that Greg occasionally seemed tense and nervous, especially in the morning.

During the first 6 weeks of sixth grade, Greg had seldom been prepared for class, and his grades declined steadily. He was often giddy and inattentive in the classroom. The teacher had contacted Greg's parents, who had expressed surprise about his grades, since he never seemed to have any homework to do. They had observed his inattention and giddiness and also an increased need for sleep at home, but had attributed these behaviors to "growing up."

Peers. Greg had always had many friends until fifth grade, when he began spending most of his time with only two other boys. Since these boys were sons of good friends of Greg's parents, this change in behavior had not alarmed them, even though the boys seemed fairly secretive about their after-school activities and seldom participated in sports or games at home.

All three boys had been involved in a shoplifting episode at a nearby toy store the summer before Greg's visit to the practitioner, but their parents had made restitution, and no charges were filed.

Emergency room visit. Greg was drowsy and incoherent immediately after being found. By the time the parents arrived at the hospital a half hour after the principal's call, it was apparent to everyone that the boy was drunk.

At the hospital, the practitioner examined Greg and told him that, although he was physically well, he was concerned about him and that they needed to talk more when Greg was fully awake. After arranging for Greg to lie down in an examining room, the practitioner spoke with Greg's parents in a nearby private room.

FATHER: Well, well, Doctor. Boys will be boys. I don't think I had my first drink until I was 18. But I really tied one on then. My head hurt for days.

MOTHER: Don't tell me you think this was his first drink.

FATHER: Well, of course it wasn't. He's had sips of my cocktails since he was about 4 years old. Didn't seem to like the taste of Scotch much, though. Always made a face and said, "Ugh."

MOTHER: I think he's been watering down the gin and vodka for years. I wondered who was doing it. Do you remember the cleaning lady who left in a huff last spring? I accused her, and she got really wild. Greg's older brother, Doctor, lived with us until September when he went to college. Of course, he's legally old enough to drink, so I didn't say anything. But now, there's only Greg at home, and the new maid is a strict teetotaler—one of the requirements for the job.

FATHER: It ought to be one of the requirements for your job.

MOTHER: Speak for yourself, Luv. I usually don't start before 4 in the afternoon. You, on the other hand, have already had four by the afternoon.

FATHER: At least I don't mix my poison with pills.

MOTHER: Aren't you lucky you don't have to go through the change?

FATHER: You've been going through the change for years.

MOTHER: You don't know how blessed you are to have me, changed or unchanged. There aren't many wives who'd tolerate your little flings and look the other way. (*Rummaging in her purse.*) You don't happen to have a cigarette do you, Luv? I ran out of the house so fast I forgot mine.

FATHER: No. I must have left my pack in the car.

MOTHER: Well, I suppose that the doctor would be just as happy if we didn't pollute the hospital. Where were we?

PRACTITIONER: Let's talk about Greg.

MOTHER: I really do think he's been drinking for a while.

FATHER: Why?

MOTHER: The gin and vodka for one thing. His funny, giggly behavior. His nervousness. His lack of appetite. Also, the school called us a couple of times last year about his poor grades. But I guess we were so sure it was just a phase that it didn't seem worth the effort to get upset. And then Greg's been borrowing a lot of money from me for months. I know he borrows more from my purse than he tells me. I've stopped leaving change around. It disappears too fast. Did you know he got caught shoplifting, Doctor? I just can't understand why. He's got everything.

PRACTITIONER: Do you think he was using his money to buy liquor?

FATHER: *(Interrupting.)* This is ridiculous. My son's not an alcoholic.

PRACTITIONER: If he isn't yet, he's well on the way to becoming one.

Discussion

Substance abuse is becoming an increasingly prevalent problem among American youth. Although thought to be confined to the middle and late adolescent age group in the mid-1960s, such abuse is now a well-defined entity among junior high and even elementary schoolchildren.

Young alcohol users point to their parents as their role models for this behavior. In fact, the child's or adolescent's first drinking experience is usually at home. Most adolescents who drink report that at least one parent also drinks. The likelihood that an adolescent will drink is increased if both parents drink. It has been reported that an adolescent's drinking pattern is similar to that of his parents. Thus, parents who drink excessively tend to have adolescent children who drink excessively (Riester and Zucker, 1968; Rosenberg, 1969; Grinder, 1973).

To a young person troubled by family tensions, alcohol or other substances offer the same kind of escape that is sought and apparently obtained by adult abusers. Even the ability to merely procure alcohol for himself and friends can enhance the child's or adolescent's feeling of self-esteem among his peers. Thus, the entire process of procurement to drunkenness can be a positively reinforcing experience for the child who receives little or no gratification from other activities.

· · ·

Greg, at 11½ years, was probably just beginning to undergo changes associated with puberty. Hormonal fluctuations can result in emotional lability, and nervousness and giddiness are not unusual. Appetite, however, is often increased in response to the demands of more rapid growth. Thus, Greg's behaviors at school and at home probably represented mild withdrawal symptoms rather than typical adolescent behavior.

Although not enough data are available to understand this family completely, it is clear that Greg's parents communicate poorly and that they have many unresolved issues between them. Whether the father's "flings" and the mother's drug use are related to midlife crises or are a result of some more intrinsic marital problem is unknown. However, both parents use alcohol and intense social activity to escape from problems, including Greg, at home.

Greg's use of alcohol may well have represented an acting-out behavior, secondary to depression about the lack of his parents' positive feeling toward and attention to him.

It is not surprising that Greg, as a preadolescent and therefore still dependent on his family and to a large extent accepting of their value systems, would choose alcohol in imitation of his parents. The fact that he only partially hid his drinking from his parents probably indicates that, on one hand, he realized they would not approve of his drinking despite their own drinking, smoking, and drug habits; on the other hand, however, he needed to have them know about his feelings. His parents' lack of response had two effects: it escalated his behavior, and it forced him to develop intensely strong peer group affiliations. His susceptibility to peer pressure and his inability to resist a dare at this age, especially one that he thought indicated grown-up behavior and that would bring him admiration, ultimately led to his participation in antisocial gang activity. Such activity is a common finding among preadolescents, especially boys.

As a first step in moving away from their family, some midadolescent children develop an "ideal family" fantasy; that is, they fantasize that they were adopted as infants and that their real parents, with whom they will eventually be reunited, are ideal individuals. As Greg moves further into adolescence, he will begin to compare his family with the families of friends and acquaintances and consider the benefits and drawbacks of alternative life-styles for himself as an adult.

Defense mechanisms/coping styles/adaptive behaviors

Greg's dependency is an indication of personal insecurity and poor self-esteem leading to depression. Although his particular method of coping with the tensions in his family and his isolation from his parents was maladaptive, it served as an effective call for help.

The parents' use of denial of their son's problems, as well as their own, is dramatic.

Intervention

Since his early morning nervousness may well be a manifestation of withdrawal, inhospital detoxification is the safest plan for Greg's care. Even if he did not display these physical symptoms, however, the denial demonstrated by the family may require that the boy be hospitalized immediately to underscore the seriousness of his problem.

Consultation from a child psychiatrist or a community mental health service offering a substance abuse rehabilitation program should be instituted immediately. Long-term follow-up that includes individual and family therapy should be arranged.

ILLNESS: Terminal illness

CONCEPTS DISCUSSED: *Physical effects of terminal illness*
Ethics of withholding treatment
Rights of minors
Quality of life
Medical neglect

Peggy, an 11-year-old fifth-grade student with known end-stage medullary cystic disease of the kidney, was admitted to the hospital for treatment of dehydration and hyponatremia associated with acute viral gastroenteritis.

Data gathering

Past history. Peggy was first diagnosed at age 3 when she experienced the onset of polyuria and polydipsia. Although examined regularly at a renal clinic, she had been hospitalized only three times before the present admission. Despite excellent medical management, she was chronically anemic and growth retarded and was at the fiftieth percentile for a 7-year-old girl for both height and weight.

During the 6 months before her current admission, she had become increasingly ill. Her parents had refused the option of dialysis and/or renal transplantation.

Family history. Peggy was the ninth of 10 living children of a 50-year-old mother who had experienced 12 pregnancies, including two miscarriages. Peggy's father was 54 years old and worked as a farmer. The four oldest siblings were married and lived away from home, but in the same community. One of Peggy's older sisters had died from the same renal disease 6 years before at age 15 after undergoing dialysis and transplantation. The youngest child, who was 8 years old, had Down syndrome. The remaining siblings were in good health and developmentally normal.

School. Peggy had attended school regularly through the third grade. In the fourth grade, she participated only in morning classes. Until a month before admission, she received home tutoring. She had always been an average student.

Peers. Peggy had few friends, primarily because of her poor school attendance and the fact that her family lived in an isolated farmhouse in a rural community. However, she got along well with her siblings.

Hospital course. Peggy was initially admitted to the intensive care unit. She was unconscious and had intermittent seizures during the first 24 hours of her admission. Within 36 hours after admission, however, her dehydration and electrolyte imbalance were corrected, and she began to have periods of lucidity. On the fourth hospital day, she was completely alert and able to take fluids orally and sit up for short periods of time. At this point she was transferred to a regular nursing unit under the care of some staff members who had known her from her previous admissions. Also at this point, the staff became aware of the parents' decision against dialysis and transplantation.

The nursing and house staff members discovered Peggy to be generally withdrawn, but occasionally very animated and engaging, especially when she was talking about her home and her new puppy. She seemed to have particular difficulty, however, talking about how she was feeling except for a superficial "fine."

The staff members asked for a conference with the attending nephrologist, explaining that they had two primary concerns: (1) the family's decision against dialysis and transplantation and their feelings about withholding such treatment, especially since it had been provided for her sister, and (2) how to treat Peggy. The nephrologist contacted Peggy's practitioner, who had cared for Peggy and all of her siblings for many years, and invited him to be present at the meeting as well.

Conference

PRACTITIONER: First, let me give you more history about the family's decision. At the time that their older daughter developed end-stage kidney disease, the parents reluctantly agreed to dialysis and transplantation because of the excellent results many children had received from these treatments of the disease. Their reluctance to participate in dialysis and transplantation at that time stemmed from their worry about inflicting pain and discomfort on their child. Although these parents are unsophisticated, they were and remain extremely caring people. As they have explained it to me, because of their familiarity with the life cycles of the farm, to hurt a person or animal is worse to them than death.

After much reassurance from us, their daughter underwent dialysis and transplantation; however, she suffered from a wide variety of complications necessitating a prolonged hospitalization, which culminated in a graft-vs.-host reaction and ultimately death 5 months after the surgery. Peggy's father sees Peggy's and her sister's illnesses as tragic occurrences but is not certain that the "quality" of life of children on dialysis or after transplantation is good enough to allow him to let his daughter Peggy be "hurt" as much as he believes his other daughter was hurt.

Peggy's mother and the other children in the family agree with Peggy's father and support his decision. They have talked about Peggy's sister's death and deny any feelings of guilt or anxiety about not agreeing to the same treatment for Peggy. As a matter of fact, I think that they are relieved about not having to go through another long, complicated hospitalization that may or may not really help Peggy.

STAFF MEMBER: I don't think the parents have a right to deny their daughter access to care that is available, and I wonder whether this constitutes medically neglectful behavior on their part.

NEPHROLOGIST: This is something we have thought about, too. The family has rigorously followed all medical regimens I have ever suggested; in my opinion, these parents are acting in what they see as the best interests of their daughter. Although I have told them that our techniques are so much better than they were 6 years ago, I cannot make them a firm promise about Peggy's response to treatment; neither can I promise them that Peggy will not die as her sister did. If I could offer them a treatment as safe and effective as, for example, penicillin for pneumococcal pneumonia or even insulin for diabetes, medical neglect would certainly be a real issue, at least in my mind. However, at this time I can't, in all honesty, make such a determination.

STAFF MEMBER: I'm ambivalent, angry, and even horrified about allowing a child to die without intervention. I feel guilty about participating in this kind of care, and I'm frustrated with the family. It seems ridiculous to me that Peggy was admitted to the intensive care unit for intensive treatment if the family's ultimate plan is to do nothing.

PRACTITIONER: I saw Peggy in my office just before her transfer to the hospital. I explained to the family that the gastroenteritis was an acute intercurrent illness that, although certainly aggravated by her underlying disease, represented a treatable complication. They had brought the child, very appropriately, to me for help and agreed in every way with the therapy that was provided by all of you here. They have told me how grateful they are, although they know that her basic disease is unchanged and perhaps even worse because of this episode.

STAFF MEMBER: But what about Peggy in all of this?

PRACTITIONER: Earlier, I told you that the children agreed with Peggy's father about the decision to withhold what they see as heroic treatment: I include Peggy when I tell you about that decision. She remembers her sister and the difficult time she had in the hospital. She knows she has the same disease. She has told me directly, both in her parents' presence and when we have talked alone, that she does not want to be in the hospital for as long as her sister was, neither does she want to be hurt as much.

STAFF MEMBER: But, really, Peggy's too young to make such decisions.

NEPHROLOGIST: Perhaps, but also perhaps not. Peggy looks like she's 7 years old because of her growth retardation, but she's really 11. In many ways, she is an old 11. By this I mean that she has had some experience with illness and death in a way that even many of us as adults have not had. She is a very quiet and private person, just like the other members of her family, and tends not to share her feelings or thoughts very readily. But I think that she is very aware of what is happening to her. You should also know that, because Peggy's younger brother has Down syndrome, he has required a lot of her parents' time and attention. Although Peggy is among the youngest children in her family and has also been quite sick, she has had to assume a lot of the responsibility for her own medical care. She has paid close attention to her diet and her fluid needs and had been totally responsible for her medications for at least the past 2 years. Thus, she is even more aware of her illness than you might imagine. I think that she is and always has been a very important member of the team in making decisions about her care.

PRACTITIONER: Let me add that this family is strongly religious. They have sought and received the support of their clergyman in their decision. The family believes fervently in a just God who rewards the good with life after death. For them, death means a reunion with those who have died before. Whether you and I share that belief is immaterial. Our job with this family is to allow them to cope with the impending tragedy as well as they can. They have thought about their decision a great deal, and I know they wonder sometimes if they are doing the right thing. They would have these concerns no matter which decision they made. But for them, now, given their experiences, their life-style, and their beliefs, I think they feel that they have made the best decision they can. Peggy understands that death is final and irreversible. We have talked, several times since her sister's death and especially during the past year, about dying. She doesn't want to die, but I think she can accept what's happening to her.

One other thing you should be aware of is that Peggy and her family would like her to be at home when she dies. The parents discussed this with Peggy about a month ago and then asked me if I would be available to them if Peggy were in pain. I have agreed to help them in any way I can.

STAFF MEMBER: I think that this family is being morbid and is preoccupied with Peggy's death.

PRACTITIONER: I understand your feelings; this is a difficult situation for all of us, but please don't misunderstand me. They have discussed Peggy's death once with her and once with me. What they told her was that they would not leave her and that they would take care of her no matter how sick she felt or how bad her kidneys became. I think she was very comforted and even relieved by their promise to stand by her and keep her comfortable.

STAFF MEMBER: Should we talk to Peggy about dying?

NEPHROLOGIST: If she wants to talk about it. I would certainly acknowledge that she is very sick and that, as she knows, her kidneys are not working properly. But please remember, Peggy is not dying yet. She still has a lot of living to do even if her living only lasts another few weeks or even days. I would like us to do everything we can to get her home as soon as possible so that she can live a while longer in the environment that she loves so much.

Peggy was discharged on her eighth hospital day, alert and oriented, but restricted to bed rest.

Follow-up. Peggy died at home a week after discharge.

Discussion

Care of the terminally ill child for whom potential intervention is available but denied is an extremely difficult and frustrating task for even the most committed professional. When intervention is denied, we must weigh whether evidence exists that the intervention, without doubt, would extend life in a way that is acceptable to the child and the family. If almost no doubt exists that the treatment would be curative and is time proven, and if the family denies treatment, then such denial may constitute medical neglect of the child. If, however, as in Peggy's case, substantial question exists about the success of the intervention, the family has a definite right to help decide whether to proceed with the intervention or whether the interests of the child are better served by protecting her from discomfort, serious side-effects, and the real possibility of an unhappy life. In such circumstances, we need to listen carefully to the family's concerns and make sure that they are as informed as possible about the consequences of whatever decision they help make.

• • •

Peggy, at age 11, had the physical characteristics of a 7-year-old and thus showed one of the stigmata of chronic renal disease: stunted growth. Adults often treat and have expectations of children who are small for their age more in keeping with their apparent age than with their actual chronological age.

Peggy had been too ill to progress with her peers in many of the usual tasks of an 11-year-old. However, she had learned to assume many of the responsibilities associated with her illness and performed her tasks in such a way that they merited praise from her health providers. She had earned the right to help make decisions regarding her care, a right that is often not recognized at all until children are much older. Certainly, the law usually does not allow for self-determination of medical care until middle or late adolescence.

At least in the area of thinking about medical care, Peggy was in the transitional stage between concrete and formal operations and showed evidence of her ability to think futuristically about her life. Her thinking closely reflected that of her family, indicating that independence of thought and movement away from her parents had not yet begun: her definition of self was very much determined by the expectations and beliefs of her family. She was also still compliant in carrying out all medical regimens, another indication of her preadolescent status.

Defense mechanisms/coping styles/adaptive behaviors

Peggy adopted two roles: that of the passively compliant patient and that of the pseudoadult child. One feels a sense of hopelessness in her acceptance of her fate. The family's repeated use of the farm analogy raises the question of whether Peggy's image of herself might be that of the damaged animal that is only worthy of slaughter. On the other hand, there is no sense of helplessness in her relationships with others: she still derives comfort from parental and familial envelopment and from the reliance she and her family placed on their religious belief in life after death.

Management

The staff has a right and an obligation to raise questions about the moral and ethical implications of a parental decision that denies a child patient access to potentially curative therapy. In turn, an advocate for the patient and family must be available to present their viewpoint if they are not able or do not wish to do so themselves.

Unless questions about ethics and morality are openly discussed, both subtle and overt interactional problems can arise between the staff and the family that can undermine the overall treatment plan for the child. Any physician, nurse, or other health care provider who maintains an ethical position that cannot be reconciled with the treatment plan requested by the family and agreed to by the responsible physician should be offered the opportunity to withdraw from the care of the child if at all possible.

Expanding technological capability in medicine makes the issue of termination of curative care increasingly difficult. One should always attempt to listen carefully to a family and offer them full information and support if they wish to help make decisions about the kind of care they believe is in the best interests of their child. Such a partnership in decision making can help to reduce feelings of guilt if complications arise during therapy or when the child dies.

Indications for referral

Professional-parent disagreements about appropriate terminal care sometimes require expert opinions from a variety of different disciplines. If parental demands appear unreasonable and seem to be based on irrational decision making, consultation from a psychiatrist may be appropriate. In addition, the legality of certain parental requests or demands may need to be reviewed by the attorney for either the hospital or the responsible physician or by a guardian appointed for the child by the court.

Follow-up of the family after the death of the child is extremely important, since parental or sibling guilt about termination of curative care may reach pathological proportions and interfere with daily living functioning for a prolonged period of time.

Chapter 10 · The adolescent from 12 to 14 years (early adolescence)

Physiological growth and development

MALES: Early pubertal changes, including testicular and penile growth. Nocturnal emissions.

FEMALES: Growth spurt near completion. Menarche.

Psychological growth and development

FREUD	Early genital stage; recrudescence of Oedipal (Electra) conflict; fleeting homosexual contacts with peers
ERIKSON	Identity vs. role confusion "Who am I?" as a physical person
PIAGET	Transitional phase: concrete operational period → early formal operational period
KOHLBERG	Conventional level
SEARS	Extrafamilial learning

The adolescent from 12 to 14 years (early adolescence)

FAMILY: Death

CONCEPTS DISCUSSED: *Loss of a parent*
Early adolescent pregnancy
Sexual activity for nonsexual purposes
Depressive equivalents

Mary Lee was a healthy 13-year-old girl who was 2 months pregnant when she was examined by her primary care practitioner for the first time in 2 years.

Data gathering

Past history. Mary Lee had been the product of an otherwise uncomplicated 34-week pregnancy when her mother was 13 years old. Mary Lee had grown and developed normally. She experienced menarche at 10 years of age; her periods became regular about a year later.

Family history. Mary Lee's mother had had chronic renal disease since childhood. In the 2 years preceding Mary Lee's pregnancy, her mother's physical condition deteriorated, and she died at age 27 awaiting renal transplantation. At the time of her mother's death, Mary Lee was placed in foster care.

Mary Lee's mother had never held steady employment; she and her daughter had always been wholly dependent on public assistance. Their extended family lived in another state and had contact with them only rarely. Mary Lee and her mother had moved often within their large metropolitan area in response to financial or social needs.

School. Mary Lee's attendance at the five schools in which she had been enrolled had always been irregular and her behavior unruly. On achievement testing, she had consistently performed one to three grade levels below expectation for her class in all subjects.

At age 11½ Mary Lee had assumed major responsibility for her mother's daily care. She was suspended from school 3 months later for absenteeism.

Peers. Mary Lee described herself as a "tomboy": someone who had always enjoyed being part of boys' rather than girls' groups in her neighborhood. However, she had one close girlfriend with whom she spent time listening to records and talking about boys.

Mary Lee began dating occasionally at age 11. She became sexually active with her current and only boyfriend at age 12, about the same time that her mother's condition had become dramatically worse.

For 6 weeks after her placement in foster care, Mary Lee did not see her boyfriend. However, she began seeing him frequently after that, although her foster parents objected strongly.

The pregnancy. Mary Lee reported that she had never considered using contraception to prevent pregnancy. On the one hand, she did not appear to understand that unprotected sexual activity could lead to pregnancy or that using contraception in the present could prevent a pregnancy in the future. On the other hand, after much denial of any feelings of loss over her mother's death, she cried, "I want my baby. I can love my baby like my mama loved me, and the baby will love me back. I am having the baby for my mama." She was vehement in her decision to keep the pregnancy and her child and refused to consider any long-range problems this might pose for her.

Mary Lee's pregnancy was medically uneventful except for the onset of premature rupture of membranes at 36 weeks. She delivered a healthy baby girl who weighed 2100 g (4 pounds 9 ounces). She named the infant after her mother.

Discussion

Sexual activity during early adolescence can be a way of fulfilling nonsexual needs for acceptance, nurturance, and support (Cohen and Friedman, 1975). Pregnancy at this age can represent an attempt to resolve depressive feelings or a means of replacing a real or fantasized loss.

• • •

Mary Lee had an early but normal menarche at 10 years of age, in contrast to the average girl who begins menstruating between 12.8 and 13.2 years of age (Root, 1973). The majority of her physical changes, including her maximum height spurt, occurred prior to her menarche. Her pregnancy confirmed that ovulation had occurred, as would be expected approximately 1 to 2 years after menarche. Mary Lee thus had all the reproductive capabilities of an adult woman.

Physical and psychological development, however, do not necessarily proceed at similar rates during adolescence. Although Mary Lee had entered the genital stage of psychosexual development, as evidenced by her heterosexual activity, she appeared to be using her relationship with her boyfriend to obtain the basic nurturance denied her by her mother's illness and death rather than to fulfill the purely genital priority articulated by Freud. Indeed, the undifferentiated state of her sexual identity is best expressed by her description of herself as a tomboy.

Mary Lee appeared not to understand the concepts related to contraception as a preventive measure against future pregnancy; however, for Mary Lee, the wish to have someone to love may be a confounding factor in interpreting her behavior. However, her lack of realistic understanding of or planning for parenthood as a long-term commitment is typical of early adolescent concrete thinking, which is very much oriented to the present rather than to the future.

Mary Lee had had neither the time nor the opportunity to experience the usual process of identity formation. Indeed, she had been forced prematurely into **role reversal** as she mothered her mother during her terminal illness. Thus, Mary Lee was deprived of both her mother's nurturance as well as her presence as a primary model for Mary Lee's future female identity. In addition, as she begins to mother her child, Mary Lee will prematurely assume an identity usually assumed in very late adolescence or in adulthood.

Often, early adolescents lack insight into their own feelings. Since her mother had died 4 months prior to Mary Lee's medical visit, one would expect that she would feel some depression. Because Mary Lee, like many 13-year-olds, was unable to verbalize her feelings, her sexual activity and pregnancy should be considered as possible **depressive equivalents** (Weiner, 1970). Similarly, boredom and restlessness, multiple somatic complaints, flight to and from people, difficulty concentrating, and acting-out behaviors can fit this category.

Mary Lee's identification with her mother, the female closest to her, and her need through her baby to maintain contact with her mother are age-appropriate. Naming the baby after her mother again reflects the concreteness of her thinking and is entirely in keeping with her developmental stage.

Defense mechanisms/coping styles/adaptive behaviors

Denial in act, word, and fantasy and identification with her mother appear to be major coping strategies for Mary Lee. She denies her feeling of loss verbally, but also tries to undo her sense of loneliness by the act of becoming pregnant and thus providing herself with a replacement object for her love. In her fantasy, she sees the infant assuming the place of her mother as someone she will love and who will love her in return. Her identification with her mother, including pregnancy at an identical age, helps her to retain a semblance of her mother's presence in her life.

Intervention

Mary Lee needs regular prepartum obstetric care and counseling. Although she is only 13 years old, with good care and particular attention to adequate nutrition, she should have no more obstetric problems than adult women of similar background. Helping her to keep regular appointments and to follow medical recommendations, however, may be more difficult. The likelihood of her delivering prematurely, as she did, is greater for girls her age than it is among older women of similar background (Elster and McAnarney, 1980).

The practitioner from whom Mary Lee first sought help can continue to advocate for both Mary Lee and then her child if Mary Lee wishes. Advocacy for Mary Lee includes (1) referral for obstetric care; (2) ongoing support to help her develop her own identity and sexual and vocational futures through individual or group counseling sessions; (3) discussion of the role of the father and/or other family members and engaging them, if appropriate, in counseling sessions; (4) health supervision of the infant; and (5) anticipatory guidance for Mary Lee as a mother (McAnarney, 1975).

As an early adolescent who has lost her mother recently, Mary Lee could be expected to fare particularly well with a nurturant female professional who would provide her with both obstetric care and a healthy female role model. A female nurse-midwife, obstetrician, or general physician would be appropriate.

Communication between Mary Lee and her caregivers must be as concrete, or explicit, as possible. Diagrams, life-sized dolls, short but complete lists, and frequent contacts to reiterate information and provide constant reinforcement will help her to perform her new tasks successfully. As in any program that seeks to modify behavior, close supervision with positive feedback is essential. In this regard, foster parents, if willing, can be particularly helpful.

A major goal for Mary Lee is to help her return to her normal adolescent activities, particularly at school. If Mary Lee is to resolve her mother's death and develop to her maximum capability, she should develop her potential for a vocation. In addition, once-pregnant adolescents who return to school after their child's birth are reported to have a lower repeat pregnancy rate during adolescence than those who do not return to school (Dickens et al., 1973).

Indications for referral

The resolution of Mary Lee's grief over the loss of her mother may or may not require formal psychiatric intervention. Although she never displayed overt depression, Mary Lee's defiance of authority and sexual activity during her foster placement might be considered depressive equivalents. A continuation or escalation of such behavior may require treatment. Engaging the foster family in counseling, as well, may help facilitate Mary Lee's transition into the new family and maintain the placement so that she will not experience yet another loss.

SCHOOL: School phobia

CONCEPTS DISCUSSED: *School refusal/withdrawal*
Homosexual panic
Somatization
Depressive equivalents
Work-related father absence

Rick was a 12½-year-old seventh-grade student whose mother called the practitioner in late January because Rick had been complaining of early morning abdominal pain for almost a month. He had been absent from school since the Christmas holidays.

Data gathering

Past history. Rick's early childhood development had been unremarkable. He had enjoyed good health and had no history of any major illnesses or trauma. He had recently started wearing glasses for myopia.

Family history. Rick was the middle child of the family. He had a 15-year-old brother and an 8-year-old sister, both of whom were healthy. His mother was 35 years old and worked as a homemaker. His father was 38 years old and worked as a traveling salesman, spending 3 out of 5 weekdays out of town. Rick's maternal grandmother, who had lived with the family for 4 years since her husband's death, was 65 years old and in good health. Although neither Rick's mother nor grandmother worked outside the home, they were active in a number of community clubs and organizations. Their participation in these activities had been limited by Rick's absence from school: at least one of them remained home to be with him during the day.

School. Rick's mother reported that of the three children, Rick had had the most difficulty adjusting to kindergarten. For several days, he had cried when she left him and had wanted to return home with her. Eventually, however, he had become acclimated to school and successfully completed kindergarten. He attended school regularly, through the fifth grade, missing only 3 or 4 days each school year because of minor illnesses. He achieved above average grades as did his siblings.

When Rick had been in the sixth grade, he had missed 15 school days. In addition, he had gone to the school nurse's office and complained of a stomachache prior to his physical education class on several occasions. At the end of 45 minutes, the duration of the gym class, he had reported feeling much better and had returned to his classroom.

Peers. Rick had several friends in the neighborhood with whom he liked to play. He often invited friends to spend the night at his home, but had never spent a night at a friend's home. He had refused to attend overnight summer camp the summer before his entrance into seventh grade.

Interviews and school contact. The practitioner asked to talk with and examine Rick alone first without his parents. Rick was engaging and articulate concerning issues unrelated to school. He also said that he had had abdominal pain that morning but that he had felt much better at noontime. He denied afternoon pain. In discussing his weekend activities, he revealed that he had no symptoms on Saturdays or Sundays.

When asked about school, he would acknowledge only that he did not want to return and looked at the floor when asked why.

Rick's physical examination was entirely normal and showed clear development of secondary sexual characteristics (Tanner stage II-III). Rick demonstrated some shyness and seemed anxious, especially during his genital examination, but asked no questions.

The practitioner then saw Rick's parents together without Rick. They both expressed their concern about Rick's refusal to return to school. His mother, in particular, wondered if his behavior were related to her husband's absences, especially since she had difficulty forcing Rick to go to school when her husband was away from home. She also wondered if it were "unhealthy" for Rick to have two women, his mother and grandmother, rather than his father, setting most of the limits for his behavior.

Rick's father acknowledged that his absences worried him somewhat but expressed surprise that Rick was having trouble with school, since his older son had done well.

The parents agreed that the practitioner could contact the school to learn from Rick's teachers and principal about his behavior, attendance, and achievement.

The practitioner then talked with Rick and his parents together. He restated his opinion that Rick was a normal, healthy boy. The practitioner told Rick that he would be contacting the school because he thought that it was important that he know more about Rick and how he was doing. He also told Rick that he wanted him to return to school the next day, but that he would give him an excuse from gym class until his next visit in a week. Although Rick expressed a willingness to return under these circumstances, the practitioner asked Rick's father to arrange his schedule so that he could help Rick get to school on time the following morning even if Rick were to develop stomach pain.

The practitioner talked with Rick's homeroom teacher, the principal, the nurse, and the physical education teacher in an after-school conference later in the week. Their consensus was that Rick's behavior in school had always seemed very appropriate. They commented on his absences from gym during the sixth grade, which had been entered on his record. They noted that Rick's particular physical education group had contained several boisterous and aggressive boys, some of whom were also in his present class. They questioned whether anything could have happened in gym or elsewhere on the school premises to upset Rick enough so that he refused to return to school.

When the practitioner saw Rick a few days later, the boy reported that he had returned to school without difficulty after his last appointment. He seemed comfortable talking about all of his classes except gym. The practitioner decided to explore Rick's feelings about physical education:

PRACTITIONER: Tell me, Rick, about some of the things you do in gym.

RICK: Oh, baseball, basketball, swimming, and stuff like that.

PRACTITIONER: Those sound like pretty strenuous activities. Do you have to wear gym clothes or can you play in your school clothes?

RICK: *(Very quietly.)* Gym clothes.

PRACTITIONER: I would guess that you can't wear your gym clothes underneath your school clothes, especially after you finish playing. Most schools have a big changing room and sometimes a large shower area that all of the boys use together. Is that the way it is at your school?

RICK: *(Head down.)* Yeah.

PRACTITIONER: Sometimes boys don't like to go to gym class because they have to change their clothes in front of everybody else.

RICK: *(No movement.)*

PRACTITIONER: Last year you visited the school nurse's office before gym and then felt better when class was over.

RICK: But my stomach hurt me.

PRACTITIONER: I understand that your stomach hurt. Sometimes when a person is upset, his stomach hurts.

RICK: *(Nods his head.)*

PRACTITIONER: I wonder whether staying home from school is connected with your feelings about gym class.

RICK: *(No response.)*

PRACTITIONER: Sometimes when boys are growing up, they compare themselves with other boys, especially boys in gym class. Everybody wants to be as fast or as good on a team as everybody else. But boys also compare how they're growing up. When you're changing your gym clothes in a big room and everybody else is undressed, too, it's easy to look and see how the other boys are growing and developing. Sometimes people don't just look, they even touch each other.

RICK: *(Becomes tearful.)*

PRACTITIONER: Rick, I see this is upsetting you, but I'm trying to find out what's happened so I can help. You are beginning to show some changes in your body. These changes are normal and mean you're becoming a man, exactly as I would expect at your age. You're developing right on schedule. I wouldn't be surprised if some of the other boys made comments or touched you or you touched them.

With much hesitation Rick reported that some of the boys in his gym class had been teasing him and had asked him to touch their genitals. He also said that they had threatened him that if he told anyone, they would beat him up.

The practitioner reassured Rick that he understood what had happened and how he felt. He said that he would ask the school to change Rick's gym class. At Rick's request, he further agreed not to tell the school personnel or Rick's parents all that Rick had told him.

The practitioner then met with Rick and his parents together. He did not reveal the details of Rick's experiences in gym class, but merely told the parents that Rick had been bullied. It was his recommendation that Rick's physical education class be changed permanently, a suggestion he promised to make to the school immediately. He requested that Rick return to school full-time at the beginning of the next week.

Follow-up. The practitioner saw the family again on two occasions within the following month to review Rick's progress and the parents' concerns about Rick's father's work and travel. Rick did well, and his attendance for the remainder of the school year was excellent.

Discussion

School phobia has also been termed school withdrawal or school refusal. When it occurs after the primary grades, it can indicate an acute withdrawal from a frightening school-related situation or a more chronic pathological state of separation anxiety (usually with regard to the mother) stemming from a hostile, but dependent relationship characterized by an intense desire to be close together (Bakwin and Bakwin, 1972).

Somatic complaints are prominent and include anorexia, nausea, vomiting, diarrhea, headache, and abdominal pain. Most symptoms occur on school day mornings and are strikingly absent later in the day and/or on weekends and holidays.

Common precipitating events that are school related include changes in the school setting, episodes of humiliation or embarrassment in the presence of teachers or classmates, and real or fantasized academic or social failure, after which return to school is difficult for the child.

The initial step in treatment is prompt return to school. Additional treatment includes a careful search for the cause of the school refusal and alterations in the school setting and/or counseling if necessary.

·   ·   ·

Rick was an early adolescent who was beginning to grow and develop rapidly. Males enter puberty on the average at 11.5 to 11.8 years of age. The first signs of puberty are testicular and penile enlargement. The adolescent growth spurt in males occurs between 12.5 and 15 years of age with the maximum velocity of growth occuring at approximately 14 years. Thus, as was corroborated by the practitioner's examination, Rick was in the midst of his physical adolescence.

Genital concerns emerge during early adolescence. Comparison of genital size in settings like physical education class is common behavior, particularly among males. Rick's withdrawal from gym class during sixth grade may have been the first indication that he was concerned about the adequacy of his body size or his physical capability in activities such as team sports.

Homosexual behavior may actually be less threatening to the undifferentiated early adolescent than is intimate heterosexual behavior. Among males, either individual or group masturbation may occur. Rick's acute withdrawal from school, in particular from the intimacy of gym class, suggests that he may have experienced **homosexual panic.**

The early adolescent may be too embarrassed to discuss his fears about homosexual behavior or sexual intimidation with parents or other adults. On the other hand, either he may not have the cognitive capacity to understand the relationship between these experiences with his peers and his refusal to go to school, or he may repress the experience altogether.

The practitioner, however, should be aware of the possibility of sexual contact, ridicule, or embarrassment as the cause of school refusal. Since it is unlikely that a young adolescent will volunteer this information, vague, open-ended questions are unproductive. Instead, the practitioner must present concrete information to which the adolescent can respond, either verbally or nonverbally by such clues as moving uncomfortably or sitting very still in his chair or nodding.

Rick's major symptom, school phobia, was a situational crisis that was satisfactorily resolved by a change in his physical education class. However, the issue of Rick's father's peripheral involvement with the family because of his job requirements deserves comment.

Rick's mother's observations that it might not be ideal for her and her mother to be setting limits for Rick is an interesting one. Regardless of the fact that Rick's father claimed that his older son did well despite his absence, this is not necessarily relevant for Rick. In fact, Rick's early history of difficulty separating from his mother is indicative of their closeness and raises the issue of whether Rick's identification with his father and his resolution of the Oedipal conflict may be somewhat tenuous.

As Rick enters midadolescence and begins to struggle with who he is, it is important that his father be present to provide Rick with appropriate role modeling and to help him to consolidate his identity formation. Rick's father may not realize the importance his consistent presence has for his adolescent sons. In fact, like many parents, he may believe that, as his children grow into adolescence, a parent's presence is less important than it was earlier.

Defense mechanisms/coping styles/adaptive behaviors

Rick used the strategies of avoidance and somatization in his attempt to manage an overwhelmingly frightening and anxiety-laden situation: homosexual panic. Somatization, or the formation of physical complaints that have no physiological basis, can be associated, for example, with perceptions of pain, limitation of movement, and paresthesia. Despite the fact that he had no underlying organic disease, it is possible that Rick's abdominal pain represented a combination of physiological and psychological processes: his anxiety about going to school, or, more, specifically, physical education class, resulted in changes in his autonomic and intestinal function, which produced stomach cramping. His lack of pain during the afternoons and on nonschool days correlates with his periods of low anxiety and, hence, low autonomic discharge, which would be expected to result in a decrease in symptoms.

Somatization in Rick's case may be considered a depressive equivalent. Another indication of his depression is his withdrawal from his peer group.

Intervention

The practitioner who undertakes management of the child experiencing school phobia needs to recognize the condition, understand it, and decide what role to assume. In their review of school withdrawal, a term they prefer to school phobia, Nader, Bullock, and Caldwell (1975) made several important points:

• School withdrawal is a great imitator of other illnesses; the initial symptoms may be physical, such as abdominal pain, and not emotional, such as overt depression.

• There are specific historical clues: a history of an increasing number of school absences, an increased number of absences in the fall and reluctance to return to school after the holidays or weekends, a decreased number of symptoms on the weekends and holidays, and a previous history of separation problems.

• School withdrawal that occurs in children and young adolescents, is of short duration, and is accepted as an emotional problem by at least one parent has a better prognosis than does that which occurs in older adolescents during high school, is of longer duration, is repetitive of the behavior of an older sibling, and is attributed by the parents solely to physical illness or the school setting.

• School withdrawal may represent an acute response to an overwhelmingly frightening event, or it may be indicative of more chronic concerns at home such as fantasied or actual parental illness or loss, strife, or aggression.

The practitioner, although considering school phobia as the diagnosis, must eliminate organic illness by a complete medical history and physical examination to reassure the child and the family. Once physical illness has been ruled out, Nader and associates suggest the following strategy for the practitioner:

• Interview the child/adolescent alone to observe how he separates from the family and to acquire any history that might be too sensitive to elicit in front of the parents.

• Interview the parents alone to discuss their candid observations about their child's behavior and to elicit any history of parental tensions and worries such as marital, in-law, financial, and/or health problems. Also observe how the parents interact and whether they communicate well or poorly.

- With parental permission and the child's knowledge, contact the school and determine which school personnel have information that is relevant to the particular child's problem. The child's school attendance, behavior, and achievement should be reviewed. Occasionally, school personnel know why a child will not go to school but do not know to whom they should communicate this information. The practitioner may want to make a school visit to discuss the child's problems at a conference.
- Decide whether you, as the practitioner, can manage the child on the basis of the following:
  1. Personal knowledge, time, and interest
  2. The prognosis of the school withdrawal based on the child's age, the duration of the symptom, previous health, the child's separation history, and the family's level of cooperation

Indications for referral

Any adolescent over the age of 13 to 14 years and/or whose symptoms have persisted for more than 4 to 6 weeks and/or who has a significant history of chronic difficulty separating from the family should be considered for an immediate mental health referral.

In conjunction with the referral, the practitioner should help the family become fully aware that the adolescent is physically healthy but that his problems require more sophisticated psychological care than the practitioner can provide. Since the members of such families have had difficulty with the issue of separation among themselves, they may have difficulty "separating" from the practitioner, or they may perceive the referral as a rejection. The practitioner should express a willingness to continue to see the adolescent for routine health maintenance and acute illness care. The psychological aspects of the school phobia syndrome, however, must be clearly stated and the appropriate lines of communication defined so that the family will not manipulate the various professionals involved in their care.

ILLNESS: Acute, self-limited illness

CONCEPTS DISCUSSED: *Hospitalization*
Regression
Behavior modification and limit setting

Alice was a 12-year-old girl who had experienced fever, cough, and lethargy for a week prior to her admission to the hospital for treatment of staphylococcal pneumonia.

Data gathering

Past history. Alice had had no major illnesses or injuries throughout her childhood. Her development had been entirely appropriate.

Family history. Alice was the older of two daughters of a 36-year-old father and a 34-year-old mother. Alice's father had been unemployed and on disability compensation since he had sustained a job-related back injury 3 years before. Alice's mother did not work outside the home. Alice's younger sister was 4 years old and in good health. As an only child for the first 8 years of her life, Alice had been "the center of attention" in her family unit and was very close to both of her parents. She had never stayed away from home overnight.

School. Alice began kindergarten uneventfully at 5 years of age. Her attendance had been excellent for the first 3 years of school. At the time of her sister's birth, Alice showed marked changes in her behavior, clung to her parents, especially her mother, and became very demanding. She refused to go to school for 2 weeks until, at the suggestion of her physician, her parents spent more time with her alone and began to allow her to participate in the care of her sister. Alice's behavior became more age appropriate almost immediately, and she returned to school within a few days.

Since then, Alice had maintained good grades, attendance, and behavior at school.

Peers. Alice was sociable and fairly outgoing. She was part of a close-knit group of a half dozen girls who spent time together in and out of school. On one or two occasions Alice had had a friend stay overnight at her home, although Alice had never spent the night at a friend's house.

Hospital course. When told by her practitioner that she had to be hospitalized, Alice, who was quite lethargic and feverish, became tearful and said that she was afraid to stay away from home overnight alone. When reassured that her mother could stay with her and that she could take one or two favorite personal items to the hospital, Alice seemed relieved and fell asleep in the family car on the way to the hospital.

Upon admission, Alice was placed on intravenous antibiotic therapy, and a chest tube was inserted. Her mother helped the staff to interpret all the procedures to Alice, and the girl performed extremely well, tolerating her pain and discomfort with few complaints.

On the sixth hospital day, Alice's chest tube was removed, and she was allowed to ambulate in her room. She was doing so well clinically that the staff suggested that her mother, who had remained in the hospital constantly since Alice's admission, should go home to sleep at night. Although Alice demanded that her mother stay, Alice's mother told her that she was exhausted and would not be back until the next day.

During the next 2 days, Alice's parents and her sister visited her often but left the hospital in the evening at the end of regular visiting hours. The staff and her parents noted that Alice was withdrawn and nonverbal and rang the bell continuously for assistance in eating, dressing, and using the bathroom, all of which she was physically capable of doing alone. Although the staff acknowledged Alice's feelings of depression about her hospitalization, her sense of loss at her mother's leaving at night, and her insecurity, Alice's behavior did not change. The nurses characterized Alice as "12 going on 2."

On the ninth hospital day, a management conference was held. The attending physician, the floor staff members, and Alice's parents were present. A plan to modify Alice's unacceptable demanding behavior and to increase her independence was developed and presented to Alice by her physician, her parents, and the nurse who provided most of Alice's care. The plan had two components: (1) a member of the staff would visit Alice every hour on the half hour for 10 minutes throughout the day to see how she was doing and offer her any assistance that she needed, and (2) in anticipation of going home, Alice would be given a daily list of things to do for *herself* (eat her meals unassisted, wash and toilet alone) and for *others* (make a key ring for her father, a change purse for her mother, and a paint-by-number picture for her sister).

Alice seemed happy about having some goals that she could work toward and that would help her to get herself ready to go home. It became apparent as she talked that she had thought that she might never get well and return to her family.

However, during the first day of the program, her behavior deteriorated even further, and a staff member called the physician to ask for other suggestions about handling her. The physician asked the staff members to continue the program for at least another 2 days. He also asked them to be particularly careful about positively reinforcing all of Alice's acceptable behavior regardless of how small the activity might be. Over the next several days, Alice became more verbal and independent. She was discharged on the sixteenth hospital day, having completed all her projects.

Discussion

Acute, self-limited illness is common in adolescence; hospitalization, however, is becoming increasingly less common. The unfamiliarity of the hospital setting and the adolescent's lack of preparation for the patient role in an acute admission can result in some unacceptable behaviors that are, nevertheless, developmentally expected for the young adolescent.

A 12-year-old girl, in her early adolescence, is often in the midst of vast physical changes, including recent or anticipated menarche. Thus, she may be uncomfortable and self-conscious with physical examinations and procedures that threaten her bodily integrity or her sense of personal privacy.

Hospitalizations that include separation from parents and family may be particularly frightening to young adolescents who are not firm in their physical or psychological identities. They are often still very attached to and dependent upon their parents, and they regress to an even more dependent state when they are ill or hospitalized.

• • •

Alice's behaviors in the hospital were typical of those seen in many 12-year-olds: demands that her mother stay with her and withdrawal and attention-seeking devices when her mother was separated from her. Youngsters of this age may have multiple reasons for wanting extra parental support at times of crisis. However, specifically in the hospital setting, intravenous feedings, surgical procedures even if relatively "minor," the use of bedpans, and other experiences may be especially threatening to the 12-year-old's need for reassurance about the basic integrity of her changing body. In this context, having her mother, rather than an unfamiliar health professional, provide care, also provides support and comfort and decreases embarrassment.

Alice was still concrete in her thinking: more concerned with the here and now than with the future. Care plans for the hospitalized early adolescent should include consideration of things in the present: comfort, the presence of family members without fostering undue dependence, and insistence on the accomplishment of the age-appropriate tasks of eating, dressing, and toileting as the patient's physical condition allows. In addition, because it may be difficult for someone of Alice's age to do so herself, others must help her to focus her attention on the end of hospitalization and her return to normal life after the completion of treatment.

Alice's response to her admission is a prime example of the misconceptions an adolescent can form about discharge. Alice felt much better at the end of her first week in the hospital. Since her continued hospitalization was necessary for the completion of parenteral antibiotic therapy rather than as a response to subjective feelings of illness, she feared that she might remain hospitalized indefinitely. She had never been able to verbalize this fear until she was asked to participate in some activities to help her prepare for going home. At that point, it became possible for her to talk about her concern, since she had been given a definite indication that her fear was unfounded.

The worsening of Alice's behavior after the management conference was held and a new plan of care was established is not uncommon. The adolescent may be confused by the change in the professionals' behavior and fantasize that this change indicates worsening of her condition. Ultimately, as she sees that the change in the professionals' behavior is a declaration that things are going well, the adolescent may feel reassured and become able to respond positively to the new demands that are made of her.

Defense mechanisms/coping styles/adaptive behaviors

Under stress, early adolescents often display regressive, dependent behaviors. Alice demonstrated her regression by refusing to eat, dress, or toilet alone even when physically able to do so. For Alice, this kind of behavior was not unexpected, since it accurately reflected the coping style she had used earlier during childhood.

Depression is frequently observed among hospitalized patients. In early adolescents, depression is often manifested by withdrawal and/or attention-seeking behaviors reminiscent of the behavior of the much younger child. Lack of insight and an inability to adequately verbalize feelings, normal characteristics of the young adolescent, are the prime determinants of such behavioral changes.

Intervention

Management should be directed toward helping the adolescent to display independence and show mastery over the challenges of the hospitalization experience.

To help the adolescent to function independently, the following must occur: (1) a great deal of family support should be offered during a period of acclimation to the hospital; (2) family support should be gradually withdrawn at the same time that other support systems are introduced; (3) while supports are being withdrawn, the child must be given adequate information, guidance, and limit setting so that she can appropriately monitor her own behavior to fulfill the expectations of hospital personnel; and (4) her attention must be focused on relinquishing the patient role in preparation for discharge and "wellness."

The staff managed Alice correctly. They encouraged her mother to leave Alice's bedside after her condition stabilized so that Alice could gain independence from her family. This is particularly important for early adolescents, whose independence may be fragile and in need of support. They further recognized that her withdrawn, nonverbal state and attention-seeking behavior were Alice's attempts to communicate the way she felt. It is often helpful for a staff member to interpret the meaning of the early adolescent's behavior directly, for example, "You're probably lonely without your family" or "The hospital can be scary." Although some early adolescents will not be able to recognize the truth of these observations about their feelings because they lack insight, most adolescents understand genuine concern on the part of the health caregiver.

A conference that includes the parents affords the staff members the opportunity to share their concerns with the family and enlist the family's support in the management of the adolescent. The leadership for calling a meeting to discuss the adolescent's behavior is usually provided by either the practitioner or a member of the ward staff.

Behavior modification programs that provide the early adolescent with structure and a clear sense of expectation are often very helpful in encouraging patients like Alice to function at their optimal developmental level. The added advantage of a behavioral modification program is that it provides members of the ward staff, who work in shifts or rotations, clear, written direction about how to respond with consistency to the adolescent's behaviors or demands.

Once a plan had been formed and presented to Alice, she knew exactly what the staff's expectations for her were. However, she also knew that someone would come to see her regularly and that she could expect positive reinforcement for appropriate behavior.

An additional feature of Alice's program was the inclusion of activities that provided her with the opportunity to make things for her family members. She thus derived a sense of closeness to them while at the same time participating in an age-appropriate and behaviorally acceptable activity.

Indications for referral

The behavior demonstrated by Alice as an inpatient is understandable after considering her history and her developmental status as an early adolescent. If her regression, depression, and attention-seeking behaviors consistently worsened, rather than improved, after the behavior modification program was instituted, a behavioral or psychological consultation might be warranted to determine if her behaviors were indeed reactive to hospitalization or indicative of a more fixed psychological problem.

Support of caregivers

Floor-based staff members need an understanding of child and adolescent development, the realization that setting clear limits and expectations for the adolescent is not punitive, and support to implement a successful behavior modification program.

If behavior modification programs are to succeed, they must be devised as a cooperative effort between the health care professionals and the family. In addition, such programs cannot include any elements that are not agreed to by all participants, including the child.

Of particular importance is attention to strict reinforcement schedules. That is, behaviors to be learned must be rewarded each time they occur. Conversely, behaviors to be extinguished must be ignored or negatively reinforced each time they occur. Otherwise, a situation of "partial reinforcement" will be created, and the plan will take much longer to become effective or will fail entirely. For example, if Alice dresses herself one morning and staff members fail to provide positive reinforcement through verbal praise (the agreed-upon "reward"), she is less likely to perform the behavior the next day. Alternatively, if she uses her assistance bell inappropriately and is "rewarded" by a visit, she will continue to ring her bell inappropriately in the hope of getting another response.

Well thought-out and implemented programs seldom require more than a few days of consistent use to significantly modify the behavior of otherwise emotionally healthy adolescents. However, they almost never work immediately. Some period of limit testing by the child is found in essentially all programs. During this time, particularly excellent communication, attention to detail, and unfailing consistency must be implemented if the program is to be ultimately effective. One well-informed staff member should be assigned to the patient each shift to optimize the chance that the program will succeed.

Chapter 11 · The adolescent from 14 to 16 years (midadolescence)

Physiological growth and development

MALES: Peak height velocity.

FEMALES: Growth nearly completed. Regular ovulatory menstrual cycles.

Psychological growth and development

FREUD	Genital stage
ERIKSON	Identity vs. role confusion "Who am I?" as a vocational person
PIAGET	Formal operational period
KOHLBERG	Early postconventional level
SEARS	Extrafamilial learning

Chapter 11

The adolescent from 14 to 16 years (midadolescence)

FAMILY: Divorce

CONCEPTS DISCUSSED: *Role reversal*
Depression
Reaction formation

John was a 15-year-old tenth-grade student whose mother referred him to his lifelong practitioner because of nightwalking, early morning awakening, anorexia, school failure, and multiple threats of running away from home during the previous 6 months. John's parents were divorced 8 months before the onset of his symptoms.

Data gathering

Past history. John had broken his left femur in a skiing accident at age 9. His recovery had been complete. His past health and developmental history were otherwise unremarkable.

Family history. John was the only child of a 38-year-old industrial engineer and a 38-year-old homemaker. John's mother had had three other pregnancies, when John was 1, 2, and 8 years old, which had ended in miscarriages.

When John was 6 years old, his paternal grandfather, who had lived with the family, had been killed in an automobile accident. John developed tantrums and school phobia for 4 weeks after his grandfather's death. Both of these symptoms had disappeared after the parents sought counseling from their practitioner.

When John was 10 years old, his father had been offered a promotion which required that he transfer to another city. John's mother had objected to leaving the town in which her entire extended family lived, and John's father had declined the transfer and the promotion.

John's parents gradually experienced other major disagreements: for example, issues such as whether John should attend a private high school and whether the family should move to a more affluent section of their community. The family decided against these changes, again at John's mother's insistence.

John often witnessed his parents' open disagreements and attempted to play the role of peacemaker, without effect. John's father began to spend increasing amounts of time away from home and also began using alcohol regularly.

John's parents separated when he was 13 years old. John continued to live in the family home with his mother, and his father rented a small apartment across town. John saw his father two or three times a week. When John's parents were formally divorced a year later, they asked him to decide with which parent he wanted to live. John initially refused to make this decision but finally yielded to their pressure: he chose to live with his father. John's mother became angry and accused John of abandoning her. John ultimately decided to stay with his mother. His mother's call for help to the practitioner came 14 months after the divorce and 6 months after the onset of John's symptoms.

School. John had entered school at age 5. He had experienced mild separation anxiety during kindergarten and first grade, which had resolved without intervention. He was an excellent student during elementary school. In junior high his grades had fallen dramatically at the time of his parents' separation but returned to average within a few weeks. Since his parent's divorce, his grades had again dropped, and his last report card showed consistent failure in every subject.

Peers. John had had many friends as a youngster. During the year his parents had been divorced, he had restricted himself to two close male friends with whom he spent most of his nonschool time. He had begun to date a girl a few months before his visit to the practitioner, but his mother had forbidden him to see the girl more than once on the weekend and never during the week. John and his girlfriend had subsequently stopped seeing each other entirely.

Office visit. The practitioner saw John and was impressed with how sad he appeared. John told the practitioner that he was feeling very lonely at home and missed his father greatly. He openly admitted to his symptoms, including his frequent threats about running away. Where he would go if he left home was unclear, but one of his thoughts was that he could live with his father and stop him from drinking. John also believed that, although his parents had some differences of opinion, they could still work these out if they tried, and he wanted to help them do so.

John expressed no conscious suicidal ideation. However, he had experienced recurrent dreams about his paternal grandfather's death in the automobile accident.

John thought that his mother had purposefully imposed overly strict limits on him and his steady girlfriend. John interpreted this as the main reason they had broken up, effectively cutting him off from one of his main sources of support.

Several times during the interview, John talked about how eager he was to leave home at age 18 and become an engineer in the Peace Corps. As he left the practitioner's office, John said that he felt better having talked with him.

Discussion

Adolescents whose parents divorce may feel angry toward one or both parents, feel guilty that they were responsible for the divorce, and/or magically think they can bring the parents back together.

•   •   •

At 15 years of age, John had probably already experienced his period of maximum physical growth, an event which usually occurs at approximately 14 years of age in males. He was also likely to have undergone most of the bodily changes associated with puberty. Thus, his physical identity was becoming solidified.

Cognitively, John was at the early formal operational stage in his thinking. His thought processes, however, were influenced by idealism and the fantasy of magical powers of omnipotence that are characteristic of midadolescents (Weiner and Elkind, 1972). It is not surprising, then, that, despite the fact that John's father continued to drink, John may have magically believed that he could reverse his father's behavior.

The recent loss of his father through divorce was particularly difficult for John as a midadolescent male. During midadolescence, young people seek like-sexed role models with whom to identify. Within families, male children usually model themselves after their fathers, and female adolescents, after their mothers. John's decision to live with his father was a logical one in light of his struggle to define "Who am I?" in the context of the male figures in his family.

John turned to his peers for support when he was under a great deal of stress or feeling particularly lonely. This is typical of the midadolescent who, seeking increased independence from the family of origin, finds comfort in peers.

John displayed behavior characteristic of the early genital stage of psychosexual development. He was interested in girls and actually had a steady girlfriend, despite the unhappiness and disagreements he had witnessed between his mother and father.

John talked openly about wanting to leave home when he was 18, become an engineer, and work in the Peace Corps. Although he was beginning to develop some future orientation in his thinking, he lacked an adequate planning strategy. For example, he stated that he wanted to become an engineer (and thus complete his identification with his father), but he was unrealistic in not including post–high school education in his plan. Last, he wanted to join the Peace Corps. This desire could represent either a means to be distanced from his family or an idealistic gesture. Both interpretations are in accord with his developmental stage. Indeed, both motivations probably contributed to his fantasy.

Defense mechanisms/coping styles/adaptive behaviors

John reacted to his parent's divorce with depression manifested by such symptoms as insomnia, anorexia, and school failure. These symptoms, which are suggestive of depression during midadolescence, are often referred to as depressive equivalents (Weiner, 1970).

John's depression was multiply determined. He was an only child. His parents were very open with him about their marital problems. At 6 years of age, he had experienced a major loss through the unexpected death of his paternal grandfather. Although his symptoms of school refusal and tantrums disappeared after his mother and father sought advice and counseling from John's practitioner to support John through his mourning process, his grief may not have been entirely resolved. The rapidly occurring events of his father's drinking problems, his parents' divorce, the reversal of his decision to live with his father, and the breakup with his girlfriend overwhelmed John to the point of depression.

In addition, John magically thought that he could reverse his father's behavior through his personal intervention. To accomplish this, he proposed to live with his father and take care of him (role reversal). To compensate for his disappointment in his father, who had displayed weakness in a number of major family decisions relative to his mother, John developed a reaction formation manifested by his overidentification (flight from mother, career choice fantasy) with his father.

Intervention

John's male practitioner had the distinct advantage of knowing John and his family for some time. His counsel regarding John's behavior when his grandfather died was successful. Thus, he already had some indication of how John handled loss and grief. In addition, the practitioner was viewed by both John and his mother as a supportive and knowledgeable resource to whom they could comfortably turn for help.

John needed a consistent adult male with whom he could relate. Although the practitioner might suggest that John's parents seek counseling for themselves or that the entire family receive psychiatric help, the practitioner could see John alone on a regular basis for a limited time (e.g., three to five sessions) to give him support, to help him in his decision making, and to provide a stable, caring male in his environment during the period of transition and loss. The length of each session might vary according to John's needs at any particular time. However, at the end of the designated number of sessions, John and the practitioner would need to re-evaluate John's status and the success or failure of treatment.

If the patient were female, a woman practitioner would be the ideal person to counsel the adolescent.

Indications for referral

If John displays ideas of self-destructive behavior (about which the practitioner may need to ask directly), becomes progressively depressed, or acts on his impulse to run away, a mental health referral should be strongly considered.

SCHOOL: Truancy

CONCEPTS DISCUSSED: *Negotiation with schools*
Improper school placement
Parental noncommunication

Martha was a 15-year-old ninth-grade student whose parents called their practitioner in early May for help with Martha's **truancy** from school.

Data gathering

Past history. Martha had been well except for bronchiolitis that required a 3-day hospitalization when she was 8 months old. Her general development was unremarkable, although her language development had been questionably delayed when she was a toddler.

Family history. Martha was the middle of three children. Her siblings were boys, ages 18 and 7 years. Her mother, age 39, was a high school graduate who worked as a beautician in their home. Her father was 42 years old, had completed the eighth grade, and worked as a truck driver.

School. Martha was a student of low average ability. She had repeated the third grade because of "immaturity." Her attendance at school, however, had been regular through the eighth grade. She had never participated in any school- or community-sponsored groups or clubs, preferring the activities of her less formal friendship group, which consisted of both neighborhood and school friends. She attended boy-girl parties but would not be allowed to "date" until she was 16.

Martha's mother wanted her to take business courses in high school and become a secretary. Martha's father wanted her to at least complete high school, regardless of the courses she chose, and had promised her a car as a graduation present.

Martha had a low D average for the first semester of the ninth grade, a distinct change from her usual C to C− work. The subjects she was scheduled to take throughout the year included earth science, English, geography, algebra, home economics, and physical education.

Martha's typical school day began at 7:30 AM when she left home. She arrived at school at 8:00 AM and was present for attendance call at 8:15. Beginning in early April, however, Martha and two of her friends were absent from earth science and English classes, the first two classes of their school day, an average of 4 mornings a week.

Martha's parents had been called by her guidance counselor after her fifth absence. They confronted their daughter, who denied any truant behavior and termed the whole affair a "mistake" on the teacher's part who "didn't like" her. Martha's parents took no further action. They assumed Martha was attending her classes despite their 7-year-old son's report a week later that Martha and her friends had been at the elementary school playground at 9:00 AM that day.

Two weeks later, Martha's mother was called by the school guidance counselor because of Martha's continued truancy and declining grades. When confronted, Martha admitted her truancy, but called the classes "boring" and implied that she had skipped class only at the instigation of her friends and "because it's spring."

Martha reluctantly agreed to talk with the practitioner.

Interviews and school contact. Martha acknowledged the history that her mother had given the practitioner by telephone but volunteered no new information. During the course of the interview, she was most animated about her father's promise of a car at graduation.

The practitioner met with Martha's parents next. The mother described herself as at a loss in dealing with her daughter. Martha's father denied knowing about the truancy until his wife asked him to attend the appointment with her practitioner. They both stated that they were surprised at Martha's behavior because she had always been a compliant and easily disciplined child. Martha's father was most concerned that she would quit school at 16, since he wanted her to have the education he had never had.

The practitioner suggested that, with Martha's knowledge and her parents' permission, she would talk with the school guidance counselor directly. The practitioner also suggested that an evaluation by the school psychologist might be necessary to help Martha select courses that were more appropriate for her level of ability and her interests.

In meeting with Martha and her parents together, the practitioner outlined her plan to contact the school the next day. She told Martha and her parents that, since adjustments in Martha's schedule would probably not be made until the following school year, they needed to come to some decision about Martha's attendance for the remainder of ninth grade. Martha's father suggested that she be grounded for a week for any class she missed. Martha immediately promised to return to her classes but expressed concern about being able to pass her subjects. The practitioner agreed to include this concern in her discussion with the guidance counselor.

When the practitioner called the school, the guidance counselor corroborated Martha's parents' history. He was very receptive to the idea of psychometric testing, since Martha's ability and vocational interests had been of concern to him as well. With Martha's parents' permission, the psychological report was forwarded to the practitioner soon after the testing was completed.

The results of Martha's testing revealed that she was functioning in the low average range (IQ, 90). In addition, she was interested in, and had a special aptitude for, the area of child care. Her educational program was reevaluated. Plans were made to place Martha in a lower-level tenth-grade group in September and also to provide her with a work-study experience at a local day-care center twice a week.

Follow-up. Martha passed English and all of her other courses except earth science, which she was required to take in summer school. In the tenth grade, she maintained a C+ average and good attendance. In addition, she received high praise for her work with infants and children and planned to continue at the day-care center during the summer after tenth grade.

Discussion

Truancy is remaining away from school without permission of the school. The variety of reasons why a child or adolescent may be truant include personal choice, parental indifference or ignorance of the law regarding compulsory school atten-dance, perceived discrimination by the teacher, real or fantasied unpopularity with other students, outside interests or conflicting obligations such as child care at home or employment, and difficulty with schoolwork. This last explanation is the most frequent cause of truancy and is the seventh leading cause of school absence (Bakwin and Bakwin, 1972).

Truancy must be differentiated from school phobia and underachievement. In truancy, the child or adolescent leaves home for school regularly but either never arrives or is absent from one or more classes during the day. Usually the parents are totally unaware of where their truant children are during the day.

The families of truants are more likely to be of the lower social classes, in which the parents have lower educational levels or aspirations. Truants often display an-tisocial behaviors such as lying or stealing. In addition, truants are often education-ally retarded and do not enjoy school. However, psychologically, they are a rela-tively normal group, and their antisocial behavior reflects the norms of their partic-ular families or peer groups, which may not conform to society-at-large (Wolff, 1969).

• • •

Martha's behavior represented truancy. She left for school regularly but was absent from specific classes, appeared to be enjoying her time away from school, and was failing. Her behavior was clearly different from that of school phobia (pp. 145 to 151), in which the child does not leave home and is depressed but is usually doing well academically. Martha's underachievement was primarily on the basis of inappropriate placement in classes that were too difficult, as contrasted to under-achievement in a bright student who lacks motivation or has some conflicting feel-ings about achievement (pp. 180 to 186).

We hear little about Martha's physical development but assume it was normal for her age; that is, she was nearing the completion of an unremarkable puberty.

From the history, Martha stated that her peers suggested she join them. The reason she did so seemed to be a result of her status as a "follower." The fact that she voluntarily gave up truancy in the face of parental authority implies that she was relatively uncommitted to the activity and probably participated because of her suggestibility.

Midadolescents are transitional between the concrete operational stage of early adolescence and the formal operational stage of late adolescence and adulthood. One might expect Martha to be somewhat less developed in her formal operational thinking than are some midadolescents, since she had a low average IQ and was having difficulty achieving at school. In addition, Martha gave no evidence of thinking futuristically and was interested in high school graduation only because of the car she would receive and not for the acquisition of knowledge that would prepare her for a career.

Not all adults reach the stage of formal operational thinking. It is not clear whether Martha's father, who finished eight grades of school, or her mother, who was a high school graduate performing a technical job, were formal operational in their thinking. However, if one assumes that their thought processes were not fully formal operational, then Martha's level of cognitive development may be limited on a genetic basis as well.

Midadolescents are in the midst of their identity struggle. Upon testing, Martha showed an interest in and an aptitude for child care. This may be a preliminary indication that she was moving toward the formation of her adult, female identity. She would be expected to use her mother as her major role model in this process, and an interest in child care would be very appropriate for her.

As she was clarifying her female identity, Martha was group dating, which is an appropriate expression of genitality during midadolescence. Group dating usually precedes dating one partner and is a setting in which the adolescent learns from peers about associating with heterosexual friends. Thus, the midadolescent is passing from the undifferentiated sexual stage of early adolescence to the differentiated sexuality of late adolescence and adulthood. The midadolescent's group dating provides a somewhat neutral format in which to learn about heterosexual interaction.

Defense mechanisms/coping styles/adaptive behaviors

Martha's truancy was a symptom of her feelings about her underachievement and her susceptibility to peer pressure. Rather than becoming overtly depressed or anxious about her school failure, she resorted to "denial by act" in its most primitive form: she ran away from the classes that were most difficult for her. She might have employed some other coping mechanism had she not been so influenced by her friends who suggested truancy to her. Thus, she was able to substitute pleasurable experiences (e.g., visits to playgrounds) at exactly the time that she would otherwise be most uncomfortable in school.

Intervention

Martha's mother contacted her practitioner to ask for help. The practitioner's role is to gather information from Martha, her parents, and the school. As an individual who is not directly involved in the parent-adolescent-school struggle, but whose main consideration is advocacy for the child, the practitioner is in an excellent position to objectively evaluate the situation.

The practitioner talked separately to Martha and her parents. Of importance is that she was open with Martha concerning what she knew about the problem. Since midadolescents are often in the midst of their battle with authority, a straightforward approach can usually avoid "games" or power struggles. For example, if the practitioner knows why the midadolescent is in the office but says, "Why are you coming in today, Martha?" Martha may reply, "I don't know." At some point, the practitioner will have to admit knowledge, to which the midadolescent may reply, "If you knew, why did you ask me?"

It is advisable to see midadolescents alone because of their self-consciousness and embarrassment in talking with adults. In addition, when faced with authority figures, the midadolescent may feel obligated to be uncooperative.

Once the history is obtained, if there is any evidence of an acute decline in school grades associated with headaches, vomiting, or lethargy, for example, and concern exists about a physical cause for these symptoms, a complete physical evaluation should be planned.

Before contacting the school officials, the practitioner should obtain parental permission, preferably in writing, so that school authorities know that the parents are in agreement with the contact. The midadolescent should know the practitioner is contacting school officials and should be encouraged to name specific personnel who might be most helpful. The adolescent should know when the practitioner will be in the school, if a meeting is planned, and where and with whom the meeting will be held. The adolescent must know that all communication is confidential and will not be discussed with anyone but the designated professionals.

Practitioners often wonder whom to call in the school. Most school authorities suggest that, out of courtesy and as a way of learning who knows the student best, the principal of the school should be contacted first. One or more other people may also be helpful: the student's guidance counselor, the school nurse, or the teachers of specific classes.

If the student appears to need psychological testing, as Martha did, the practitioner may rely on school personnel to develop the consultation or may contact the psychologist directly for discussion. For example, Martha needed intellectual testing and vocational planning. This request can be made directly to the school psychologist, much as the practitioner would request a hematologist, after consultation, to perform a bone marrow aspiration or biopsy in a youngster in whom aplastic anemia is suspected.

If practitioners spend significant time in school contacts, they should charge for their services. Although most families are pleased that the practitioner will provide this service, it should be clearly stated that a specific fee will be charged.

Occasionally, parents prefer to use the practitioner's recommendations as a basis for carrying out their own negotiations with the school. Although we have stressed that direct contact with the school by the practitioner is our preferred management plan, the parent-school alternative is a viable one if it promotes better communication and results in the needed services. However, sometimes parents are not successful in obtaining help because of large backlogs of students in need of psychological services. Professional-professional contact, especially if the practitioner has already brought some definition to the problem through her own assessment, as in Martha's situation, can often expedite school evaluation. In either plan, follow-up with the family after 3 to 6 weeks is essential to ensure that the adolescent is being appropriately managed.

Indications for referral

Martha's truancy and underachievement were related. The practitioner was able to participate in the definition of Martha's problem and its ultimate solution by a concerted effort that included Martha, her parents, and school officials. A mental health referral might be made if the truant adolescent were depressed. A referral to Family Court should be considered if the adolescent is reluctant or demonstrates evidence of major **sociopathic disturbance** without depression. In some cases, referrals to both sources of help may be appropriate.

ILLNESS: Terminal illness

CONCEPTS DISCUSSED: *Adolescent view of death*
Experimental behaviors
Depression
Support of the caregiver

Eleanor, a 16-year-old high school junior with known acute myelogenous leukemia (AML) for a year, was admitted to the hospital in relapse following a short remission.

Data gathering

Past history. Eleanor's childhood health had been excellent, and her development completely normal. Although independent and carefree, she had never presented any major behavioral problems during her childhood.

Family history. Eleanor was the youngest of eight siblings, the oldest of whom was 35 years old. Eleanor was the only child living at home. Her next oldest sibling was 20 and attended college out of town. Her father was a 56-year-old self-employed plumber. Her mother was 54 years old and had worked as an aide in a day-care center for 12 years.

School. Eleanor had always been an above-average student in school. She had participated in a number of student council community outreach projects and had been in the school band.

Peers. Eleanor had many friends, including a few close ones. She had just begun dating her steady boyfriend when she became ill.

Family's response. At the time of Eleanor's diagnosis, the family had experienced shock and disbelief. Her parents expressed some guilt, as well, about having been "too old" when she was conceived. Her siblings were anxious about Eleanor's illness, being most concerned that she would suffer and be in pain.

At the suggestion of Eleanor's practitioner and the pediatric oncologist, Eleanor had been told her diagnosis at the time of her first admission to the hospital. Her poor prognosis was touched on, but most of the discussion focused on hope for a remission. Although she had cried, she had said little else. She had asked only a few questions then and almost none in the subsequent months of treatment.

Early in the course of her illness, Eleanor had been compliant but somewhat withdrawn. The effect that disfigurement from treatment, especially alopecia, would have on her peer relationships concerned her greatly, but she wore a wig or kerchief and seemed to adapt well. Indeed, she returned to all of her former activities and added others to her busy schedule as well.

During the 2 months preceding her current admission, Eleanor became increasingly noncompliant with medications, began swearing and shouting at her parents, and was defiant of the limits they set for her regarding dating and staying out at night.

Hospital course. Upon admission, Eleanor refused to give a medical history, permit a physical examination, or cooperate in any laboratory or therapeutic procedures. That evening, her practitioner, her oncologist, a staff nurse, Eleanor, and her parents met together.

The health professionals were sensitive to Eleanor's feelings of fear and discouragement concerning the exacerbation of her disease and the necessity for rehospitalization. However, they also made it clear to her that, although they wanted to help her get better, they could not do so without her cooperation.

Eleanor was asked to list for the staff the things she disliked most about hospital routine and her treatment regimen so that they could make changes or compromises where possible or give her explanations for procedures or rules that were not flexible.

Eleanor immediately mentioned four items: hospital food, clothing, visitation, and procedures. It was agreed that, since she was not on a restricted diet, she could have complete control over her menu and she could also ask her family to bring in food she especially liked as long as she ate at least 1500 calories a day. It was further agreed that she could wear street clothes and have visits from her friends any time during visiting hours if no major procedures were planned. In addition, she could decide when her intravenous medication would be given or procedures performed as long as the dosage schedule or procedure was not delayed for more than 30 minutes. Thus, if she were engaged in an activity or had a friend visiting, she could finish her business rather than be interrupted.

After these negotiations had taken place, Eleanor was encouraged to think of other items that concerned her and to mention them to the practitioner who planned to visit at least four times a week. The option for further negotiation with the practitioner as someone who was in authority but was not actually involved in her antileukemia therapy was thus open to Eleanor.

Eleanor became increasingly more compliant with the staff members. Gradually and indirectly, she also began to express her fears about dying to her practitioner. She said that she felt that her body was no longer hers, since it was constantly intruded upon by intravenous feedings, blood tests, and bone marrow aspirations and would be disfigured again by medication. She expressed worry about her parents who looked older and more weary to her and also about her 20-year-old sister who often had tears in her eyes when she visited. She admitted to not taking her medications prior to her admission but stated, "They won't make any difference anyway." She expressed unhappiness and guilt over disobeying her parents but said that she had only wanted to have some fun "before it's too late." She did not want to talk with her family about her feelings because she thought that her mother and father were already too upset.

Eleanor began to show signs of depression manifested primarily by hour-long periods of withdrawal during which she stayed in bed, her shades and drapes drawn, crying. Occasionally she talked to a hospital friend with cystic fibrosis. Usually she asked to be left alone.

Discussion

Terminal illness during midadolescence may be particularly difficult for the patient, family, and professional. Midadolescence is the time when youth think they are immortal and are just beginning to feel a sense of freedom and independence from family and authority. They are energetic and daring, often recklessly so. The diagnosis of a terminal illness during this stage can be devastating and can accentuate the characteristic behaviors of midadolescents that are difficult for adults to cope with even under "normal" circumstances: struggle with authority, experimentation with drugs or sex, and forced, premature independence.

· · ·

Eleanor, like most females 16 years of age, had completed the majority of her physical development. She was more comfortable with her physical being than is an early adolescent but not quite as comfortable as a late adolescent or an adult eventually becomes. This discomfort with their bodies may make midadolescent girls particularly sensitive to physical examinations and procedures that are intrusive: for example, intravenous feedings and bone marrow aspirations. Midadolescent girls are often extremely conscious of their appearance and the style of their hair in particular. Thus, loss of hair or any other actual or fantasied bodily disfigurement may be particularly stressful to them.

During midadolescence young people begin to pair off and date individuals of the opposite sex. Heterosexual experimentation, like experimentation with driving, drinking, and smoking, is common. Terminally ill midadolescents like Eleanor may think they will never grow into adulthood and may thus experiment more recklessly than will healthy adolescents. For example, they may engage in sexual intercourse without protection, particularly if they believe they will not live long enough to have to worry about the consequences. Some experimental behaviors of terminally ill adolescents may border on self-destructive behavior and serve as a "cry for help" for underlying depression and despair.

Eleanor had moved into the genital stage of midadolescence. Since she had not complied with the limits set by her parents on dating, one should be concerned about her heterosexual experimentation and the possibility of an unwanted pregnancy. Despite a patient's terminal illness and shortened life span, practitioners must be aware of the terminally ill midadolescent's burgeoning sexuality and perhaps greater need for intimacy, which may result in more intense experimentation. The adolescent's response to a frank discussion about the prevention of unwanted pregnancies will depend partially on her cognitive development (particularly the ability to think in the future and to understand cause-and-effect relationships) and her level of depression (as manifested by her degree of willingness to indulge in reckless behavior and chance taking).

Although adolescents share the adult concept of death as a universal and inevitable process, it is common for midadolescents to think that they are immortal. They firmly believe that disaster cannot befall them. However, as a terminal illness progresses, some understanding may be achieved and lead to reality-based depression, similar to Eleanor's.

Clarification of one's sexual and vocational identities is an important task begun in midadolescence. In addition, terminally ill adolescents are struggling to incorporate a sense of the "sick self." Although the adolescents may have several "well" models, there may be no adult models in the environment who are similar to the "sick self." Thus, when terminally ill adolescents are hospitalized, they sometimes befriend other chronically or terminally ill adolescents who have similar concerns and who they think understand the struggle for identity. The importance of peers in identity formation is nowhere better illustrated than in relationships that are developed among ill midadolescents.

Defense mechanisms/coping styles/adaptive behaviors

Eleanor initially responded to her illness by denying it. She refused to talk about it, except as it obviously affected her by, for example, changing her appearance. As she felt increasingly better, she denied her illness by developing an even fuller academic and social schedule than she had had before the onset of her illness. Such denial is a useful tool in helping a life-threatened individual to live fully while the opportunity exists. The danger in such denial, however, is that it can lead to reckless, and possibly self-destructive, behavior. Not having died at the time of diagnosis, the adolescent may develop a sense that "nothing can harm me."

Eleanor's acting-out behaviors were a manifestation of her depression, which she was unable to adequately share with anyone verbally. Her inability to share her worries arose, in part, from the fear that her devastating concerns about death might be confirmed by her confidante. Eleanor, however, also isolated herself from her parents. She did this first by trying to alienate them. Later, she felt guilty about their obvious distress and was afraid to add to it by sharing herself and her burden with them. Although she may have gained some relief from talking with her practitioner and her chronically ill friend, it was also necessary for her to do some of her grief work alone.

Intervention

Eleanor needed to know that her family and the staff members understood how she was feeling and cared about her. In fact, she needed to know that they cared enough to set limits on her behavior and clarify what was expected of her in the management of her illness. Eleanor was given control over rules and regulations specific to the hospital setting that did not compromise her medical care: she was allowed to wear her own clothes to reinforce her identity, and she was given back some measure of her tenuous independence.

Eleanor was also provided a person with whom she could talk confidentially and who would help her to talk more effectively with the other people who cared for her.

Indications for referral

Eleanor displayed increasingly overt depression during her hospitalization: a normal and expected response to her terminal illness. The goal of psychological work with Eleanor was to help her to transfer the trust she developed in her practitioner to her family, especially her parents, and to help them feel freer to express their feelings to her. To successfully accomplish this task, it might be necessary to involve a family therapist who is skilled in fostering "open communication" (Spinetta, 1978) among family members.

Support of the caregiver

Professionals who provide care for terminally ill children and adolescents often experience frustration and anger at their inability to cure the patient's disease. As the patient becomes increasingly physically ill and depressed, the professionals may experience similar feelings. Professionals need to be aware of their feelings and understand how these can affect patient care. Patients, on the other hand, need to know that their health providers are human and can experience the full range of human emotion.

When few medications remain to help cure the illness, the patient needs to know that the practitioner can still provide comfort care, in its broadest sense, through both medication to ease pain and a willingness to sit and listen to the individual's most personal and terrifying fears.

It is important for health caregivers to realize that terminally ill patients have limited energy for forming relationships and thus may be very open with one or two professionals or family members but cut themselves off from all others, sometimes to the point of hostility. That a child or adolescent is either talking to someone or seems to be at peace with himself should be ample indication that the situation is in hand.

Some persons generally cope with stress verbally, whereas others do not. Lifelong characteristics seldom change even in the face of terminal illness. Helping professionals should not think that lack of verbalization, in and of itself, indicates that an adolescent is not coping adequately.

Caring for terminally ill adolescents can be a stressful, tiring process for the professional. Thus, colleague, family, and/or religious support of the caregiver is of paramount importance to excellent and sustained care of the dying patient.

Chapter 12 • The adolescent from 16 to 18 years (late adolescence)

Physiological growth and development

MALES: Growth completed late in this period; increasing comfort with physical self.

FEMALES: Growth completed early in this period; comfort with physical self.

Psychological growth and development

FREUD	Genital stage; progression toward mature sexuality and commitment to a single partner
ERIKSON	Identity vs. role confusion "Who am I?" as a sexual person
PIAGET	Formal operational period
KOHLBERG	Postconventional level
SEARS	Extrafamilial learning

Chapter 12

The adolescent from 16 to 18 years (late adolescence)

FAMILY: Move

CONCEPTS DISCUSSED: *Anorexia nervosa*
The late adolescent's role in family decision making

Joyce was a 17-year-old high school senior who was referred to her practitioner in January because of a 9 kg (20-pound) weight loss in the 4 months since her parents' decision to accept a promotion for her father and move the family across the country.

Data gathering

Past history. Joyce had enjoyed excellent health throughout childhood and early adolescence, although she had been chubby when she was in the sixth and seventh grades. Her development had been normal.

She had experienced menarche at $13^{1}/_{2}$ years and had completed her growth by age 15. She was at about the sixtieth percentile for height and at slightly less than the fiftieth percentile for weight during her last routine physical examination at age 16.

Family history. Joyce was the oldest of three daughters of a 44-year-old physicist and a 41-year-old professional artist. Her sisters were 11 and 9 years old. The family had lived in their current home for almost 5 years.

School. Joyce was a "straight-A" student. She was active in extramural activities and was the president of the honor society and the school orchestra. She planned to enroll in a music conservatory after high school and ultimately become a concert cellist.

Peers. Except for a period of about 6 months when she moved into her current school district in seventh grade and had some difficulty adjusting to her new setting, Joyce had been reasonably popular with her peers. Despite her mild aloofness, her teachers considered her a natural leader. She had dated one boy for almost a year, said she was serious about him, and planned to marry and have a family in "5 or 6 years" after she completed her music studies. Her boyfriend, who was also a high school senior, had already been accepted into the college of his choice and was planning to major in physics. Joyce described him as intense and serious about his studies, but very gentle and caring with her. She had commented once that his feelings about her were like the feelings her father used to have about her.

History of the present illness. The decision in favor of Joyce's father's transfer, which involved a substantial promotion, had been made by her parents without discussing it with the children the September preceding Joyce's referral to her practitioner. When Joyce learned about the transfer, which was scheduled for early April of her senior year in high school, she cried hysterically. She accused her parents, especially her mother, who Joyce believed had never really liked their present home and wanted to move at any cost, of being totally insensitive to her needs and opinions. She received no support, however, from her siblings, who were looking forward to the move.

Joyce tried to negotiate with her parents about her staying in her hometown with her boyfriend's family so that she could complete high school and attend a local music conservatory. Although her parents refused to discuss this alternative plan, Joyce thought that they would ultimately give in to her wishes. She was initially so certain of this eventuality that, although she discussed her father's transfer with friends, she denied that she would be moving.

Over the course of the succeeding month, however, it became clear to Joyce that her parents were inflexible in their decision despite the fact that her father's transfer was a constant theme for her whenever she talked with her parents. In early October, she began to eat irregularly and by early November she was eating only very small meals, consisting mostly of salads, which she usually vomited. She also skipped some meals entirely. She showed a moderate increase in her interest in cooking and on several occasions independently prepared rather elaborate dinners for her family, which she, however, did not join them in eating.

During the Thanksgiving holiday, she joined a health club and began swimming 2 to 3 miles each day. At home, she was routinely doing 200 push-ups before going to sleep. Her new schedule gave her less time to spend with her boyfriend. Whereas they had studied together at least twice a week and had dated on both Friday and Saturday nights, they now rarely saw each other except in class.

In early December, Joyce was noticeably thinner and paler and had become amenorrheic. Her parents observed that she was very irritable and angry. In January, when they discovered that she had lost 20 pounds (15% of her usual body weight) and had been amenorrheic for 2 months, they contacted their practitioner.

Discussion

Eating behavior and the communications in families around food are basic to relationships and the expression of nurturance. Anorexia nervosa is one of the eating disorders of adolescence. It is more prevalent among females than males. It is most common among early and middle adolescent girls, but it also occurs in late adolescents and, rarely, adult women. The illness can be fatal (Bruch, 1973).

Features of anorexia nervosa include anorexia, sometimes to the point of aversion to food; vomiting; weight loss; emaciation; pallor; menstrual irregularity or frank amenorrhea; and signs of a hypometabolic state including hypotension, bradycardia, and hypothermia. Paradoxically, some patients display intermittent bulimia. This behavior is followed, however, by vomiting or purging resulting in an overall weight loss. Increased strength and stamina, manifested by a raised activity level, are often seen early in the illness but may be replaced by weakness and general fatigue as weight loss increases.

Individuals with anorexia nervosa are typically tense, hyperactive, rigid, perfectionistic, extremely ambitious, overachieving especially in the school setting, sensitive, and unsure of themselves. In addition, they are dependent on their families (especially their mothers), fearful of the separation from the family that is associated with maturation, and extremely anxious about heterosexual relationships.

Events that can precipitate anorexia nervosa include a chance remark about weight that leads to excessive, compulsive dieting and/or heightened anxiety about sex roles, which can lead to slimming to the point of sexual unattractiveness, and/or the onset of open discord between the adolescent and the parent, usually the mother, especially when they face separation and the ensuing independence of the adolescent.

Treatment regimens vary but usually include attention to the symptom of anorexia per se as well as to the deeper psychological features of the illness.

• • •

Joyce's childhood was uneventful. Like many preadolescents, she experienced an increase in weight prior to her growth spurt, making her somewhat chubby during the late elementary and early junior high school years. Her menarche had occurred uneventfully at age 13^1/$_2$. One would expect that ovulation and therefore the ability to reproduce began about 1 to 2 years later. Her physical growth at age 17 was complete and normal for the late adolescent.

Joyce had progressed extremely well scholastically. Evidence that she had attained the cognitive level of formal operations was apparent from two sources: academic excellence in college-oriented high school courses requiring the ability to abstract and her well-defined career and marriage plans indicating her future orientation and realistic strategy-planning ability.

Joyce showed some evidence of having achieved the genital stage of psychosexual development in that she had been dating seriously for almost a year. However, evidence also existed that she had not yet completely resolved those aspects of the Oedipal (Electra) conflict which tend to resurface during adolescence; the reemergence of the girl's sexual feelings for her father that are finally resolved by her identification with her mother and her selection of a heterosexual partner who is like her father.

Although we know little of the personality characteristics of Joyce's father and her boyfriend, there is an undercurrent of similarity between them concerning careers and personality style that is suggestive of incomplete resolution of Joyce's feelings about her father. In addition, like many middle and late adolescent girls, Joyce had particular difficulty communicating with her mother, another indication of some adolescent Oedipal conflict. Identity formation will finally be completed when Joyce develops a sense of herself as an individual who is like, but not identical to, her mother.

In this context, when faced with the possiblity that she might be separated from her own family, it is of interest that Joyce offered her boyfriend's family as a surrogate for her own. It is also of interest that, as she and her family became less able to communicate, she also drew away from her boyfriend. One might hypothesize that, since she denied, to herself and to her friends, the possibility that her parents would ultimately force her to move with them, she was also convinced that they might actually acquiesce to her demand that she live with her boyfriend and his family. If her sexual identity were tenuous and she were anxious about her sex role, such a possibility might have been very frightening and have added to her wish to both avoid her boyfriend and make herself less attractive to him.

The inability of the family to communicate about their move and Joyce's feelings or to negotiate compromises led to her anorexia as a "cry for help." That is, she expressed her feelings of loneliness and isolation by refusing any nurturance (food) whatsoever from her family.

Defense mechanisms/coping styles/adaptive behaviors

Depression, anxiety, and fear of separation were among the most prominent features of Joyce's illness.

Denial was a major defense for her, particularly early in her illness. She also employed a form of isolationism: by being very "busy," she left herself little time or energy for personal relationships. As another example, although she prepared meals for her family, she did this alone before dinnertime and then withdrew from the family during the act of eating together.

The formation of her symptom, anorexia, was her only means of communication with her family.

Intervention

The symptoms of Joyce's eating disorder were directly precipitated by her family's plans to move. None of the other hypothesized psychological reasons for her disorder was, in and of itself, abnormal. In other words, partial resolution of the Oedipal (Electra) conflict, anxiety regarding sexual identity, and fear of separation can all be *normal* occurrences in late adolescence as long as they do not result in dysfunction. Had the family not planned a precipitous move that introduced the possibility of premature separation, and had Joyce not selected her boyfriend's family as a possible surrogate, she may never have overtly or consciously experienced such psychological turmoil. For example, her separation from her family would have eventually taken place in September of her first year at the conservatory as a positively anticipated and gradual event, especially since she was planning to attend a school close to home. Her feelings of closeness to her present or a future boyfriend who ultimately might have become her husband, would have developed gradually, as well, over "5 or 6 years," the length of time she designated before considering marriage.

In the initial evaluation of an adolescent with anorexia, both psychological and physical causes must be considered. As a first step, the practitioner should interview Joyce and her parents separately. A late adolescent, who is struggling for independence and individuation from parents, should be treated like an adult and see the practitioner alone to express personal concerns about psychological turmoil as well as possible physical illness.

After an interview with the parents, in which they should be encouraged to be frank in their observations and feelings, the entire family should be seen together. This family meeting provides an opportunity for the practitioner to gain further history and observe how the family members interact and communicate.

As the next step, the practitioner must perform a thorough physical examination and a selective laboratory evaluation to be assured that the adolescent's weight loss is a response to a developmental crisis and not a physical problem such as a malignancy, an intestinal disease, or an infectious illness.

A weight loss of 15% or less, by itself, does not demand hospitalization. Other factors must be considered:

1. Hypometabolic state: hypotension, bradycardia, and hypothermia
2. Electrolyte imbalance: hypochloremia from vomiting, hypokalemia from purging with laxatives
3. Suspected organic etiology that warrants inhospital evaluation, such as a suspected central nervous system lesion
4. Suspected psychological cause such as psychosis for which observation of behavior and formal psychological evaluation are warranted
5. The need for observation of the adolescent's eating habits and behavior, especially when conflicting historical data are presented by the patient and family
6. Development of a crisis in the family

Suspected anorexia nervosa can be fully evaluated and diagnosed on an outpatient basis. However, such a workup may not be nearly as expedient or focus the family's attention as successfully as an inpatient evaluation.

If Joyce were to gain weight merely because of hospitalization and the consequent separation from her parents, the practitioner may be the person to see the family as a group and aid them in a decision in Joyce's best interests. For example, some families, under similar circumstances, have found that the parents and the late adolescent can agree to the adolescent's remaining in the original city if the parents think that the place where she would stay is acceptable, such as the home of a relative or close friends who can provide guidance and supervision similar to that of the biological family. Joyce, who is articulate, should be given the opportunity to express herself in the presence of her parents. However, she may need an advocate who can assist her and support her feelings as well as those of her parents.

Indications for referral

If Joyce does not gain weight merely by a separation from her family through hospitalization, her eating disorder may represent a graver and more deep-seated disturbance. The practitioner should seek formal psychological consultation for Joyce and her family. The practitioner's role then becomes one of monitoring Joyce's weight. Some practitioners have found that a behavioral modification program, which includes a "formal contract" between the physician and the patient, can be very helpful. Usually, the patient is initially restricted to her hospital room with no privileges, including no bathroom privileges, television, or visitors. For each half or full pound gained, the patient earns a given privilege. Discharge is normally contingent on attaining a specific, previously determined weight. Readmission occurs when the patient's weight falls below the weight agreed upon for discharge from the hospital. During the weeks after hospitalization, weight goals are gradually increased until the patient is stable at a mutually acceptable weight (Hoekelman and Munson, 1978).

The role of the mental health consultant in this management plan is to help the adolescent patient express herself verbally rather than through her symptom and to work with her and her family toward resolution of the conflict between them.

SCHOOL: Underachievement

CONCEPTS DISCUSSED: *Delayed physical development*
Psychosocial immaturity
The education- and career-oriented family

Paul was a $16^{4}/_{12}$-year-old high school senior whose mother called the practitioner in November for advice about her son's declining school grades.

Data gathering

Past history. Paul had been well except for multiple episodes of otitis media during infancy and toddlerhood requiring the insertion of pressure-equalizing tubes at $3^1/_2$ years of age. He had been well since then, and audiometric testing at $4^1/_2$ and 10 years of age had been normal. His developmental milestones had been achieved appropriately.

During a summer camp physical examination when he was $14^{11}/_{12}$ years old, he was observed to have early evidence of secondary sexual changes (early Tanner stage II).

Family history. Paul was the only child of a 55-year-old father who was a banker and also the president of the board of education in the affluent suburban town in which his family lived and a 56-year-old mother who was a college graduate and active in volunteer activities but not otherwise employed outside the home. Paul's father was 175 cm (5 feet 9 inches) tall and weighed 74 kg (163 pounds); his growth spurt had occurred at age 15. Paul's mother was 157 cm (5 feet 2 inches) tall, weighed 56 kg (123 pounds), and had had her menarche at age 14.

School. Paul's early school history revealed that he had maintained an A average in elementary school. He had undergone group psychometric testing as part of his school's routine evaluation of students in the sixth grade. His IQ, as measured in that examination, was 130, a fact that was known to his parents.

Paul maintained a B+ average through his junior year in high school. The first report from his senior year revealed that he had received mostly C's and D's.

Peers. Paul had a number of friends from his town and the neighboring urban area. Most of his friends were interested in motorcycles, and more than half owned cycles. Paul's father had made it clear that he did not want to meet these friends and that they were not welcome in his home. On several occasions, he had urged Paul to play tennis or golf, swim at their country club, or associate with other classmates who "aspire to something after high school."

Paul's mother liked the girl Paul had dated occasionally since the summer, and Paul and his girlfriend sometimes spent time talking with his mother after school before his father came home from work. His father had met the girl on one or two occasions and had said little about her except that he was glad she was planning to go to college.

The practitioner suggested that Paul and his parents come to his office for an evaluation.

Interviews and physical examination. The practitioner began by talking alone with Paul, whom he had known for almost 15 years:

> PRACTITIONER: Your mother has already told me about your falling grades in school. Both of your parents are concerned and are looking for some answers. I'm sure you've given the matter some thought. Tell me about it.
>
> PAUL: I don't really know what to think. The work is easy, and I know I can do it, but I just don't want to. And my dad bugs me constantly. You know, it's very hard to have my dad as a father. He's older than most fathers, pretty successful and on top of that, president of the board of education. He wants me to be just like him. I can't, and I don't want to be. I want to be myself.

PRACTITIONER: Aside from school, how do the two of you get along?

PAUL: I'm really not sure. He's not happy about my grades. He's not happy about my friends because they have long hair and ride motorcycles. He's not happy about the way I spend my time. There's not much left, is there? He just doesn't understand. He judges people on who they are and what they have instead of what they're really like as people. He always wants me to be with the "right" people who do the "right" things.

PRACTITIONER: What about your mother? How do the two of you get along?

PAUL: She'd never think of contradicting my father. But she seems to like the girl I'm dating, and she's nice to her.

PRACTITIONER: You've painted a pretty bleak picture of how your father sees you; maybe a slightly better picture of your mother's feelings. But what about Paul? What do you think about yourself?

PAUL: Not great. A lot of the seniors have already applied to college, and I haven't, even though my dad's been strongly hinting that I should. I'm not sure I want to go to college next year. All the kids seem interested in something, but I just can't get focused. I like motorcycles, but I guess that's because they're fast and make a lot of noise. But my father won't let me get a cycle, and I always seem to be tagging along when the guys with cycles get together. Actually, that's my problem—tagging along. I'm the youngest and the smallest in the class. I'm not big enough to be good at sports. My dad says I should try an individual sport like tennis or golf, but they're just not my thing.

PRACTITIONER: Does it have anything to do with your father being very good at tennis and golf?

PAUL: Probably. It's part of his master plan to make me exactly like him. That's what he'd like me to be, you know: a clone of himself. I wish he'd leave me alone and let me do my own thing.

PRACTITIONER: Do you ever just sit down and talk with your father?

PAUL: Never. He doesn't listen. He won't listen. All he ever says is that I'm lazy and misdirected by my friends. He hates my friends. He probably hates me too because I'm going to be a failure.

PRACTITIONER: How would you feel about talking with your father right now?

PAUL: Oh, no.

PRACTITIONER: I'll be with you. I'll ask your mother to join us, too.

Paul's parents were invited into the practitioner's office. Paul's father began immediately:

FATHER: Paul's a bright boy, Doctor. He should be able to get into the best college in the country. He's lazy and hanging around with the wrong group. He embarrasses us. He doesn't listen to us. Maybe he should have gone to military school and learned to be a man.

MOTHER: I see things differently. Paul is bright and likes to read. I think he'd like to go to college but doesn't know exactly what he wants to do, what he wants to major in. He often talks about his plans for the future—a good job and a family, but I think Paul isn't quite sure how to get what he wants. The girl Paul is dating is very concerned about him. She'll be leaving for college next fall. She seems more mature and settled than Paul. But then, Paul's the youngest in his class and he's very sensitive about being short. Rather than thinking about military school, I sometimes wonder if we shouldn't have started Paul in school a year later than we did. He always was and still is very bright. My husband and I really haven't talked about this, but it's been on my mind for some time that we may have made a mistake 12 years ago. I hope it isn't too late.

PRACTITIONER: Paul, do you want to say anything?

PAUL: *(Silence.)*

PRACTITIONER: Paul, you said some very important things to me when we were alone. I hope you'll share your thoughts with your parents.

FATHER: Speak up, Paul. The doctor asked you to speak.

PAUL: I need time to think about what I want to do after high school. I don't want to leave home in September. I want more time to look at colleges and talk to people. I've been thinking about getting a job in June and taking some English literature courses at the community college at night next fall. I always thought I'd like to teach English, but I really don't know. Dad, I need time. If I didn't feel so much pressure to decide everything right now, I think I could start concentrating on the schoolwork I have to do just to graduate.

FATHER: None of my friends has a son who didn't go to college right after high school.

MOTHER: Dear, I think you're forgetting the Thompson boy who eventually went to law school and Jean and Bob's son. I remember Jean talking about how awful they felt when their son went to work as a stock boy at the supermarket for a year. But then I also remember her telling me a couple of years later that it had been the best thing he could have done because he really matured into a young man who knew what he wanted to do with his life.

FATHER: *(Silence.)*

PRACTITIONER: Time off for Paul next year sounds like a possibility the three of you need to talk about at home. Paul, I think your mother has some positive feelings about it. Your dad might consider it favorably, too, after he's had a chance to do some more thinking.

Since Paul's height was of concern to him, the practitioner followed up the interviews with a review of Paul's growth chart and a complete physical examination. Paul's growth chart showed that he had consistently been in the twenty-fifth percentile for height and weight during childhood but, because he was almost a year younger than his classmates, seemed much shorter. Paul's physical examination revealed midpubescent penile and scrotal growth (Tanner stage III), indicating that Paul's growth spurt was imminent. Paul had a few questions about sexual development that the practitioner answered.

After interpreting Paul's physical examination findings to him privately, the practitioner gave the same information to Paul's parents in Paul's presence. The practitioner suggested that the family meet with him again in 2 weeks after they had had time to discuss the issues Paul had raised.

Follow-up. At a meeting 2 weeks later, Paul and his parents showed evidence of making some progress in their discussions about Paul's "year out." Paul returned again about a month later "just to talk." In late May the practitioner saw Paul for his work physical. His height at that time had increased almost 2 inches in 6 months. Paul successfully completed high school in June.

Discussion

School underachievement may represent an innate inability to do the work, as in mental retardation; an uncompensated perceptual defect, as in a learning disability; classroom boredom in students with superior intelligence who are not adequately challenged; or a behavioral expression of underlying frustration, anger, or depression.

Diagnostic procedures include psychometric testing and psychosocial evaluation. Treatment is specific to the underlying cause.

· · ·

Paul was the youngest student in his class; in addition, he was relatively short for his chronological age. The nonpathological causes of short stature include the following:
1. Constitutional (genetic) short stature
2. Delayed pubescence
3. An unrealistic perception of oneself as short because of an inappropriate comparison group

Investigation of short stature includes a thorough medical history, including the heights and weights of family members and their ages at puberty (menarche for females, maximum height velocity for males); a complete physical examination, including Tanner staging of sexual hair and genital development; and a careful plotting of all available height and weight measurements from birth.

Since height is genetically determined and appears to be derived from genes from both parents, Paul would be expected to attain an ultimate adult height that is low average. Both of Paul's parents had experienced their pubescent changes somewhat later than the average adolescent, consistent with the finding that Paul, at age $16^4/_{12}$, had not yet undergone his growth spurt. However, by objective evidence (Tanner staging), he was maturing appropriately even if slowly.

In Paul's case, all three of the nonpathological causes of short stature were operative. His parents were relatively short, his pubescence was delayed but normal, and his basis for comparison was a substantially older peer group at a period in his life when age can be significantly related to size. Clarification of this issue was of critical importance to Paul, for whom shortness and self-concept appeared to be intimately related.

The role model with whom Paul would most closely identify was his father, who was successful and older and more established than many fathers of adolescent sons. In addition, Paul's father had clear ideas he wished to impress on his son about what constituted masculinity: a clean-cut appearance, association with the "right" people, and interest and high achievement in school and sports. However, Paul, like most adolescents, was strongly influenced by his peers, especially since his concept of himself as an adequate teenage boy was so poor.

As is often the case, Paul and his father were operating at different levels of moral judgment of people. Paul's attention to the intrinsic value of an individual as a basis for judgment reflects level III postconventional (principled) reasoning. His father, on the other hand, tended to be more conventional in his judgments, reflecting a bias toward social acceptance or "law and order" as the motivating force in his decision making. Since debate exists about whether postconventional reasoning is necessarily a "higher" form of judgment, one is left with the feeling that both father and son may be equally justified in their separate approaches to people, an example of the seemingly irresolvable conflicts often found between parents and children.

We have only a little information about Paul's relationship with his mother. However, they clearly felt warmly toward one another, and Paul's mother could be protective of her son. There is a possibility that the adolescent Oedipal conflict had not yet been resolved in this family.

Paul had dated one girl, occasionally, as a step in the direction of mature genitality. Of note, however, is that this girl was "very concerned" about him, indicating a maternal rather than a peer interest in Paul and consistent with his general level of social immaturity.

Paul was fortunate in being articulate enough to verbalize his insecurity and cognitively developed enough to have some insight into his feelings and those of his parents. However, although Paul had some vocational and personal aspirations for the future, these were somewhat nebulous and idealized. An overall impression of Paul is that he was somewhat developmentally young for his 16 years but certainly young compared with those of his classmates who were much more successful in making decisions about the future than he was.

Defense mechanisms/coping styles/adaptive behaviors

Paul's depression and anxiety over his lack of a comfortable physical or psychological identity and his anxiety over his impending separation from his parents led to his academic underachievement: failure during his senior year might result in his having to repeat the year or at least substantially diminish his chances of being accepted into college. The underachievement also represented one of Paul's most potent weapons against his father, who valued academic success so highly.

Intervention

The practitioner's management was excellent. Interviewing Paul alone first gave Paul the sense that his observations and feelings were of primary importance and that he was not being seen merely to rebut his parent's impressions.

The practitioner then spoke with Paul's parents in Paul's presence. Although sometimes it may be necessary to interview the parents of a late adolescent alone, it is preferable to see them with the patient so that open communication is fostered.

The practitioner did not speak for Paul despite having much information about the boy's perception of the problem. However, he assisted Paul in taking on his new task of direct communication with his father. Having accepted what Paul said in private and having indicated that he had reasonable and legitimate concerns, the practitioner gave Paul a sense of security in presenting himself. The practitioner did not make any value judgment about Paul's plan for his future, but rather let the family negotiate that decision in private.

The practitioner requested that the family return after 2 weeks, primarily so that he could evaluate the progress they had made on their own and make a decision about the possible need for a referral to a mental health specialist.

Paul's third visit, a month later, was made at his own request so that he could discuss some issues with the practitioner and get some direction on how to present them to his father.

Indications for referral

It was fairly clear that Paul's poor self-concept was at least partly the result of a situational factor (delayed pubescence) that was about to be resolved without intervention. In addition, there was no indication that Paul's underachievement signified severe psychological disturbance, since, with support, the family was able to negotiate a mutually satisfactory solution to their crisis situation.

If the family had not been able to negotiate such a solution, or if Paul had continued to fail, immediate referral to a family therapist would have been indicated at the time of the follow-up visit.

ILLNESS: Chronic illness

CONCEPTS DISCUSSED: *Hidden disability*
Adaptive denial

This was the sixth hospital admission for Michael, an 18-year-old high school senior with known cystic fibrosis (CF) since 3 years of age. Michael was admitted at the request of his practitioner for a biosocial evaluation: pulmonary toilet, antibiotic therapy, and a review of his current developmental-behavioral status because of parental concerns about his depression and denial of his illness.

Data gathering

Past history. Michael was well as an infant and preschooler except for three episodes of "pneumonia" and very mild growth failure. He was diagnosed as having CF as part of a routine family screening following the diagnosis of CF in his younger sister. After diagnosis, he was placed on a low-fat diet and enzyme replacement therapy and received prompt outpatient treatment for his respiratory infections. Michael's treatment was managed by his primary care practitioner in consultation with the CF center director, although Michael was seen annually at the center for a full evaluation including pulmonary function tests.

Michael had fared extremely well as a child and required no hospitalizations until age 15 when he began to experience increasing respiratory difficulties. Since that time, he had been hospitalized four times, the most recent hospitalization occurring 4 months prior to his present admission.

Michael experienced his growth spurt at age $14^{1}/_{2}$ and underwent full sexual development. His growth was completed by age $17^{1}/_{2}$, and he was found to be just above the tenth percentile in height and weight. He experienced the onset of noticeable digital clubbing and increasing anteroposterior chest diameter at age 16.

Family history. Michael was the third of five children and the only male child. His younger sister had died when she was 12 years old, 5 years before his present admission. None of the other children in the family had CF.

Michael's father was 48 years old and a high school principal. His mother was 44 years old and taught in elementary school.

The family lived in a medium-sized town about 80 km (50 miles) from the medical center.

School. Michael had always been an A student and maintained this average in high school despite his frequent illnesses and hospitalizations. He prided himself on being labeled the "brain" in his class. He was active in several academic clubs and was editor of the school newspaper. He liked sedentary sports and was an excellent chess player.

He had been given a full tuition scholarship to an out-of-state college (his parents' alma mater) 400 km (250 miles) from home. He planned to attend this college the following September.

Peers. Michael had one close male friend who knew about his illness. When other students asked him about his chronic cough, he told them that he had "walking pneumonia" or laughed the symptom off entirely without discussing it.

Michael's only date had been for the junior prom the spring before his current admission.

Hospital course. Early in the hospitalization, Michael was told by the CF center director that his pulmonary function test results showed definite deterioration during the 4 months since his last admission. Michael countered with a discussion of his plans to attend college out-of-state and for the first time mentioned his ultimate plans for applying to medical school. The CF director addressed himself to Michael's college plans rather than his career goal. He explained that Michael needed close follow-up wherever he chose to attend college. Thus, Michael had two options: he could either be referred to another CF center, near the college, or attend college close to home and continue to receive care through the center he presently attended. The physician presented both of these alternatives as reasonable and easily arranged from the medical point of view.

After their talk, Michael seemed to be on a high. He was much more talkative and even flamboyant. He asked the physician to pursue the possibility of referral, talked increasingly about going to medical school, and also mentioned his plans for marriage and his desire for five children, despite knowing, from many discussions, that he was probably sterile.

Michael's parents were alarmed by his behavior and asked for a family conference with the CF director. At this conference, the physician presented the actual data from Michael's pulmonary function tests. Michael seemed to suddenly recognize the progressive severity of his illness. He began crying, "I know I'm going to die just like my sister did. I can't stand being here. All I want to do is get as far away from everyone as I can, so they won't be hurt again."

Immediately after his outburst, Michael's parents moved closer to him. His mother took his hand, and his father put his arm around his shoulder. The physician encouraged the parents to let Michael know how they felt as well. Both talked about loving him, their fears about losing him, and their intense desire to help him make the decisions that were best for him.

After Michael and his parents became more composed, the physician again presented to Michael, as well as to his parents, the alternatives available to Michael regarding college. The physician told them that he would investigate the possibility of referral, but that in the meantime they, as a family, needed to talk about Michael's future and discuss his options openly.

Follow-up. After his discharge from the hospital, Michael's physical condition stabilized. He visited his primary care practitioner weekly for a month for physical examinations. During the visits, they also talked about Michael's future goals of college, medical school, marriage and a family and Michael's growing desire to remain close to his family.

Over the next few months, Michael made the decision to attend a college only 16 km (10 miles) from home, although he planned to live in a dormitory. His parents agreed to this plan.

During his college physical examination, Michael expressed many feelings of depression and asked to be referred for counseling. The practitioner agreed to do so and also encouraged Michael to join the young adults' cystic fibrosis group that met at the medical center. Michael decided to pursue both individual and group counseling.

Discussion

A chronic illness that becomes life threatening in adolescence can seriously interfere with the adolescent's ability to consolidate his personal identity. In addition, a long period of acclimation to the disease and its restrictions on daily living activities can lead to unrealistic planning and expectations for the future when the course of the illness becomes more severe.

Since adolescence is generally the time for individuation and, thus, poor communication within families, reality-based fears of ultimate separation through death may be so painful that they are not expressed except through behavioral aberrations or a premature "running away." The late adolescent often has good insight into his motivations but needs the assistance and support of someone outside the family to help him share this insight with his parents, other relatives, and friends.

●　　●　　●

The late adolescent's physical growth is usually complete or nearing completion. Acceptance of his physical body is an important aspect of accepting and understanding himself.

Some young people with chronic illness have a physical disability or disfigurement that is apparent to any passerby at a glance. Thus, the "visible" handicap becomes integrated into the viewer's impression of the young person, who must then work strenuously to prove that the handicap "doesn't matter."

Michael's physical self, on the other hand, was close to normal despite the fact that he had cystic fibrosis. The external signs of the disease, such as clubbing, cyanosis, an increased anteroposterior chest diameter, diminished growth, and a constant cough were relatively mild in his case until midadolescence. Thus, he had a "hidden" disability that may have made his lack of stamina in vigorous exercise in physical education class or his constant hacking cough throughout the day and night more difficult for him to explain and for his peers to accept. Children and young people with hidden handicaps may actually be at a greater disadvantage than those with visible handicaps (McAnarney et al., 1974). For example, because they look well, those with hidden handicaps may not receive needed services promptly or at all. Or they may spend a great deal of physical or psychological energy keeping the handicap hidden, thereby depriving themselves of appropriate supports and assistance.

Cognitively, Michael was at the stage of formal operational thinking. He was able to think about the future and to consider his educational needs in light of his planned vocation. He also displayed insight into his feelings when he admitted depression and asked for help in making the critical decisions that lay before him. In addition, he was aware of his family's feelings of sadness about his deteriorating condition, especially in view of their relatively recent loss of his sister.

Michael's identity was fairly well defined, and he seemed comfortable with it. He recognized himself as a "cerebral" person: an excellent student and an outstanding sedentary sportsman who used his brain rather than his brawn.

He talked of going to his parents' alma mater and to medical school. Thus, he identified educationally with his parents and vocationally with his physicians. He talked about fatherhood in considering his sexual identity. He expressed a desire to have five children, the same number his father had, suggesting his identification, in the psychosexual sense, with his father.

The fact that Michael had dated only once is a common finding among chronically ill adolescents, who tend to not date for a variety of reasons, such as illness, which may force them to miss social events; physical immaturity, which may make them uncomfortable in boy-girl settings; and realistic concerns about potency. Despite this apparent inexperience, they may have a paradoxically good understanding of their sexual selves because of the additional attention they have had to give to determining their adult roles.

The chronically ill adolescent must also clarify another identity—that of the chronically ill person, specifically one who is facing deteriorating health and the rapid progression of disease. Such a confrontation with the possibility of death is difficult for anyone, regardless of age. It may be particularly difficult for the late adolescent who, at the same time, is shaping his vocational and sexual identities out of the vast array of opportunities before him: in essence, the moment when he can be "anyone and anything." Impending death, at some premature age, forces the adolescent to give up some of his wonderful expectations of long-awaited adulthood. Thus, death is often vigorously denied and actively defied.

Defense mechanisms/coping styles/adaptive behaviors

Michael coped with his illness by denying it within the confines of his limitations. Thus, such denial during his childhood and early adolescence helped him develop a characteristic style and personality type. He became a "brain" and a chess wizard. It is impressive that Michael did *not* deny his illness to the extent that he insisted on playing vigorous team or individual sports. Rather, he limited his sphere of physical and social activity to within medically indicated limits. This adaptive behavior allowed him to be thoroughly successful and to derive a great deal of satisfaction from his pursuits. It also allowed him to share with no one, except a single friend, the terrifying secret of his life.

Although one could question the benefit of his denial when it led to perhaps unrealistic expectations about his ability to care for himself far away from home or to be accepted into medical school, we must guard against prematurely burying those with threatened lives. With proper referral, Michael could have gone to the college of his choice away from home. His compromise decision, which stipulated that he would, indeed, live away from home throughout the week and perhaps on weekends, still required the same arrangement for his daily care (such as pulmonary toilet) as would have been necessary farther from home. In addition, although it is fairly certain that his life span is limited, should he, a priori, be denied the right of applying to medical or any other graduate school?

Michael's denial became maladaptive only when it interfered with his ability to reason about his options and to make judgments that would be in his best interests and when it precluded honest dialogue with his parents.

Showing Michael the actual data about his condition broke through his denial. Predictably, since denial was an excellent and long-used defense for him, he became angry—"I can't stand being here"—and then he became depressed. His depression probably resulted from the recognition that he, too, might die as his sister had, perhaps a painful and lingering death; that his plans for college might be altered or never realized; that his plans for adulthood might also be modified and/or thwarted; and that his family would experience the loss of another child just as he would experience the loss of them.

Intervention

Management of the chronically ill, late adolescent is a challenging responsibility that in many cases is shared by a number of professionals, including the primary care practitioner. Optimal management requires excellent communication and close attention to detail so that the information given to the patient and the family is consistent and accurate.

Honesty is an important element in caregiving. The late adolescent has, or almost has, reached the age of majority when he legally has control over his medical care. Thus, the information given must allow the adolescent to help make reasonable choices based on factual knowledge.

Fostering independence is also important, but must be tempered by a realistic appraisal of the adolescent's need for support from family and friends. The maintenance of hope is essential if the patient is to comply with medical regimens, keep appointments, and exercise care in daily living. Giving up can lead to despair and either recklessness or suicide.

An opportunity to go beyond "How are you?"–"I'm fine" and to discuss the dilemmas the adolescent faces can be the particular strength of his relationship with his primary practitioner. This was certainly true for Michael.

Michael had a reality-based depression; that is, he was faced with the totally realistic possibility of his death. He needed someone who understood the nature and prognosis of his illness, who was honest in his appraisal of the situation, and who encouraged him to view all his options before deciding on a course of action. The encounters that he had with his practitioner may have lasted only 10 or 15 minutes and most likely included some judgment about respiratory status as well, since this was an important element in his day-to-day decision making. The time, however, was well spent in honest talk.

The fact that Michael requested a referral for counseling indicated his receptivity to this approach and his trust in his physician to direct him appropriately.

Indications for referral

Although life-threatened patients are dealing with reality-based anxiety resulting from progressive organic disease, they can sometimes fear that they are "going crazy." The foundation that the practitioner lays for an understanding of this anxiety is extremely important for the patient, who then has the option of handling the anxiety with the help of either the practitioner or a mental health specialist.

It is important to recognize that such reality-based anxiety may take many forms including such states as agitated depression, profound grief reactions, or suicidal ideations among others. Any indication that the individual is seriously contemplating suicide requires immediate mental health referral. Depression and grief reactions may or may not require referral.

Treatment modalities include individual, peer group, and family counseling. The primary advantage of individual counseling is that it allows the patient, whether adolescent or adult, to discuss such intimate matters as concerns about death and dying and sexuality in the context of a confidential relationship.

Group counseling is often especially beneficial for chronically ill adolescents and young adults. Peer interaction and acceptance are hallmarks of adolescence; thus, feelings of being supported and accepted can be developed through contacts with a group of people who share a chronic illness and have many of the same medical problems and psychological difficulties. The parents of chronically ill adolescents may also benefit from a similar group experience.

At times, family counseling is warranted, especially if communication among family members is poor. However, late adolescents, particularly those who are chronically ill, may be struggling for their independence. Thus, decisions about family therapy should be carefully considered and discussed privately with the adolescent before such a referral is made.

Glossary

acceleration Overall process of further or continued growth and development.

accommodation *(Piaget)* The individual's tendency to change by developing new processes (behaviors, skills) in response to environmental demands.

achievement tests *(Piaget)* Measures of the amount of information or skill an individual has acquired from past learning.

adaptation General principle of functioning that describes an organism's ability to fit the environment through modification; accomplished through the processes of accommodation and assimilation.

anal stage *(Freud)* Developmental period in toddlerhood in which the anus is the primary erogenous zone: pleasure is derived from elimination and/or withholding.

animism *(Piaget)* Belief that inanimate objects are alive as people are alive; characteristic of preoperational thinking.

anorexia nervosa Once known as hysterica apepsia, an eating disorder of adolescence characterized by severe loss of appetite, aversion to food, and weight loss.

anticipatory goal response *(learning theory)* Appearance of a learned response too early in a situation in which the response is otherwise appropriate.

aptitude test Scale designed to determine the ability of an individual to learn tasks or skills in some occupation or to succeed in higher education.

artificialism *(Piaget)* Belief that all things are made for a purpose; characteristic of preoperational thinking.

assimilation *(Piaget)* The individual's ability to deal with an environmental event using already available processes (behaviors, skills).

attention-seeking behavior *(learning theory)* Behavior that attracts the notice of some other individual.

autonomy vs. shame and doubt *(Erikson)* Second age of man, during which the task of the individual is to develop feelings of autonomy and to overcome feelings of self-doubt about personal ability and shame for past enjoyment of dependence; analogous to the anal stage in Freudian psychology.

basic trust vs. basic mistrust *(Erikson)* First age of man, during which the infant develops a trusting, open approach and overcomes an uncertain, mistrusting approach to new experiences.

behavior modification Treatment modality using reinforcement techniques to alter behavior patterns; based on S-R psychology.

behaviorism School of psychology that stresses the study of observable actions and reactions of organisms.

bell-shaped curve Symmetrical frequency distribution that results when half the area falls under the curve to the right and half to the left of the mean. The mean, median, and mode are identical.

blended family A family that has been formed by the marriage of two persons who bring their respective children into the marriage.

"brittle" diabetes Poorly controlled or difficult-to-control diabetes characterized by recurrent ketoacidosis or hypoglycemic crises that require repeated hospitalization. The role of psychological factors is unknown but thought to be significant, particularly in young diabetics.

castration anxiety *(Freud)* Oedipal boy's fears that, if he persists in antagonism toward his father, he may be physically harmed through castration.

castration complex *(Freud)* Penis envy in females and castration anxiety in males.

cathexis *(Freud)* Investment of psychic energy in

an idea, external object, person, or some aspect of the self.

cell maturation Developmental process whereby new or different functions are performed on a molecular level by existing cells.

cell replacement Developmental process whereby old, injured, or nonfunctional cells are replaced by new cells.

centration *(Piaget)* Cognitive inability to consider several aspects or dimensions of a situation simultaneously; a characteristic of preoperational thinking.

classical conditioning *(learning theory)* Sometimes known as Pavlovian conditioning; process by which (1) a naturally occurring stimulus (food) that elicits a particular response (salivation) is paired with a neutral stimulus (bell); (2) after a number of pairings, the same or a very similar response (now referred to as the conditioned response) is elicited by the neutral stimulus (now referred to as the conditioned stimulus).

cognition Process of acquiring and using knowledge.

cognitive-intellectual theory Represented by the works of Piaget and Kohlberg, this approach provides a framework for understanding the development of knowledge, thought, and reasoning about the world, both physical and social, in children and adolescents.

competence What a person can optimally do at a given developmental stage.

concrete operational period *(Piaget)* Developmental period that extends from approximately 7 to 12 years of age and is distinguished by the appearance of logical thinking about physically present (concrete) problems.

conditioned response *(learning theory)* Response elicited by a conditioned stimulus; similar, but not always identical, to the unconditioned response.

conditioned stimulus *(learning theory)* Stimulus that is initially neutral and causes no direct effect or response, but upon repeated pairings with an unconditioned stimulus comes to elicit the response.

conditioning See *classical conditioning* and/or *instrumental conditioning*.

conscience *(Freud)* The part of the superego that is the child's conception of what his parents consider to be morally bad.

conservation *(Piaget)* Ability to understand that changes in shape or appearance do not affect

equivalency in quantity, substance, weight, or volume; developed during the concrete operational period.

conventional (moral) level *(Kohlberg)* Level of moral reasoning characterized by the performance of good or right roles and the fulfillment of social expectations.

critical periods Circumscribed periods of time during which the organism displays heightened responsivity to a particular environmental stimulus.

culture Concepts, habits, skills, and institutions characteristic of a group of people during a given period.

culture-fair tests Intelligence tests that avoid cultural bias.

deceleration Decline in size or certain abilities or an unlearning of formerly appropriate responses that have become inappropriate; a normal part of the growth and development continuum.

defense mechanisms *(Freud)* Methods employed by the ego that deny, falsify, or distort reality to alleviate anxiety.

denial *(Freud)* Defense mechanism that allows perception of the world as one wants it to be rather than as it actually is.

dependency anxiety *(social learning theory)* State of apprehension about feelings of need for, or reliance on, others; can lead to a fierce sense of independence manifested by a refusal to communicate with or behave affectionately toward others, especially parents.

depressive equivalents Behaviors displayed by an individual in response to depression that are not generally regarded as indicating depression, for example, acting out or flight to or from people.

development Maturation or differentiation; usually measured by evaluating complexity of functioning or degree of performance skill.

discrimination *(learning theory)* Limiting a response to specific stimuli by selective reinforcement.

disengaged family Family characterized by rigidity and inflexibility of subsystem boundaries in which communication across subsystems is difficult or nonexistent, thus handicapping the protective function of the family.

displacement *(Freud)* Defense mechanism that allows repressed impulses to be disguised to achieve satisfaction.

drive motivation *(learning theory)* Organism's degree of readiness to respond to a stimulus.

ego *(Freud)* Executive function of the personality

or the intermediary between the id, the super-ego, and the external world; governed by the reality principle.

egocentrism *(Piaget)* Cognitive inability to take another person's viewpoint; the young child's feeling that he is the origin of all actions in his world; characteristic of preoperational thinking.

ego-ideal *(Freud)* The part of the superego that is the child's conception of what his parents consider to be morally good.

ego-instincts Instincts concerned with self-preservation, for example, hunger, thirst, and escape from pain.

ego integrity vs. despair *(Erikson)* Eighth age of man, during which an individual approaching the final phase of life and reflecting on his existence and experiences develops the sense that life has been good, thus forming a positive appreciation of self-integrity and overcoming the feeling that life was lived inadequately (despair).

Electra conflict *(Freud)* Mother-daughter conflict that results from the girl's love of her father and her jealousy of her mother as initiated by penis envy; characteristic of the phallic stage.

enmeshed family Family characterized by free permeability across subsystem boundaries where there is little or no distance between family members, no privacy, and no autonomy.

environment Physical and psychological milieu; source of nurturance or training.

erogenous zone *(Freud)* Region of the body where localized tensions can be reduced through manipulation.

external aim *(Freud)* Overt behavior or action that satisfies an instinctual drive.

extinction *(learning theory)* Process of "undoing" a behavior by repeatedly failing to reinforce it.

failure to thrive See *nonorganic failure to thrive.*

fixation *(Freud)* Defense mechanism that inhibits progression to the next developmental phase.

formal operational period *(Piaget)* Developmental period that extends from early adolescence through adulthood and is distinguished by the appearance of abstract thought.

gender identity Sameness, unity, and persistence of one's individuality as male, female, or ambivalent, to some degree, particularly as it is experienced in self-awareness and behavior.

generalization *(learning theory)* Process of eliciting a response with a variety of similar stimuli.

generativity vs. stagnation *(Erikson)* Seventh age of man, during which the task of the individual is to establish and maintain a social structure conducive to the growth of the next generation and to overcome personal and social stagnation.

genital stage *(Freud)* Developmental period, beginning in adolescence, in which the genitalia are the primary erogenous zone: pleasure is derived from mature sexual attraction to a love object.

genotype Actual gene composition as determined by deoxyribonucleic acid (DNA) sequencing.

"good boy"–"nice girl" orientation *(Kohlberg)* Good behavior is viewed as that which is approved by others; characteristic of the conventional level of moral reasoning.

growth Increase in size, usually assessed by measuring such parameters as length, weight, breadth, or depth.

habit *(learning theory)* Strength of a learned response directly related to the number of times it has been reinforced.

habit-family hierarchy *(learning theory)* More than one sequence of behaviors elicited by a single stimulus and resulting in an identical reward.

heredity Genetic endowment that defines, within broad limits, an individual's basic overall potential and predisposition.

homosexual panic Fear or anxiety experienced when one's sexual behavior or drive is directed toward members of the same sex rather than toward those of the opposite sex.

id *(Freud)* Foundation of personality, whose sole function is to avoid pain and seek pleasure; the inaccessible part of the personality, closer in touch with the body and its processes than with the external world; retains its infantile character throughout life.

identification *(Freud)* Incorporation of the qualities of another person into one's personality.

identity vs. role confusion *(Erikson)* Fifth age of man, during which the individual seeks to establish his identity independent from his family and overcome a sense of confusion about his role in society.

imaginary audience Feature of adolescent egocentrism in which the young person feels that he is being constantly evaluated and judged by others.

imitation See *observational learning.*

individuality Constellation of innate characteristics and learned behaviors that distinguish one person from another.

industry vs. inferiority *(Erikson)* Fourth age of man, during which school-age children are motivated to learn tasks, improve their skills and knowledge, and overcome a sense of inferiority if mastery is not achieved.

inhibition *(learning theory)* Counteracting the expression of a behavior in order to avoid punishment.

initiative vs. guilt *(Erikson)* Third age of man, during which preschoolchildren are constantly challenged to new activity and purpose and to overcome a sense of guilt if the goals and actions they plan and carry out are in conflict with the autonomous activity of others.

instincts *(Freud)* Inborn impulses or conditions that impart direction to psychological processes.

instrumental conditioning *(learning theory)* Learning or strengthening of correct responses through reinforcement.

instrumental-relativistic orientation *(Kohlberg)* Pragmatic concepts of fairness, reciprocity, and sharing; characteristic of the preconventional (premoral) level of moral reasoning.

integrity vs. despair *(Erikson)* See *ego-integrity vs. despair*.

intellectualization *(Freud)* Defense mechanism consisting of focusing only on the cognitive aspects of a situation and thus attaining a purely nonaffective appreciation of a problem.

intelligence Capacity to perceive and understand facts and propositions and their relations and to reason about them.

intelligence quotient *(IQ)* Ratio of maturational age (as defined by standardized tests) to chronological age multiplied by 100 (IQ = MA/CA × 100); commonly used measure of functional cognitive ability.

intelligence tests Measures of an individual's level of cognitive functioning.

internal aim *(Freud)* Reduction of excitation or achievement of satisfaction of an instinctual drive.

intimacy vs. isolation *(Erikson)* Sixth age of man, during which young adults develop feelings of closeness and commitment to partnership and overcome feelings of distance from other people.

irreversibility *(Piaget)* Lack of appreciation of successive changes or transformations; lack of cognitive ability to attend simultaneously to more than one relevant dimension or understand compensation and reciprocity; characteristic of preoperational thinking.

isolation (of affect) *(Freud)* Defense mechanism that allows the repression or lack of awareness of a feeling associated with an idea but not the idea itself.

juxtaposition *(Piaget)* Cognitive inability to perceive causality, resulting in a listing of events without specifying relationships among them; characteristic of preoperational thinking.

latency See *psychosexual latency*.

"law and order" orientation *(Kohlberg)* Emphasis on authority and fixed rules; characteristic of the conventional level of moral reasoning.

learning theory An approach to development, represented by the work of Sears and others, that provides a framework for understanding the behavior of the child as it is learned and maintained by association, reinforcement, and observation.

libido *(Freud)* Sex drive concerned with species preservation; motivating life force that includes a drive to maturity.

magical thinking *(Piaget)* Cognitive process of equating thought and fantasy with action; the feeling that one's wish causes some external event; characteristic of preoperational thinking.

maturational age Functional ability of the individual, compared with normative behavior of other individuals at specified ages, as determined by standardized testing.

nature Inherent or innate biological, physical, and psychological characteristics of the individual.

nonorganic failure to thrive Poor growth in the absence of medical illness sufficient to account for the degree of observed growth deficiency; seen in children suffering from stimulus deprivation (neglect).

normal variation Within the limits of "normality"; growth or developmental characteristics that are normally distributed *and* that fall within two standard deviations of the group mean.

nurturance Positive environmental conditions and experiences to which the individual is exposed; training.

object *(Freud)* Any external person or thing that must be involved in some way for the individual to achieve gratification.

object concept *(Piaget)* Understanding, usually developed during infancy, that things exist independently of a person's perception of them.

object permanence See *object concept*.

observational learning *(learning theory)* Modification of old behaviors or introduction of new behaviors as a result of the individual's watching other peoples' behaviors or attitudes.

Oedipal conflict *(Freud)* Father-son conflict that arises from the boy's drive for exclusive sexual possession of his mother and his jealousy and rivalry with his father; characteristic of the phallic stage.

Oedipus complex *(Freud)* Universal, unconscious, incestuous fantasy that children experience during the phallic stage: young boys fall in love with and sexually desire the mother and wish the father's death, whereas young girls sexually desire the father and are jealous of the mother. Name derived from the mythological Greek figure, Oedipus.

oral stage *(Freud)* Developmental period during infancy in which the mouth is the primary erogenous zone: pleasure is derived from tactile stimulation and biting.

organization *(Piaget)* Tendency common to all organisms to integrate processes, which may be either physical or psychological, into higher-order systems or processes.

overachievement Performance that is higher than measured ability.

partial reinforcement *(learning theory)* Inconsistent, random reinforcement that increases the amount of time necessary to learn a behavior and decreases the likelihood that a behavior will be extinguished.

participation *(Piaget)* Belief that a continuing connection or interaction exists between human actions and natural processes; characteristic of preoperational thinking.

penis envy *(Freud)* Young girl's awareness that she does not have a penis, which results in her stronger love for her father, who possesses the desired organ; characteristic of the phallic stage.

performance What an individual may actually or habitually do under ordinary circumstances; to be distinguished from the individual's level of competence, which represents optimal functioning.

personal fable Feature of early adolescent egocentrism by which the young person believes that his feelings are unique and he is immortal.

phallic stage *(Freud)* Developmental period during the preschool years in which the genitals form the primary erogenous zone: pleasure is derived from self-stimulation.

phenotype Morphological and physiological characteristics of a given individual as determined by the expression or suppression of certain gene compositions or combinations.

pleasure principle *(Freud)* Tendency to avoid pain and find satisfaction or pleasure, which motivates id functioning.

postconventional (principled) level *(Kohlberg)* In-dividual, personal conformity to moral principles that have validity in application apart from social authority and convention.

preconcepts *(Piaget)* Early, inconstant, and idiosyncratic understandings of abstract ideas (concepts), especially as related to the definition and use of words.

preconventional (premoral) level *(Kohlberg)* Moral reasoning that rightness or wrongness resides in an action's external, physical consequences.

preoperational period *(Piaget)* Period of cognitive development, extending from about 2 to 7 years of age, characterized by the child's acquisition of language and the appearance of initial reasoning.

primary process *(Freud)* Internal imaging of a tension-reducing object; characteristic of id functioning.

primary sexual characteristics Physical characteristics that distinguish between males and females and are directly involved with reproduction.

projection *(Freud)* Defense mechanism that attributes a dangerous drive motivation or an undesirable characteristic to the external world so that it becomes an objective anxiety and is therefore easier for the ego to master.

psychic energy *(Freud)* Form of energy that operates the three systems of personality and performs psychological work such as perceiving, thinking, and remembering.

psychoanalytic theory Conceptual framework for understanding the development of intrinsic personality structure and the development of the individual as a member of society who must encounter and resolve interpersonal conflicts as they relate to his functioning in the world. Two major developmental theories are subsumed within this school: psycho*sexual* development (Freud) and psycho*social* development (Erikson). The name psychoanalytic is derived from the primary method of investigation and treatment: psychoanalysis.

psychosexual latency *(Freud)* Developmental period during the elementary school-age years in which sexual impulses are repressed.

psychosocial dwarfism Growth failure thought to result from functional hypopituitarism caused by a disturbed emotional environment.

punishment-obedience orientation *(Kohlberg)* Perception of rules as absolutes without any consideration of motive or intent; characteristic of the preconventional level of moral reasoning.

rationalization *(Freud)* Defense mechanism by

which an unacceptable act is justified by changing its nature to make it more acceptable.

reaction formation *(Freud)* Defense mechanism by which an anxiety-producing instinct is repressed by concentrating on its opposite: unacceptable, unconscious feelings are masked by opposite, acceptable feelings; can result in overcompensation.

reality principle *(Freud)* Accurate perception of what exists in the external world, which guides ego functioning.

regression *(Freud)* Defense mechanism that allows retreat to an earlier developmental stage in the face of anxiety or fear.

reinforcement *(learning theory)* A consequent (reinforcer) to a behavior, which influences the probability that the behavior will occur again; may be positive or negative.

repression *(Freud)* Defense mechanism by which anxiety-producing experiences, memories, and ideas are buried in the unconscious and forced away from awareness.

reversibility *(Piaget)* Cognitive process of transforming objects or quantities from similar to dissimilar states and back again while maintaining the concept of an invariant unit; characteristic of concrete and formal operational thinking.

role reversal Interaction pattern established, temporarily or permanently, between two individuals, each of whom adopts the role or social expectations usually associated with the partner. For example, a child may adopt the parental role to care for the parent.

school phobia Form of emotional or behavioral maladjustment characterized by a persistent refusal to attend school, usually accompanied by vague complaints of physical ailments; observed in elementary schoolchildren and adolescents; may represent a fear of separation from parent(s) or home or a situational anxiety associated with a person or event at school.

school refusal See *school phobia*.

secondary gain Unconsciously desired benefits or indirect effects or consequences of a behavior.

secondary process *(Freud)* Discovering or producing a desired reality by a plan of action developed through thought and reason; characteristic of ego functioning.

secondary sexual characteristics Physical characteristics that distinguish between males and females but are not directly involved with reproduction.

secular trend Epidemiological term referring to

change noted in a population over time; in adolescent development, the change in age of onset of puberty observed during the past century.

self-esteem The positive or negative value that one places on oneself.

semiotic function *(Piaget)* Cognitive ability to make something (object or mental symbol) stand for or represent something else that is not present; developed during the preoperational stage of thinking.

sensorimotor period *(Piaget)* First stage of cognitive development characterized by the infant's use of his senses to gain information and the use of his increasing motor capabilities to seek out new experiences and modify his environment.

sequencing As it applies to physical development at adolescence, the predictable order of appearance of sexual characteristics.

sexual instinct See *libido*.

shaping *(learning theory)* Reinforcement of successive approximations of a desired behavior until the desired behavior is attained.

sibling rivalry Competitive and hostile negotiations carried out by the children within a family in defining their relationships and responsibilities to one another as peers within the family heirarchy.

social-contract, legalistic orientation *(Kohlberg)* Right action is defined in terms of general individual rights; a clear awareness exists of the relativism of personal values and opinions; characteristic of the postconventional level of moral reasoning.

socialization Process whereby a society trains children to behave like the adults of that society.

socioeconomic status Family characteristic defined by income, extent of education, and occupational level of the heads of the family.

sociopathic disturbance Disorder characteristic of chronically antisocial persons who seem unable or unwilling to live within established social and moral frameworks and who do not form stable and intimate interpersonal relationships.

somatization Formation of physical complaints that have no physiological basis but can be associated with perceptions of real pain or limitation of function.

source *(Freud)* Excitation, need, or impulse arising in some part of the body.

stimulus-response psychology Psychological theory based on the principle that all predictable behavior (response) is elicited by a stimulus, thereby providing a framework for understanding and modifying behavior as it is related to external events.

sublimation *(Freud)* Defense mechanism that robs an instinctual drive of its primitive character and transforms its expression into an activity that is socially acceptable.

substance abuse Consistent reliance upon alcohol or drugs to provide escape from psychological stress at the cost of impairment to health, judgment, or functioning.

superego *(Freud)* Moral or judicial function of the personality representing the ideal rather than the real.

syncretism *(Piaget)* Tendency to group several apparently unrelated objects or events together into a confused whole; characteristic of preoperational thinking.

temperament Psychological component of phenotype; the apparently innate, characteristic or habitual inclination or mode of emotional response to stimuli idiosyncratic to an individual that is displayed beginning in early infancy.

test bias Result of measures (e.g., intelligence tests) that do not adequately evaluate a function (e.g., mental ability) as independent from learning or social or economic factors.

transduction *(Piaget)* Reasoning from a particular to a particular, for example, seeing a relationship between two particular objects where there

is none; characteristic of preoperational thinking.

transitional object Object associated with a familiar or secure setting that provides a sense of comfort to an individual in an unfamiliar or anxiety-provoking setting, for example, the toy from home that a child takes with him to the hospital

transitional period Interval spanning the end of one developmental stage and the beginning of the next during which the individual's characteristics and abilities are not completely representative of either stage but show definite tendency toward progression.

truancy Act of remaining away from school without permission of the school.

trust vs. mistrust See *basic trust vs. basic mistrust*.

unconditioned response Automatic response to a specific stimulus.

unconditioned stimulus Stimulus that automatically elicits a specific response.

underachievement Performance that is lower than measured ability.

universal-ethical-principled orientation *(Kohlberg)* Conscience and self-chosen ethical principles are preeminent in moral decision making; characteristic of postconventional moral reasoning.

wish fulfillment *(Freud)* Feeling of satisfaction derived from the formation of a tension-reducing image through primary process.

Suggested readings for parents and children

The following annotated bibliography presents books that may be of interest to parents, children, or adolescents facing certain developmental issues. The approximate cost is provided for most titles.

CHILD DEVELOPMENT

Buxbaum, E. 1974. *Your Child Makes Sense: A Guidebook for Parents*. New York: International Universities Press. $4.95.

   Approaches parenting from the viewpoint of the physical, emotional, and intellectual development of the child. A classic.

Conger, J. 1979. *Adolescence*. New York: Harper & Row, Publishers, Inc. $4.95.

   Easy-to-read book on adolescent development that many parents will find helpful and enjoyable reading. Topics of interest include physical and mental growth; relationships with parents and peers; and sex, drug, and psychological problems.

Chess, S., Thomas, A., and Birch, H. G. 1972. *Your Child is a Person: A Psychological Approach to Parenthood Without Guilt*. New York: The Viking Press. $2.95.

   Supportive of the parents' struggle with the parent-child relationship. Offers practical techniques for coping. Describes personality development as an interaction between the child, with his unique temperament and the total environment, including the child's parents.

Duvall, E. M. 1974. *Family Development* (4th ed.). Philadelphia: J. B. Lippincott Co. $14.95.

   Designed as a textbook for preprofessionals, but parents often find material on family development helpful.

Fraiberg, S. 1959. *The Magic Years*. New York: Charles Scribner's Sons. $4.95.

   Sensitive and understanding approach to the trials and tribulations of childhood and parenthood written from a psychoanalytic viewpoint. Very readable and helpful descriptions of the emotional development of children. Uses specific examples to explain particular concepts and to relate to a parent's own experiences. Covers early childhood and the preschool years.

Gesell, A., Ilg, F. L., Ames, L. B., and Rodell, J. L. 1974. *Infant and Child in the Culture of Today: The Guidance of Development in Home and Nursery School*. New York: Harper & Row, Publishers, Inc. $15.95.

   Presents norms and standards for physical and emotional development with allowances for individual variation. Designed to help new parents learn about child behavior.

Hymes, J. L. 1963. *The Child Under Six*. Englewood Cliffs, N. J.: Prentice-Hall, Inc. $8.95.

   Will help parents acquire more understanding of young children and how they develop.

Ribble, M. 1955. *The Personality of the Young Child*. New York: Columbia University Press.

   Summarizes early child development from a psychoanalytic perspective.

Salk, L. 1970. *Your Child from 1 to 12*. New York: Signet. $1.50.

   Developmental approach for parents of toddlers, early school-age children, and young adolescents. Tells why children behave as they do at particular ages. Answers basic questions; helps parents learn about nutrition, school readiness, child health, and other relevant topics.

Schowalter, J. E., and Anyan, W. R. 1979. *The*

200

Family Handbook of Adolescence. New York: Alfred A. Knopf, Inc. $10.95.

Complete information on all aspects of adolescence, such as conflicts with parents, sex, normal and abnormal development, diet, exercise, drinking, and drugs, with full descriptions of common physical and psychological problems, plus advice on care and treatment.

Teenagers and parenting

Gordon, S., and Wollin, M. M. 1975. *Parenting: A Guide for Young People*. New York: W. H. Sadler.

Designed as a text for school courses on parenting. Written in a readable style.

Howard, M. 1975. *Only Human: Teenage Pregnancy and Parenthood*. New York: The Seabury Press, Inc. $8.95.

Uses three different parenting situations to illustrate the problems and answer the questions of young parents. Extremely helpful to parents of school-age children: relates directly to their needs and interests. Highly recommended.

CHILD REARING

Arnstein, H. S. 1964. *What to Tell Your Child about Birth, Illness, Death, Divorce, and Other Family Crises*. New York: Pocket Books. $2.25.

Briefly discusses wide range of topics. Good general reference.

Axline, V. M. 1969. *Play Therapy*. New York: Ballantine Books, Inc. $2.25.

Presents the basic principles of play therapy through which the adult can help the child experience self-exploration, self-expansion, and self-expression. Includes implications for education. Rewarding for parents, teachers, and anyone who comes in contact with children.

Babcock, D. E., and Keepers, T. D. 1976. *Raising Kids O.K.* New York: Avon Books. $1.95.

Transactional analysis framework for approaching issues of parenthood, including being an OK parent, child ego, punishment, toilet training, the school years, sexuality, marriage and remarriage, disability, and illness. Presents down-to-earth, practical advice in a readable, interesting format.

Bettleheim, B. 1962. *Dialogues with Mothers*. New York: Avon Books. $2.25.

Psychoanalytic approach to child care that helps parents understand, respect, and respond to the day-to-day problems of children.

Brazelton, T. B. 1974. *Toddlers and Parents*. New York: Delacorte Press. $6.95.

Discusses major parenting issues such as working and single parents and describes how to cope with hyperactive, demanding, and withdrawn toddlers. Well-written text, in tune with the feelings of parents, accompanied by excellent pictures.

Button, A. D. 1969. *The Authentic Child*. New York: Random House, Inc.

Stresses the importance of parental acceptance, honesty, and willingness to be human. Will help parents see beauty in their children and experience joy in a mutual, nonpower relationship. Rejects pat solutions in parent education in favor of developing open relationships with children.

Callahan, S. C. 1974. *Parenting: Principles and Politics of Parenthood*. Baltimore: Penguin Books. $1.95.

Presents the cultural, psychological, theoretical, and practical aspects of child rearing in this country in an interesting and enjoyable way. Provides a helpful and relevant critique of "how-to-parent" books.

Corsini, R. J., and Painter, G. 1975. *The Practical Parent*. New York: Harper & Row, Publishers, Inc. $10.95.

Excellent approach for parents about how to raise responsible children. Teaches practical application through the use of vignettes. Enlightening, encouraging, full of common sense, humorous.

Dodson, F. 1970. *How to Parent*. New York: Nash Publishing Corp. $1.95.

Practical approach to parenting based on psychological theory and practice. Enjoyable and helpful.

Duvall, E. M. 1974. *Handbook for Parents*. Nashville, Tenn.: Broadman Press. $4.95.

Discusses the responsibilities of parenthood as well as child-rearing experiences parents are likely to face as their children develop from infancy through adolescence. Sensitive, helpful, and thoroughly readable.

Faber, A., and Mazlish, E. 1974. *Liberated Parents, Liberated Children*. New York: Avon Books. $2.25.

Based on Haim Ginott's theory of child rearing and family life. Candidly shows how parents can create a loving atmosphere in the home and aid their children in developing insight and responsibility.

Gersh, M. 1973. *How to Raise Children at Home in Your Spare Time*. New York: Stein & Day Publishers. $1.75.

Combines humor with sound advice to help parents cope with the trials and tribulations of child rearing. Enables parents to stop feeling guilty and enjoy parenthood. An added feature is a section that deals with poisoning by common house and garden plants.

Ginott, H. G. 1964. *Between Parent and Teenager*. Toronto: Macmillan Co. of Toronto, Ltd. $2.25.

Addresses the conflict parents face when they realize that their children are growing up and becoming independent of them. Outlines a new approach to praise and criticism and shows how to express anger without insult. Includes sections on teenage sex, drinking, driving, and drugs and on the freedom and limits of social life.

Ginott, H. G. 1965. *Between Parent and Child*. New York: Avon Books. $2.50.

Discusses how to talk with children and to communicate effectively. Describes the use and impact of praise and criticism. Teaches parents how to avoid self-defeating patterns of parent-child interaction. Sections on jealousy and anxiety in children should prove very helpful in understanding the kinds of stress children face as they grow up. Sex education, sexual roles, and social functioning are discussed. The last two chapters describe the kinds of children and parents who may benefit from professional help. The presentation is direct and easy to understand. Illustrates advice by dialogue and anecdotes.

Gordon, T. 1970. *Parent Effectiveness Training*. New York: Peter H. Wyden, Inc. $5.95.

Interesting, informative, and helpful for parents of both young children and teenagers. Considers communication an extremely important element of the parent-child relationship. One chapter discusses how to change unacceptable behavior by changing the environment. Describes inevitable parent-child conflicts, but shows how parents can prevent some conflicts by modifying themselves.

Gordon, T. 1976. *P.E.T. in Action*. New York: Peter H. Wyden, Inc. $2.75.

Provides case histories and in-depth reports that illustrate how individual families handled real problem situations. A readable, helpful accompaniment to *Parent Effectiveness Training*.

Gould, S. 1977. *Teenagers: The Continuing Challenge*. New York: Hawthorn Books, Inc. $3.95.

Valuable advice and information for parents on the issues of management, trust, and respect, communication, conflict, stepparenting.

Group for the Advancement of Psychiatry. 1973. *The Joys and Sorrows of Parenthood*. New York: Charles Scribner's Sons.

Describes the stages of parenthood. Answers many of the questions commonly asked by parents. A valuable resource, easy to read.

Kelly, M., and Parsons, E. 1975. *The Mother's Almanac*. New York: Doubleday & Co. Inc. $4.95.

Explores parenthood from the mother's viewpoint.

Klein, C. 1975. *The Myth of the Happy Child*. New York: Harper & Row, Publishers, Inc. $8.95.

Thoughtful; contributes to an understanding of the feelings of children and the kinds of guilt they engender in their parents that compound parenting difficulties.

Larrick, N. 1975. *A Parent's Guide to Children's Reading*. New York: Bantam Books, Inc. $8.95.

Includes sections on dictionaries, encyclopedias, poetry, children's magazines, and the effect of television on children's reading. A helpful and informative guide for parents who wish to stimulate their child's motivation for reading.

LeShan, E. 1973. *How to Survive Parenthood*. New York: Warner Books, Inc.

The material in this volume was enthusiastically received on educational television because it deals with specific questions that worry many parents and makes suggestions for coping with them.

Levine, M. I., and Seligmann, J. H. 1978. *The Parents' Encyclopedia of Infancy, Childhood, and Adolescence* (Rev. ed.). New York: Harper & Row, Publishers, Inc. $3.95.

Everything from A (accident-prone children) to M (masturbation) to T (toys and other play materials). A handy, easy-to-use reference.

Missildine, W. H. 1963. *Your Inner Child of the Past*. New York: Simon & Schuster, Inc. $9.95.

Highlights how one's childhood influences adult parenting attitudes and skills. Offers suggestions for coping with one's "inner child" and freeing oneself to live and parent effectively. Excellent.

Neill, A. S. 1960. *Summerhill*. New York: Hart Publishing Co., Inc. $4.95.

One approach to child rearing.

Salk, L. 1973. *What Every Child Would Like His Parents to Know to Help Him with the Emotional Problems of His Everyday Life*. New York: Warner Books, Inc. $1.95.

How to approach problems from the child's point of view.

Salk, L., and Kramer, R. 1969. *How to Raise a Human Being: A Parents' Guide to Emotional Health from Infancy through Adolescence*. New York: Random House, Inc. $6.95.

Describes the nature of mothering and the feeding relationship during the early months, how the preschoolchild learns to be a person, language and play, and living with others. The discussion of how to set limits should be helpful to parents who want to discipline yet not control their children.

Spock, B. M. 1962. *Problems of Parents*. New York: Fawcett Publications, Inc.

Empathetic answers to the questions most frequently asked by parents. Very helpful.

Spock, B. M. 1974. *Raising Children in a Difficult Time*. New York: W. W. Norton & Co., Inc. $1.95.

Addresses the problems faced by parents today, from rebellion and drugs to sexual identification. Practical, understandable, and thought provoking.

Spock, B. M. 1976. *Baby and Child Care* (Rev. ed.). New York: Pocket Books. $1.95.

One of the most widely recommended and best-read handbooks for parents. Presents psychological and developmental concepts in readable and understandable language. Most importantly, Dr. Spock is able to communicate with parents and to help them believe in themselves.

Talbot, N. B. 1976. *Raising Children in Modern America*. Boston: Little, Brown & Co. $8.95.

Discusses the responsibilities of parents and society in the growth and development of our children. Identifies children's needs that are not being met and offers suggestions for improvement.

Weisberger, E. 1979. *Your Young Child and You: How to Manage Growing up Problems in the Years from One to Five*. New York: E. P. Dutton & Co., Inc. $4.95.

Commonsense solutions to child-rearing problems in toilet training, discipline, and sex education. Also includes a discussion of problems children may face, including hospitalization, death, and divorce. Interesting and helpful.

Discipline

Baruch, D. W. 1943. *New Ways in Discipline*. New York: McGraw-Hill Book Co., Inc. $8.95.

One of the most widely read books for parents. Written in simple style. Illustrates use of active listening. Deals with problems of reward and punishment. Shows how parents can apply methods of play therapy at home.

Bernhardt, K. S. 1964. *Discipline and Child Guidance*. New York: McGraw-Hill Book Co.

Attempts to apply knowledge of child development to formulate principles about discipline. Presents a philosophy of discipline that takes into consideration the nature of the child, the kind of world in which the child is being reared, and the goals the parents have. Presents everyday situations and illustrates how the principles of discipline can be applied. Gives a developmental view of the use of discipline from infancy through adolescence. Presents discipline as a form of training and stresses the positive approach.

Dodson, F. 1978. *How to Discipline with Love*. New York: Signet Books. $2.50.

Guides parents in dealing with misbehaviors from infancy through adolescence. Discusses the pros and cons of spanking. Includes special sections devoted to the child-rearing issues that concern working mothers and single parents. Excellent.

Dreikurs, R. 1948. *Coping with Children's Misbehavior*. New York: Hawthorn Books, Inc., Publishers. $3.95.

Explains why children misbehave as well as effective methods of discipline. Offers practical solutions to trying situations such as tantrums or poor school performance.

Dreikurs, R., and Grey, L. 1970. *A Parents' Guide to Good Discipline* (Rev. ed.). New York: Hawthorn Books, Inc. $3.50.

Offers a constructive, supportive approach to parenting. Discusses the importance of discipline and identifies ways of acheiving it.

Dreikurs, R., and Soltz, V. 1964. *Children: The Challenge*. New York: Hawthorn Books, Inc., Publishers. $4.95.

Stresses human dignity, freedom, and responsibility. Discusses four reasons for misbehavior: to attract attention, to gain power, to retaliate, and to respond to inadequacy. Teaches how to encourage children and how to use the principles of behavior modification. Stresses that responsible parents raise responsible chil-

dren and that mistakes can be profitable learning experiences. Appropriate reading for parents of children of all ages.

Kiley, D. 1978. *Keeping Kids out of Trouble*. New
York: Warner Books, Inc. $2.50.

Shows parents how and when to take action
in dealing with child misbehavior. Simple, direct approach to child rearing presented in an
entertaining and sensitive manner. For parents
of children in early childhood through adolescence.

Behavior modification

Becker, W. C., and Becker, J. W. 1974. *Successful Parenthood: How to Teach Your Child Values, Competence, and Responsibility*. Chicago:
Follett Publishing Co.

Application of reinforcement theory to child-
rearing practices. Provides parents with knowledge about how to use rewards and punishments to influence children's behavior and to
change problem behavior. Discusses the development of self-control and describes the problems children may have in social interactions.
Addresses the special concerns of working parents.

Krumboltz, J. D., and Krumboltz, M. B. 1972.
Changing Children's Behavior. Englewood
Cliffs, N.J.: Prentice-Hall, Inc. $8.95.

Gives many everyday examples of appropriate
and inappropriate behavior. Emphasis is on positive reinforcement. Covers such topics as
scheduling rewards to develop persistence,
teaching a child to avoid harm, and preventing
fears. Also gives examples of how people reinforce unacceptable behaviors without realizing
they are doing so.

Patterson, G. R. 1975. *Families*. Champaign, Ill.:
Research Press. $4.95.

Intended to give family members the skills
they need to interact more appropriately. Applies a social learning model to family life.

Patterson, G. R. 1979. *Living with Children: New
Methods for Parents and Teachers* (Rev. ed.).
Champaign, Ill.: Research Press. $3.95.

Gives parents and teachers a practical, effective technique to deal with children's misbehaviors. Written in down-to-earth language.

FAMILY LIFE
The black family

Comer, J. P., and Poussaint, A. F. 1976. *Black
Child Care*. New York: Simon & Schuster, Inc.
$10.95.

Describes how to raise a psychologically and
emotionally healthy black child in America.
Theoretically and practically sound advice. Well
written and very helpful.

Harrison-Ross, P., and Wyden, B. 1974. *The
Black Child: A Parent's Guide to Raising Happy
and Healthy Children*. New York: Berkeley
Publishing Corp.

Developmental approach designed to help
parents help their children grow up liberated.
A sensitive, readable account of black dimensions of discipline and sex.

McLaughlin, C. J. 1976. *The Black Parent's
Handbook*. New York: Harcourt Brace Jovanovich, Inc. $3.95.

Everything black parents want to know about
conception, pregnancy, birth, and child care.

Fathers

Biller, H. B., and Meredith, D. 1975. *Father
Power*. New York: Anchor Books. $3.50.

Defines father power as "the use of your profound, natural influence to help your child become what he or she wants to be." Delineates
the father's role and offers ideas for strengthening this role.

Dodson, F. 1974. *How to Father*. New York: Signet Books. $2.25.

Sequel to *How to Parent* in which the author
provides advice tailored to the unique aspects of
fathering. Also includes material on the older
child.

Gatley, R. H., and Kovlack, D. 1979. *Single Father's Handbook*. New York: Anchor Press.
$4.95.

Useful guide for separated and divorced fathers. Discusses common concerns from custody and visitation to socializing your children.
Offers helpful advice on everything from feeding children to what to do when children get
sick. Should be very helpful to fathers who want
to play an active role in child rearing and are
interested in improving their relationships with
their children.

Kahan, S. 1978. *For Divorced Fathers Only*. New
York: Monarch Press. $3.95.

Gives advice and strategies for handling the
emotional, legal, and financial consequences of
divorce.

Working mothers

Callahan, S. C. 1972. *The Working Mother*. New
York: Paperback Library.

Explores issues relating to substitute mothering and the problems of mothers who work outside the home.

Cotten, D. W. 1965. *The Case for the Working Mother*. New York: Stein & Day Publishers.

Designed for both mothers and helping professionals who have ambivalent feelings about mothers who work and the adequacy of their parenting.

Curtis, J. 1976. *Working Mothers*. New York: Doubleday & Co., Inc. $2.95.

Updates and sensitively discusses the important issues relating to the working mother.

Harrell, J., and Pizzo, P. 1973. *Mothers in Paid Employment*. Washington, D.C.: Day Care and Child Development Council.

Excellent series of articles dealing with problems faced by the working mother.

Single parents

Hope, K., and Young, N. 1976. *Momma: The Sourcebook for Single Mothers*. New York: Plume. $4.95.

Presents the kind of helpful, practical information crucial to the survival of the single mother.

Klein, C. 1973. *The Single Parent Experience*. New York: Avon Books. $2.50.

Sensitively and realistically deals with the special problems of raising a child without a partner, such as day care, dating, and sexual problems; men as mothers; homosexuals as parents.

Divorce

Despert, J. L. 1953. *Children of Divorce*. New York: Doubleday & Co., Inc. $2.50.

Offers insightful suggestions to parents coping with the impact of divorce on their children. A classic—highly recommended.

Gardner, R. 1971. *The Boys and Girls Book About Divorce*. New York: Jason Aronson, Inc. $1.95.

Helpful and effective approach for both children and parents of divorce. An invaluable aid to providing appropriate answers to children's questions about divorce.

Grollman, E. A. 1969. *Explaining Divorce to Children*. Boston: Beacon Press. $4.95.

Presents readings by 9 experts who answer the question of how parents can help children understand a divorce and what it means to them. Contains valuable information for parents who want to prevent their divorce from becoming their children's tragedy.

Grollman, E. A. 1975. *Talking about Divorce: A Dialogue between Parent and Child*. Boston: Beacon Press. $2.95.

Helpful guide to communicating with children on their own level about the sensitive, painful topic of divorce.

Le Shan, E. 1978. *What's Going to Happen to Me? When Parents Separate or Divorce*. New York: The Four Winds Press. $6.95.

Touches on many of the concerns children may or may not be able to verbalize.

Stuart, I., and Abt, L. E. 1972. *Children of Separation and Divorce*. New York: The Viking Press.

Book of articles by many authors on the psychological and developmental effects of divorce. Informative, practical, and thoroughly understandable.

Death

Bernstein, E. J. 1977. *Loss and How to Cope with It*. New York: The Seabury Press, Inc.

Practical and simple discussion of the topic of death. Contains a bibliography of fiction and nonfiction titles plus a listing of nonprint materials that are available commercially.

Cook, S. S. 1973. *Children and Dying*. New York: Health Sciences Publishing Corp. $4.95.

Essays on the child's perception of death.

Grollman, E. A. 1967. *Explaining Death to Children*. Boston: Beacon Press. $4.50.

Specialists in psychology, psychiatry, sociology, biology, religion, and children's literature offer help in easing a child' first confrontation with the death of a loved one.

Grollman, E. A. 1976. *Talking About Death: A Dialogue between Parent and Child*. Boston: Beacon Press. $3.95.

Wise and useful guide to communicating about death on the child's level. Sensitively illustrated.

Sahler, O. J. Z. (Ed.) 1978. *The Child and Death*. St. Louis: The C. V. Mosby Co. $14.95.

Although originally designed for a medical professional readership, many chapters are appropriate for educators, clergy, and parents. Presents the development of the concept of death in children and their reactions to personal death and the death of others. Includes a comprehensive annotated bibliography of books about death for children, young adults, and parents.

Schiff, H. S. 1977. *The Bereaved Parent*. New York: Penguin Books. $2.95.

Written for parents of a child who has died.

Sensitive, understanding style. Gives genuine comfort to survivors of this tragedy. Offers guidelines and practical step-by-step suggestions to help parents cope with every stage of grief, from facing the funeral to rebuilding a marriage.

Vogel, L. J. 1975. *Helping a Child Understand Death*. Philadelphia: Fortress Press. $2.50.

Offers practical help for parents who seek information on helping their children cope with death.

Wolfstein, M. 1969. *Children and the Death of a President*. Magnolia, Mass.: Peter Smith.

Based on research done after the assassination of President Kennedy. Offers excellent suggestions about how to approach the topic of death with children. Advocates a change of attitude toward death in our society.

Death: written for children

Fassler, J. 1977. *My Grandpa Died Today*. New York: Human Sciences Press, Inc. $6.95.

Recounts the conversations between a child and his grandfather as the grandfather approaches and accepts his own death. Will help children think about and deal with the emotional aspects of death.

LeShan, E. 1976. *Learning to Say Good-By: When a Parent Dies*. New York: Macmillan, Inc. $5.95.

Appropriate for children in late elementary school but highly recommended for adults as well. Touches on such topics as the stages of grief, fear of abandonment, and guilt and acceptance, including new relationships in the future.

Smith D. B. 1973. *A Taste of Blackberries*. New York: Scholastic Book Services. 85¢.

Classic first-person narrative recounting a young friend's feelings about the sudden death of Jamie. Appropriate for preadolescent children.

Stein S. B. 1974. *About Dying: An Open Family Book for Parents and Children Together*. New York: Walker & Co. $4.50.

A book of photographs, each of which is accompanied by two narratives. The narrative for parents explains the child's understanding of loss and concept of death. The narrative for children depicts one child's reaction to the deaths of his grandfather and his pet. Excellent, well written, practical. Appropriate for children ages 4 years and older.

SCHOOL AND LEARNING

Brutten, M., Richardson, S. O., and Mangel, C. 1979. *Something's Wrong with My Child: A Parent's Book about Children with Learning Disabilities*. New York: Harcourt Brace Jovanovich, Inc. $3.95.

Includes a discussion about detecting a learning disability, finding appropriate professional help, dealing with the inevitable tensions that arise at home. Well written, informative, and practical.

Friedman, R. 1973. *Family Roots of School Learning and Behavior Disorders*. Springfield, Ill.: Charles C Thomas, Publisher. $11.

Focuses on family influences on the school learning process of children. The various authors, all experienced clinicians, provide a rational framework for the diagnosis and treatment of the family's role in a learning disorder problem regardless of the specific cause or therapeutic modality used.

Glasser, W. 1969. *Schools without Failure*. New York: Perennial Library. $2.25.

Maintains that faulty education, not faulty children, is the main cause of school failure. Details the shortcomings of current education and proposes a provocative new program to reduce school failure. Short and easy to read.

Holt, J. 1964. *How Children Fail*. New York: Dell Publishing Co., Inc. $2.75.

Provides a penetrating analysis of what teachers and classes do to children to cause them to fail—even children who achieve good grades. Explores the effects of evaluation, boredom, fear, and confusion. Parents, as well as teachers, will find this book fascinating.

Holt, J. 1969. *The Underachieving School*. New York: Pitman Publishing Corp. $1.25.

Discusses how evaluation and authoritarian control may seriously interfere with a child's learning. Will help parents acquire new insights about how children should be treated and educated.

Illich, I. 1971. *Deschooling Society*. New York: Harper & Row, Publishers, Inc. $1.95.

Raises basic questions about our educational philosophies and schooling in our society. Especially useful to parents and teachers.

Kozol, J. 1967. *Death at an Early Age*. Boston: Houghton Mifflin Co. $1.95.

Describes the difficulties of minority groups in inner-city schools where teachers may lack an understanding of their students' problems.

Helpful to parents who wish to establish better communication with their children's teachers.

Miller, M. S., and Baker, S. S. 1976. *Straight Talk to Parents: How You can Help your Child Get the Best out of School*. New York: Stein & Day Publishers. $2.95.

Treats parenting from the viewpoint of home and school relations; discusses the parent-child-teacher relationship. Offers encouraging and constructive suggestions for parents who want to develop an open communication system.

HEALTH, ILLNESS, AND HOSPITALIZATION

Apgar, V., and Beck, J. 1973. *Is My Baby All Right?* New York: Pocket Books. $1.95.

Sensitive, practical style. Will give parents the guidance, courage, and understanding needed to care for a child afflicted with such problems as cerebral palsy, cystic fibrosis, hearing loss, spina bifida, tumors, phenylketonuria, and cleft palate.

Gyulay, J. 1978. *The Dying Child*. New York: McGraw-Hill Book Co. $8.95

Written by a pediatric nurse, this book examines death as another facet of the life experience. Informative and clearly written; discusses reactions to grief, the children (young, older, and those with problems and special needs), their families, and the nursing process. Although written for health care personnel, helpful and easy to read for parents as well.

Johnson, F. L., and Miller, M. 1975. *Shannon: A Book for Parents of Children with Leukemia*. New York: Hawthorn Books, Inc. $6.95.

Compelling narrative reveals the life-style, joys, and heartaches of a little girl suffering from leukemia. Presents medical information about the course of treatment as well as family concerns and coping in a readable and informative style.

Moore, C. B., and Morton, K. G. 1976. *A Reader's Guide for Parents of Children with Mental, Physical, or Emotional Disabilities*. U.S. Department of Health, Education, and Welfare Publ. No. (HSA) 77-5290. Washington, D.C.: U.S. Government Printing Office.

Provides parents with information that will facilitate surveying the current literature, selecting what is of particular interest, locating it in the libraries, or ordering it from publishers.

Schulman, J. L. 1976. *Coping with Tragedy: Successfully Facing the Problem of a Seriously Ill Child*. Chicago: Follett Publishing Co.

Sensitive and positive book for parents who are faced with the reality of a seriously ill child. How do they tell the child and explain the situation to relatives and friends? How do they change their life-style? Interviews parents who have had to cope with this tragedy and highlights how families have managed successfully. Deals with the guilt some parents feel when they must make decisions about their child's life or death. Discusses a variety of illnesses, including leukemia, cystic fibrosis, spina bifida, mental retardation, and muscular dystrophy.

U.S. Department of Health, Education, and Welfare. 1976. *When Your Child Goes to the Hospital*. DHEW Publ. No. 76-30092. Washington, D.C.: U.S. Government Printing Office. 85¢.

Practical, helpful guide that provides straightforward answers to parents' frequently raised questions. Explains how to choose a physician and hospital and how to prepare oneself and one's child for the hospital experience.

Health, illness, and hospitalization: written for children

Bemelmans, L. 1967. *Madeline*. New York: Penguin Books. $2.50.

Describes a little girl's visit to the hospital to have her appendix removed. Parents will find that the story can serve as an excellent way to talk with their children about a forthcoming hospital experience.

Clark, B. 1973. *Going to the Hospital*. New York: Random House, Inc. $3.95.

Interesting and comforting style. Will help parents prepare their child for the hospital experience: recognizing and dealing with the emotional needs of children before an operation can contribute to a more positive, less emotionally damaging hospital experience.

Gelman, R. G., and Buxbaum, S. K. 1977. *OUCH! All about Cuts and Other Hurts*. New York: Harcourt Brace Jovanovich, Inc. $6.95.

Organized alphabetically; enables a child, parent, or teacher to locate a particular injury and read a simply written, informative description. Fun; will help children learn about what happens to their bodies when they are bumped, scratched, or cut.

Meeker A. M. 1962. *How Hospitals Help Us*. Chicago: Benefic Press. $3.20.

Informs children about emergency and x-ray rooms, staying at the hospital, operations, and going home. Will familiarize children with the language of hospitalization as a way to help prepare them for the experience.

Rey, M., and Rey, H. A. 1966. *Curious George Goes to the Hospital*. Boston: Houghton Mifflin Co. $1.95.

Written especially for young children facing their first stay at the hospital. Parents will find the book invaluable in preparing a child for the hospital experience. The book's appeal to young children is demonstrated by one preschoolchild who, upon entering the hospital library, ran to the bookshelf, picked out this book, and exclaimed gleefully, "Mommy, Mommy, my favorite book!"

Rogers, F. 1974. *Mister Rogers Talks about Going to the Doctor*. New York: Platt & Munk Publishers. $3.95.

Helps parents prepare young children for their first visit to the doctor.

Shay, A. 1969. *What Happens When You Go to the Hospital*. Chicago: Reilly & Lee. $4.50.

For children ages 3 to 10. Clear, comforting description of what happens in hospitals and why.

Sobol, H. L. 1975. *Jeff's Hospital Book*. New York: Henry Z. Walck, Inc. $6.95.

Tells all about the things that happen to Jeff when he goes to the hospital to have an operation. Includes pictures of his tests and shots and of the doctors and nurses who take care of him. Deals with hospital procedures and the child's normal anxieties about them.

Stein, S. B. 1974. *A Hospital Story: An Open Family Book for Parents and Children Together*. New York: Walker & Co. $6.95.

Will help parents and children share the often frightening experience of a first visit to the hospital. The adult text of this book explains ways that children between 3 and 8 years normally make sense of difficult events in their lives. Highly recommended.

References

Adelson, J. 1975. The development of ideology in adolescence. In S. E. Dragastin and G. H. Elder (Eds.), *Adolescence in the life cycle: psychological change in social context*. New York: John Wiley & Sons, Inc.

Adelson, J., and O'Neill, R. R. 1966. Growth of political ideas in adolescence: the sense of community. *Journal of Personality and Social Psychology* 4:295-306.

Allmond, B. W., Buckman, W., and Gofman, H. F. 1979. *The family is the patient: an approach to behavioral pediatrics for the clinician*. St. Louis: The C. V. Mosby Co.

Alpert, A. 1941. The latency period. *American Journal of Orthopsychiatry* 11:126-133.

Alport, G. W. 1961. *Pattern and growth in personality*. New York: Holt, Rinehart & Winston.

Apley, J., and MacKeith, R. 1968. *The child and his symptoms* (2nd ed.). Oxford, England: Blackwell Scientific Publications Ltd.

Asher, S. R., Oden, S. L., and Gottman, J. M. 1977. Children's friendships in school settings. In L. G. Katz (Ed.), *Current topics in early childhood education*. Norwood, N. J.: Ablex.

Ausubel, D. P., Montemayor, R., and Svajian, P. 1977. *Theory and problems of adolescent development*. New York: Grune & Stratton, Inc.

Ayllon, T., Smith, D., and Rogers, M. 1970. Behavioral management of school phobia. *Journal of Behavior Therapy and Experimental Psychiatry* 1:125-138.

Bakwin, H., and Bakwin, R. M. 1972. *Behavior disorders in children*. Philadelphia: W. B. Saunders Co.

Baldwin, A. L. 1955. *Behavior and development in childhood*. New York: The Dryden Press.

Baldwin, A. L. 1967. *Theories of child development*. New York: John Wiley & Sons, Inc.

Bandura, A. 1969. *Principles of behavior modification*. New York: Holt, Rinehart, & Winston.

Bandura, A. 1969. The stormy decade: fact or fiction? In R. E. Grinder (Ed.), *Studies in adolescence*. Toronto: Collier Macmillan Canada, Ltd.

Bandura, A. 1972. The role of modeling processes in personality development. In C. Lavatelli and F. Stendler (Eds.), *Readings in child behavior and development*. New York: Harcourt Brace Jovanovich, Inc.

Bandura, A., and Walters, R. H. 1959. *Adolescent aggression*. New York: The Ronald Press Co.

Banks, W. C., McQuates, G. V., and Hubbard, J. L. 1978. Toward a reconceptualization of the social-cognitive bases of achievement orientations in Blacks. *Review of Educational Research* 48:381-397.

Bartel, N. R. 1971. Locus of control and achievement in middle- and lower-class children. *Child Development* 42:1099-1107.

Baumrind, D., and Black, A. E. 1967. Socialization practices associated with dimensions of competence in preschool boys and girls. *Child Development* 38:291-327.

Baver, D. H. 1977. An exploratory study of developmental changes in children's fears. In S. Chess and A. Thomas (Eds.), *Annual progress in child psychiatry and child development*. New York: Brunner/Mazel, Inc.

Bayley, N., and Tuddenham, R. D. 1944. Adolescent changes in body build. In *National Society for the Study of Education forty-third yearbook*. New York: The Society.

Becker, D., and Margolin, F. 1976. How surviving parents handled their young children's adaptation to the crisis of loss. In R. H. Moss (Ed.), *Human adaptation: coping with life crises*. Lexington, Mass.: D. C. Heath & Co.

Becker, W. C. 1964. Consequences of different kinds of parental discipline. In M. L. Hoffman and L. W. Hoffman (Eds.), *Review of child development research* (Vol. 1). New York: Russell Sage Foundation.

Bell, R. Q. 1960. Relations between behavior manifestations in the human neonate. *Child Development* 31:463-477.

Bell, R. Q. 1975. Reduction of the stress in child-rearing. In L. Levi (Ed.), *Society, stress and disease* (Vol. 2). London: Oxford University Press.

Bernstein, D. M. 1972. After transplantation—the child's emotional reactions. In S. Chess and A. Thomas (Eds.), *Annual progress in child psychiatry and child development*. New York: Brunner/Mazel, Inc.

Bernstein, J. E. 1977. Helping young children cope with death. In L. G. Katz (Ed.), *Current topics in early childhood education* (Vol. 1). Norwood, N.J.: Ablex.

Beuf, A. H. 1979. *Biting off the bracelet: a study of children in hospitals*. Philadelphia: University of Pennsylvania Press.

Bijou, S. W., and Baer, D. M. 1961. *Child development* (Vol. 1). New York: Appleton-Century-Crofts.

Bijou, S. W., and Baer, D. M. 1966. Operant methods in child behavior and development. In W. K. Honig (Ed.), *Operant behavior: areas of research and application*. New York: Appleton-Century-Crofts.

Biller H. B. 1968. A note on father absence and masculine development in young lower-class Negro and white boys. *Child Development* 39:1003-1006.

Biller, H. B. 1970. Father absence and the personality development of the child. *Developmental Psychology* 2:181-201.

Biller, H. B. 1971. Father absence and the personality development of the male child. In S. Chess and A. Thomas (Eds.), *Annual progress in child psychiatry and child development*. New York: Brunner/Mazel, Inc.

Blackham, G. J., and Silberman, A. 1975. *Modification of child and adolescent behavior* (2nd ed.). Belmont, Calif.: Wadsworth Publishing Co., Inc.

Blom, G. E. 1958. The reactions of hospitalized children to illness. *Pediatrics* 22:590-600.

Blos, P. 1967. The second individuation process of adolescence. *Psychoanalytic Study of the Child* 22:162-186.

Blos, P. 1971. The young adolescent. *Daedalus* 100:961-978.

Bornstein, B. 1972. On latency. In C. Lavatelli and F. Stendler (Eds.), *Readings in child behavior and development*. New York: Harcourt Brace Jovanovich, Inc.

Boulette, T. R. 1977. Parenting: special needs of low-income Spanish-surnamed families. *Pediatric Annals* 6:95-107.

Bowen, G. L. 1977. Death education with kindergarten–first grade groups. *Journal of Pediatric Psychology* 2:77-78.

Bowlby, J. A. 1958. The nature of the child's tie to his mother. *International Journal of Psychoanalysis* 39:350-373.

Bricklin, B., and Bricklin, P. M. 1967. *Bright child—poor grades: the psychology of underachievement*. New York: Delacorte Press.

Bronson, W. C., and Purkey, W. B. 1977. The evaluation of early individual differences in orientation toward peers. Presented at the meeting of the Society for Research in Child Development, New Orleans, March.

Brooks, M. 1957. Constructive play experience for the hospitalized child. *Journal of Nursing Education* 12:7-13.

Brophy, J. E. 1977. *Child development and socialization*. Chicago: Science Research Associates, Inc.

Brophy, J. E., and Good, T. L. 1970. Teachers' communications of differential expectations for children's classroom performance: some behavioral data. *Journal of Educational Psychology* 61:365-374.

Bruch, H. 1973. *Eating disorders*. New York: Basic Books, Inc., Publishers.

Burke, R. J., and Weir, T. 1978. Sex differences in adolescent life, stress, social support, and well-being. *Journal of Psychology* 98:277-288.

Buxbaum, E. 1951. A contribution to the psychoanalytic knowledge of the latency period. *American Journal of Orthopsychiatry* 21:182-198.

Buxbaum, E. 1959. Psychosexual development: the oral, anal, and phallic phases. In M. Levitt (Ed.), *Readings in psychoanalytic psychology*. New York: Appleton-Century-Crofts.

Cain, A. C., Fast, I., and Erickson, M. E. 1976. Children's disturbed reactions to the death of a sibling. In R. H. Moos (Ed.), *Human adaptation: coping with life crises*. Lexington, Mass.: D. C. Heath & Co.

Campbell, E. Q. 1969. Adolescent socialization.

In D. A. Goslin (Ed.), *Handbook of socialization theory and research*. Chicago: Rand McNally & Co.

Caplan, G. 1955. *Emotional problems of early childhood*. New York: Basic Books, Inc., Publishers.

Carey, W. B., and Sibinga, M. S. 1973. Avoiding pediatric pathogenesis in the management of acute minor illness. In S. Chess and A. Thomas (Eds.), *Annual progress in child psychiatry and child development*. New York: Brunner/Mazel, Inc.

Carlsmith, L. 1964. Effect of early father-absence on scholastic aptitude. *Harvard Educational Review* 34:3-21.

Chamberlin, R. W. 1977. Parenting styles, child behaviors, and the pediatrician. *Pediatric Annals* 6:50-63.

Chandler, M. J., Paget, K. F., and Koch, D. A. 1978. The child's demystification of psychological defense mechanisms: a structural and developmental analysis. *Developmental Psychology* 14:197-205.

Charney, E. 1972. Patient-doctor communication: implications for the clinician. *Pediatric Clinics of North America* 19:263-279.

Chenoweth, L. B. 1937. Increase in height and weight and decrease in age of college freshmen. *Journal of the American Medical Association* 108:354-356.

Chess, S. 1968. Temperament and learning ability of school children. *American Journal of Public Health* 58:2231-2239.

Chess, S., and Thomas A. 1977. Temperament and the parent-child interaction. *Pediatric Annals* 6:26-45.

Chilman, C. S. 1980. *Adolescent sexuality in a changing society*. U.S. Department of Health, Education, and Welfare Publ. No. 79-1426. National Institutes of Health. Washington, D.C.: U.S. Government Printing Office.

Chodoff, P., Friedman, S. B., and Hamburg, D. A. 1964. Stress, defenses and coping behavior: observations in parents of children with malignant disease. *American Journal of Psychiatry* 120:743-749.

Clarke-Stewart, K. A. 1978. Popular primers for parents. *American Psychologist* 33:359-369.

Clausen, J. A. 1966. Family structure, socialization, and personality. In L. W. Hoffman and M. L. Hoffman (Eds.), *Review of child development research* (Vol. 2). New York: Russell Sage Foundation.

Clausen, J. A. 1975. The social meaning of differential physical and sexual maturation. In S. E. Dragastin and G. H. Elder (Eds.), *Adolescence in the life cycle: psychological change in social context*. New York: John Wiley & Sons, Inc.

Cliquet, R. L. 1968. Social mobility and the anthropological structure of populations. *Human Biology* 40:17-43.

Coelho, G. V., Hamburg, D. A., and Adams, J. E. 1974. *Coping and adaptation*. New York: Basic Books, Inc., Publishers.

Cohen, M. W., and Friedman, S. B. 1975. Nonsexual motivation of adolescent sexual behavior. *Medical Aspects of Human Sexuality*, September, pp. 8-31.

Coleman, J. S. 1961. *The adolescent society*. New York: The Free Press.

Conger, J. J. 1971. A world they never knew: the family and social change. *Daedalus* 100:1105-1138.

Conger, J. J. 1977. *Adolescence and youth: psychological development in a changing world*. New York: Harper & Row, Publishers, Inc.

Connolly, K. J., and Bruner, J. S. 1974. *The growth of competence*. New York: Academic Press, Inc.

Cooke, R. E. 1967. Effects of hospitalization on the child. In J. A. Naller (Ed.), *The hospitalized child and his family*. Baltimore: The Johns Hopkins University Press.

Coopersmith, S. 1967. *The antecedents of self-esteem*. London: W. H. Freeman & Co. Ltd.

Cowan, P. A. 1978. *Piaget: with feeling*. New York: Holt, Rinehart & Winston.

Cowen, E. L., Zax, M., Klein, R., Izzo, L. D., and Trost, M. A. 1965. The relation of anxiety in school children to school record, achievement, and behavioral measures. *Child Development* 36:685-695.

Crandall, V. C. 1967. Achievement behavior in young children. In W. W. Hartup and N. L. Smothergill (Eds.), *The young child: reviews of research*. Washington, D.C.: National Association for the Education of Young Children.

Crandall, V. C., Dewey, R., Katovsky, W., and Preston, A. 1964. Parents' attitudes and behaviors and grade-school children's academic achievements. *Journal of Genetic Psychology* 104:53-66.

Crandall, V. C., Katovsky, W., and Crandall, V. J. 1965. Children's beliefs in their own control of reinforcements in intellectual-academic achievement situations. *Child Development* 36:91-109.

Crandall, V. J. 1963. Achievement. In H. W. Stevenson, J. Kagan, and C. Spiker (Eds.), *Child psychology: the sixty-second yearbook of the National Society for the Study of Education* (Part I). Chicago: University of Chicago Press.

Crawford, J. D., and Osler, D. C. 1975. Body composition at menarche: the Frisch-Revelle hypothesis revisited. *Pediatrics* 56:449-458.

Danilowicz, D. A., and Gabriel, H. P. 1972. Postoperative reactions in children: "normal" and abnormal responses after cardiac surgery. In S. Chess and A. Thomas (Eds.), *Annual progress in child psychiatry and child development*. New York: Brunner/Mazel, Inc.

Deutsch, M., Katz, I., and Jensen, A. R. 1968. *Social class, race and psychological development*. New York: Holt, Rinehart & Winston.

Dickens, H. O., Mudd, E. H., Garcia, C. R., Tomar, K., and Wright, D. 1973. One hundred pregnant adolescents: treatment approaches in a university hospital. *American Journal of Public Health* 63:794-800.

Dinkmeyer, D. C. 1965. *Child development: the emerging self*. Englewood Cliffs, N. J.: Prentice-Hall, Inc.

Dollard, J., and Miller, N. E. 1959. Critical training situations in childhood. In L. Gorlow and W. Katkovsky (Eds.), *Readings in the psychology of adjustment*. New York: McGraw-Hill Book Co.

Douvan, E., and Gold, M. 1966. Modal patterns in American adolescence. In L. W. Hoffman and M. L. Hoffman (Eds.), *Review of child development research* (Vol. 2). New York: Russell Sage Foundation.

Dragastin, S. E., and Elder, G. H. 1975. *Adolescence in the life cycle: psychological change and social context*. New York: John Wiley & Sons, Inc.

Duncan, J. D. 1978. Medical, psychological, and legal aspects of child custody disputes. *Mayo Clinic Proceedings* 53:563-568.

Durfee, J. T., and Lee, L. C. 1973. Infant-infant interaction in a day-care setting. Presented at the meeting of the American Psychological Association, Montreal, August.

Eckenhoff, J. E. 1953. Relationship of anesthesia to postoperative personality changes in children. *American Journal of Diseases of Children* 86:587-591.

Elkind, D. 1961. The child's conception of his religious denomination. I: The Jewish child. *Journal of Genetic Psychology* 99:209-225.

Elkind, D. 1962. The child's conception of his religious denomination. II: The Catholic child. *Journal of Genetic Psychology* 101:185-193.

Elkind, D. 1963. The child's conception of his religious denomination. III: The Protestant child. *Journal of Genetic Psychology* 103:291-304.

Elkind, D. 1966. Conceptual orientation shifts in children and adolescents. *Child Development* 37:493-498.

Elkind, D. 1973. Borderline retardation in low and middle income adolescents. In R. M. Allen, A. D. Artazzo, and R. P. Tolster (Eds.), *Theories of cognitive development*. Coral Gables, Fla.: University of Miami Press.

Elkind, D. 1974. *Children and adolescents: interpretive essays on Jean Piaget* (2nd ed.). New York: Oxford University Press.

Elkind, D. 1975. Recent research on cognitive development in adolescence. In S. E. Dragastin and G. H. Elder (Eds.), *Adolescence in the life cycle: psychological change and social context*. New York: John Wiley & Sons, Inc.

Elkind, D. 1976. Cognitive development and psychopathology: observations on egocentrism and ego defense. In E. Schopler and R. J. Reichler (Eds.), *Psychopathology and child development*. New York: Plenum Publishing Corp.

Elkind, D. 1978. *A sympathetic understanding of the child: birth to sixteen*. Boston: Allyn & Bacon, Inc.

Elkind, D. 1979. *The child and society*. New York: Oxford University Press.

Elkind, D., Barocas, R., and Johnson, P. 1969. Concept production in children and adolescents. *Human Development* 12:10-21.

Elkind, D., and Deblinger, J. 1969. Perceptual training and reading achievement in disadvantaged children. *Child Development* 40:11-19.

Elkind, D., Medvene, L., and Rockway, A. S. 1969. Representational level and concept production in children and adolescents. *Developmental Psychology* 2:85-89.

Elster, A. B., and McAnarney, E. R. 1980. Medical and psychosocial risks of pregnancy and childbearing during adolescence. *Pediatric Annals* 9:89-94.

Erikson, E. H. 1940. Studies in the interpretation of play. I: Clinical observation of play disruption in young children. *Genetic Psychology Monographs* 22:557-671.

Erikson, E. H. 1950a. *Childhood and society*. New York: W. W. Norton & Co., Inc.

Erikson, E. H. 1950b. Growth and crises of the healthy personality. In M. J. E. Senn (Ed.),

Symposium on the healthy personality. New York: Josiah Macy, Jr. Foundation Publications.

Erikson, E. H. 1951. A healthy personality for every child: a fact finding report: a digest. In Midcentury White House Conference on Children and Youth. Raleigh, N.C.: Health Publications Institute.

Erikson, E. H. 1956. The problem of ego identity. *Journal of the American Psychoanalytic Association* 4:56-121.

Erikson, E. H. 1958. Play interviews for four-year-old hospitalized children. *Monographs of the Society for Research in Child Development* **23**(3).

Erikson, E. H. 1960. *Identity and the life cycle*. New York: International Universities Press, Inc.

Erikson, E. H. (Ed.). 1965. *The challenge of youth*. Garden City. N.Y.: Doubleday & Co., Inc.

Erikson, E. H. 1968. *Identity, youth, and crisis*. New York: W. W. Norton & Co., Inc.

Erlenmeyer-Kimling, L., and Jarvik, L. F. 1963. Genetics and intelligence: a review. *Science* **142**:1477-1479.

Eveleth, P. B., and Tanner, J. M. 1976. *Worldwide variation in human growth*. London: Cambridge University Press.

Fagot, B. I. 1978. Reinforcing contingencies for sex role behaviors: effect of experience with children. *Child Development* **49**:30-36.

Faust, M. S. 1960. Developmental maturity as a determinant in prestige of adolescent girls. *Child Development* **31**:173-184.

Felice, M., and Friedman, S. B. 1978. The adolescent as a patient. *Journal of Continuing Education/Pediatrics*, October, pp. 15-28.

Findlay, I. I., Smith, P., Graves, P. J., and Linton, M. L. 1969. Chronic disease in childhood: a study of family reactions. *British Journal of Medical Education* **3**:66-69.

Fine, B. 1967. *Underachievers*. New York: E. P. Dutton.

Finesinger, J. E. 1959. Psychological factors in adolescent behavior. In L. Gorlow and W. Katkovsky (Eds.), *Readings in the psychology of adjustment*. New York: McGraw-Hill Book Co.

Flavell, J. H. 1977. *Cognitive development*. Englewood Cliffs, N.J.: Prentice-Hall, Inc.

Forbes, G. B. 1978. Prevention of obesity. In R. A. Hoekelman, S. Blatman, P. Brunell, S. B. Friedman, and H. M. Seidel (Eds.), *Principles of pediatrics: health care of the young*. New York: McGraw-Hill Book Co.

Foster, R. M. 1977. Parenting the child with a behavior disorder: a family approach. *Pediatric Annals* **6**:29-43.

Fraiberg, S. 1959. *The magic years*. New York: Charles Scribner's Sons.

Francis, V., Korsch, B. M., and Morris, M. J. 1969. Gaps in doctor-patient communications. Patients' response to medical advice. *New England Journal of Medicine* **280**:535-540.

Freeberg, N. E., and Payne, D. T. 1968. Parental influence on cognitive development in early childhood: a review. In S. Chess and A. Thomas (Eds.), *Annual progress in child psychiatry and child development*. New York: Brunner/Mazel, Inc.

Freud, A. 1946. *The ego and the mechanisms of defense*. New York: International Universities Press, Inc.

Freud, A. 1947. *Psychoanalysis for teachers and parents*. New York: Emerson Books, Inc.

Freud, A. 1952. The role of bodily illness in the mental life of children. *Psychoanalytic Study of the Child* **7**:69-81.

Freud, A. 1963. The concept of developmental lines. *Psychoanalytic Study of the Child* **18**: 245-265.

Freud, A. 1965. *Normality and pathology in childhood*. New York: International Universities Press, Inc.

Freud, A. 1966. *The ego and the mechanisms of defense* (Vol. II). New York: International Universities Press, Inc.

Freud, A. 1969. Adolescence as a developmental disturbance. In G. Caplan and S. Lebovici (Eds.), *Adolescence: psychosocial perspectives*. New York: Basic Books, Inc.

Freud, A. 1972. Identification with the aggressor. In C. Lavatelli and F. Stendler (Eds.), *Readings in child behavior and development*. New York: Harcourt Brace Jovanovich, Inc.

Freud, S. 1907. The sexual enlightenment of children. In S. Freud (Ed.), *Collected papers* (Vol. II). London: The Hogarth Press.

Freud, S. 1908. On the sexual theories of children. In S. Freud (Ed.), *Collected papers* (Vol. II). London: The Hogarth Press.

Freud, S. 1909. Analysis of a phobia in a five-year-old boy. In S. Freud (Ed.), *Collected papers* (Vol. III). London: The Hogarth Press.

Freud, S. 1917a. The development of the libido and the sexual organizations. In J. Strachey (Ed.), *The complete psychological works of Sigmund Freud* (Vol. XVI). London: The Hogarth Press.

Freud, S. 1917b. The sexual life of human beings. In J. Strachey (Ed.), *The complete psychological works of Sigmund Freud* (Vol. XVI). London: The Hogarth Press.

Freud, S. 1920. Associations of a four-year-old child. In J. Strachey (Ed.), *The complete psychological works of Sigmund Freud* (Vol. XVIII). London: The Hogarth Press.

Freud, S. 1924. The passing of the Oedipus-complex. In S. Freud (Ed.), *Collected papers* (Vol. II). London: The Hogarth Press.

Freud, S. 1925. Some psychological consequences of the anatomical distinction between the sexes. In S. Freud (Ed.), *Collected papers* (Vol. V). London: The Hogarth Press.

Freud, S. 1931. Female sexuality. In J. Strachey (Ed.), *The complete psychological works of Sigmund Freud* (Vol. XXI). London: The Hogarth Press.

Freud, S. 1935. Children's dreams. In J. Riviere (Ed.), *A general introduction to psychoanalysis*. New York: Liveright Publishing Corp.

Freud, S. 1938. Infantile sexuality. In S. Freud (Ed.), *The basic writings of Sigmund Freud*. New York: Random House, Inc.

Freud, S. 1947. *The ego and the id*. London: The Hogarth Press.

Freud, S. 1949. The development of the sexual function. In S. Freud (Ed.), *An outline of psychoanalysis*. New York: W. W. Norton & Co., Inc.

Friedman, A. S., and Friedman, D. B. 1977. Parenting: a developmental process. *Pediatric Annals* 6:564-572.

Friedman, S. B. 1974. Psychological aspects of sudden unexpected death in infants and children. *Pediatric Clinics of North America* 21:103-111.

Fries, M. D. 1959. Review of the literature on the latency period with special emphasis on the so-called "normal case." In M. Levitt (Ed.), *Readings in psychoanalytic psychology*. New York: Appleton-Century-Crofts.

Frisancho, A. R., Sanchez, J., Pallardel, D., and Yanez, L. 1973. Adaptive significance of small body size under poor socio-economic conditions in Southern Peru. *American Journal of Physical Anthropology* 39:255-262.

Frisch, R. E. 1974. A method of predication of age of menarche from height and weight at ages 9 through 13 years. *Pediatrics* 53:384-390.

Frisch, R. E., and Revelle, R. 1970. Height and weight at menarche and a hypothesis of critical body weights and adolescent events. *Science* 169:397-399.

Frisch, R. E., Revelle, R., and Cook, S. 1971. Height, weight and age at menarche and the critical weight hypothesis. *Science* 174:1148-1149.

Galdston, R. 1973. The burning and the healing of children. In S. Chess and A. Thomas (Eds.), *Annual progress in child psychiatry and child development*. New York: Brunner/Mazel, Inc.

Garber, B., and Polsky, R. 1970. Follow-up study of hospitalized adolescents. *Archives of General Psychiatry* 22:179-187.

Garn, S. M. 1966. Body size and its implications. In L. W. Hoffman and M. L. Hoffman (Eds.), *Review of child development research* (Vol. 2). New York: Russell Sage Foundation.

Gaudry, E., and Spielberger, D. C. 1971. *Anxiety and educational achievement*. Sydney, Australia: John Wiley & Sons Australasia Pty. Ltd.

Gelfand, D. M., and Hartmann, D. P. 1975. *Child behavior: analysis and therapy*. Elmsford, N.Y.: Pergamon Press, Inc.

George, C., and Main, M. 1979. Social interactions of young abused children: approach, avoidance and aggression. *Child Development* 50:306-318.

Gesell, A. 1928. *The mental growth of the preschool child: a psychological outline of normal development from birth to the sixth year*. New York: The Macmillan Co.

Gesell, A., Ilg, F. L., and Ames, L. B. 1956. *Youth: the years from ten to sixteen*. New York: Harper & Brothers.

Gesell, A., Ilg, F. L., Ames, L. B., and Bullis, G. E. 1946. *The child from five to ten*. New York: Harper & Brothers.

Gesell, A., Ilg, F. L., Ames L. B., and Rodell, J. L. 1974. *Infant and child in the culture of today* (Rev. ed.). New York: Harper & Row, Publishers.

Ginsburg, H., and Opper, S. 1979. *Piaget's theory of intellectual development* (2nd ed.). Englewood Cliffs, N.J.: Prentice-Hall, Inc.

Gofman, H., Buckman, W., and Schade, G. H. 1957. The child's emotional response to hospitalization. *American Journal of Diseases of Children* 93:157-164.

Gold, D., and Andres, D. 1978. Developmental comparisons between ten-year-old children with employed and nonemployed mothers. *Child Development* 49:75-84.

Goldstein, H. 1971. Factors influencing the height

of seven-year-old children—results from the National Child Development Study. *Human Biology* **43**:92-111.

Green, M., and Solnit, A. J. 1964. Reactions to the threatened loss of a child: a vulnerable child syndrome. *Pediatrics* **34**:58-66.

Grey, M. J., Genel, M., and Tamborlane, W. V. 1980. Psychosocial adjustment of latency-aged diabetics: determinants and relationship to control. *Pediatrics* **65**:69-73.

Greydanus, D. E., and Hofmann, A. D. 1979a. A perspective on the brittle teenage diabetic. *Journal of Family Practice* **9**:1007-1012.

Greydanus, D. E., and Hofmann, A. D. 1979b. Psychological factors in diabetes mellitus. *American Journal of Diseases of Children* **133**:1061-1066.

Grinder, R. E. 1969. *Studies in adolescence* (2nd ed.). London: Macmillan & Co. Ltd.

Grinder, R. E. 1973. *Adolescence*. New York: John Wiley & Sons, Inc.

Grinder, R. E. 1975. The concept of adolescence in the genetic psychology of G. Stanley Hall. In R. E. Grinder (Ed.), *Studies in adolescence*. New York: The Macmillan Co.

Gruber, H., and Voniche, J. J. 1977. *The essential Piaget*. New York: Basic Books, Inc., Publishers.

Grumbach, M. M. 1975. Onset of puberty. In S. S. Berenberg (Ed.), *Puberty*. Leiden, The Netherlands: Stenfert-Kroese.

Grumbach, M. M., Roth, J. C., Kaplan, S. L., and Kelch, P. P. 1974. Hypothalamic-pituitary regulation of puberty: evidence and concepts derived from clinical research. In M. M. Grumbach, G. D. Grave, and F. E. Mayer (Eds.), *Control of the onset of puberty*. New York: John Wiley & Sons, Inc.

Gurman, A. S. 1970. The role of the family in underachievement. *Journal of School Psychology* **8**:48-53.

Hall, C. S. 1954. *A primer of Freudian psychology*. New York: The World Publishing Co.

Hamburg, B. A., and Hamburg, D. A. 1975. Stressful transitions of adolescence—endocrine and psychosocial aspects. In L. Levi (Ed.), *Society, stress and disease* (Vol. 2). London: Oxford University Press.

Hammil, P. V., Johnson, F. E., and Lameshow, S. 1972. *Height and weight of children: socioeconomic status: United States*. U.S. Department of Health, Education, and Welfare Publ. No. 73-1601. Washington, D.C.: U.S. Government Printing Office.

Hardgrove, C. B., and Dawson, R. B. 1972. *Parents and children in the hospital*. Boston: Little, Brown & Co.

Harris, F. R., Wolf, M. M., and Baer, D. M. 1967. Effects of adult social reinforcement on child behavior. In W. W. Hartup and N. L. Smothergill (Eds.), *The young child* (Vol. 1). Washington, D.C.: National Association for the Education of Young Children.

Harris, J. A., Jackson, C. M., Patterson, D. G., and Scammon, R. E. 1930. *The measurement of man*. Minneapolis: University of Minnesota Press.

Harrison, S. I., Davenport, C. W., and McDermott, J. F. 1976. Children's reactions to bereavement: adult confusions and misperceptions. In R. N. Moos (Ed.), *Human adaptation: coping with life crises*. Lexington, Mass.: D. C. Heath & Co.

Harrison-Ross, P. 1977. Parenting the black child. *Pediatric Annals* **6**:84-94.

Hartup, W. W. 1970. Peer interaction and social organization. In P. H. Mussen (Ed.), *Carmichael's manual of child psychology* (3rd ed., Vol. 2). New York: John Wiley & Sons.

Hartup, W. W. 1976. Peer interaction and the behavioral development of the individual child. In E. Schopler and R. J. Reichles (Eds.), *Psychopathology and child development*. New York: Plenum Publishing Corp.

Heider, G. M. 1966. Vulnerability in infants and young children: a pilot study. *Genetic Psychology Monographs* **73**:1-216.

Heisel, J. S., Ream, S., Raitz, R. R., Rappaport, M, and Coddington, R. D. 1973. The significance of life events as contributing factors in the diseases of children. *Journal of Pediatrics* **83**:119-123.

Hemenway, J. E. 1978. Where is God? In O. J. Z. Sahler (Ed.), *The child and death*. St. Louis: The C. V. Mosby Co.

Henry, N. B. 1944. *Adolescence: the forty-third yearbook of the National Society for the Study of Education* (Part I). Chicago: University of Chicago Press.

Herbert, M. 1974. *Emotional problems of development in children*. London: Academic Press, Inc. (London) Ltd.

Herbert, M. 1978. *Conduct disorders of childhood and adolescence*. Chichester, England: John Wiley & Sons Ltd.

Herron, R. E., and Sutton-Smith, B. 1971. *Child's play*. New York: John Wiley & Sons, Inc.

Hersov, L. A. 1960. Persistent nonattendance at school. *Journal of Child Psychology and Psychiatry* 1:130-136.

Hess, R. D. 1970. Social class and ethnic influences on socialization. In P. H. Mussen (Ed.), *Carmichael's manual of child psychology* (3rd ed., Vol. 2). New York: John Wiley & Sons, Inc.

Hetherington, E. M. 1966. Effects of paternal absence on sex-typed behaviors in Negro and white preadolescent males. *Journal of Personality and Social Psychology* 14:87-91.

Hetherington, E. M. 1972. Effects of father absence on personality development in adolescent daughters. *Developmental Psychology* 7: 313-326.

Hetherington, E. M. 1979. Divorce: a child's perspective. *American Psychologist* 34:851-858.

Hetherington, E. M., Cox, M., and Cox, R. 1978. Family interaction and the social, emotional and cognitive development of children following divorce. Presented at the Symposium on the Family: Setting Priorities, Washington, D.C.

Hetherington, E. M., and McDermott, J. F. 1968. Parental divorce in early childhood. *American Journal of Psychiatry* 124:118-125.

Hill, K. T. 1972. Anxiety in the evaluative context. In W. W. Hartup (Ed.), *The young child*. Washington, D.C.: National Association for the Eucation of Young Children.

Hill, K. T., and Sarason, S. B. 1966. The relation of test anxiety and defensiveness to test and school performance over the elementary-school years: a further longitudinal study. *Monographs of the Society for Research in Child Development* 31 (Serial No. 104).

Hoekelman, R. A., and Munson, S. 1978. Anorexia nervosa. In R. A. Hoekelman, S. Blatman, P. Brunell, S. B. Friedman, and H. M. Seidel (Eds.), *Principles of pediatrics: health care of the young*. New York: McGraw-Hill Book Co.

Hoffman, L. W. 1974. Effects of maternal employment on the child: a review of the research. *Developmental Psychology* 10:204-228.

Hoffman, L. W. 1979. Maternal employment: 1979. *American Psychologist* 34:859-865.

Hoffman, L. W., and Hoffman, M. L. 1966. *Review of child development research*. New York: Russell Sage Foundation.

Hoffman, M. L. 1970. Moral development. In P. H. Mussen (Ed.), *Carmichael's manual of child psychology* (3rd ed., Vol. 2). New York: John Wiley & Sons, Inc.

Hollingworth, L. S. 1928. *The psychology of the adolescent*. New York: Appleton & Co.

Holman, G. H. 1972. Learning from each other: pediatricians and teachers. *Childhood Education* 48:240-243.

Holt, J. 1964. *How children fail*. New York: Pitman Publishing Corp.

Holt, K. S. 1977. *Developmental paediatrics*. London: Butterworth & Co. (Publishers) Ltd.

Horn, J. L. 1978. The nature and development of intellectual abilities. In R. T. Osborne, C. E. Noble, and N. Weyl (Eds.), *Human variation: the biopsychology of age, race, and sex*. New York: Academic Press, Inc.

Howell, M. C. 1973. Effects of maternal employment on the child. II. *Pediatrics* 52:327-343.

Humphreys, L. G. 1972. *Theory of intelligence*. Unpublished manuscript, Psychology Department. Urbana: University of Illinois.

Ilg, F. L., Ames, L. B., Haines, J., and Gillespie, C. 1978. *School readiness*. New York: Harper & Row, Publishers, Inc.

Illingworth, R. S. 1972. *The development of the infant and young child: normal and abnormal* (5th ed.). Baltimore: The Williams & Wilkins Co.

Inhelder, B., and Piaget, J. 1964. *The early growth of logic in the child*. New York: W. W. Norton & Co., Inc.

Iscoe, I., and Stevenson, H. W. 1960. *Personality development in children*. Austin: University of Texas Press.

Jackman, J. A. 1978. The rites of death: thoughts of a funeral director. In O. J. Z. Sahler (Ed.), *The child and death*. St. Louis: The C. V. Mosby Co.

Jackson, K., Winkley, R., Faust, O., Cermak, E. G., and Burtt, M. M. 1953. Behavior changes indicating emotional trauma in tonsillectomized children: final report. *Pediatrics* 12:23-27.

Jenkins, G. G. 1979. For parents particularly. II. *Childhood Education* 55:157-159.

Johnston, F. E., Malina, R. M., and Galbraith, M. A. 1971. Height, weight, and age at menarche and the "critical weight" hypothesis. *Science* 174:1148.

Jones, H. E., and Conrad, H. S. 1933. The growth and decline of intelligence: a study of a homogeneous group between the ages of ten and sixty. *Genetic Psychology Monographs* 13:223-298.

Jones, M. C., and Bayley, N. 1950. Physical maturity among boys as related to behavior. *Journal of Education Psychology* **41**:129-148.

Jones, M. C., and Mussen, P. H. 1958. Self-conceptions, motivations, and interpersonal attitudes of early- and late-maturing girls. *Child Development* **29**:491-501.

Jordan, F. L., and Massey, J. 1969. *School readiness survey* (2nd ed.). Palo Alto, Calif.: Consulting Psychologists Press, Inc.

Josselyn, I. M. 1952. *The adolescent and his world*. New York: Family Service Association of America.

Josselyn, I. M. 1959. The psychoanalytic psychology of the adolescent. In M. Levitt (Ed.), *Readings in psychoanalytic psychology*. New York: Appleton-Century-Crofts.

Kagan, J., and Coles, R. 1972. *Twelve to sixteen: early adolescence*. New York: W. W. Norton & Co., Inc.

Kagan, J., and Moss, H. A. 1960. The stability of passive-dependent behavior from childhood through adulthood. *Child Development* **31**: 577-591.

Kagan, J., and Moss, H. A. 1962. *Birth to maturity: a study in psychological development*. New York: John Wiley & Sons, Inc.

Kaluger, G., and Kaluger, M. F. 1979. *Human development: the span of life* (2nd ed.). St. Louis: The C. V. Mosby Co.

Katovsky, W., Crandall, V. C., and Good, S. 1967. Parental antecedents of children's beliefs in internal-external control of reinforcements in intellectual achievement situations. *Child Development* **38**:765-776.

Kelly, J. B., and Wallerstein, J. S. 1976. The effects of parental divorce: experiences of the child in early latency. *American Journal of Orthopsychiatry* **46**:20-32.

Kenny, T. J., and Clemmens, R. L. 1975. *Behavioral pediatrics and child development: a clinical handbook*. Baltimore: The Williams & Wilkins Co.

Kent, M. W., and Rolf, J. E. 1978. *Primary prevention of psychopathology* (Vol. 3). *Promoting social competence and coping in children*. Hanover, N.H.: University Press of New England.

Kessen, W., and Kuhlman, C. (Eds.). 1970. *Thought in the young child*. Chicago: University of Chicago Press.

Kessler, J. W. 1977. Parenting the handicapped child. *Pediatric Annals* **6**:62-72.

Kestenbaum, C. J., and Stone, M. H. 1976. The effects of fatherless homes upon daughters: clin-ical impressions regarding paternal deprivation. *Journal of the American Academy of Psychoanalysis* **4**:171-190.

King, S. H. 1973. Coping and growth in adolescence. In S. Chess and A. Thomas (Eds.), *Annual progress in child psychiatry and child development*. New York: Brunner/Mazel, Inc.

Kinsbourne, M. 1973. School problems. *Pediatrics* **52**:697-710.

Kinsey, A. C., Pomeroy, W. B., Martin, C. E., and Gebhard, P. H. 1953. *Sexual behavior in the human female*. Philadelphia: W. B. Saunders Co.

Klatskin, E. H. 1972. Developmental factors. In I. R. Stuart and L. E. Abt (Eds.), *Children of separation and divorce*. New York: Grossman Publishers.

Kohlberg, L. 1963. Moral development and identification. In H. W. Stevenson (Ed.), *Child psychology: the sixty-second yearbook of the National Society for the Study of Education*. Chicago: University of Chicago Press.

Kohlberg, L. 1964. Development of moral character and moral ideology. In M. L. Hoffman and L. W. Hoffman (Eds.), *Review of child development research* (Vol. 1). New York: Russell Sage Foundation.

Kohlberg, L. 1966. A cognitive-developmental analysis of children's sex-role concepts and attitudes. In E. E. Maccoby (Ed.), *The development of sex differences*. Stanford, Calif.: Stanford University Press.

Kohlberg, L. 1967. The development of children's orientations toward a moral order (Part 2). *Social experience, social conduct, and the development of moral thought*. Unpublished manuscript.

Kohlberg, L. 1968a. Early education: a cognitive-developmental view. *Child Development* **39**: 1013-1062.

Kohlberg, L. 1968b. Moral development. In *International encyclopedia of the social sciences*. New York: Crowell Collier & Macmillian, Inc.

Kohlberg, L. 1969. Stage and sequence: the cognitive-developmental approach to socialization. In D. A. Goslin (Ed.), *Handbook of socialization theory and research*. Chicago: Rand McNally & Co.

Kohlberg, L. 1973a. *Collected papers on moral development and moral education* (Unpublished vol.). Rochester, N.Y.: University of Rochester Library.

Kohlberg, L. 1973b. Continuities and discontinuities in childhood and adult moral development revisited. In P. B. Baltes and K. W. Schaie (Eds.), *Life-span developmental psychology: research and theory*. New York: Academic Press, Inc.

Kohlberg, L. 1975. Moral education in the schools: a developmental view. In R. E. Grinder (Ed.), *Studies in adolescence*. New York: Macmillan Publishing Co.

Kohlberg, L. 1977. The cognitive-developmental approach to moral education. In H. F. Clarizio, R. C. Craig, and W. A. Mehrens (Eds.), *Contemporary issues in educational psychology*. Boston: Allyn & Bacon, Inc.

Kohlberg, L., and Gilligan, C. 1971. The adolescent as a philosopher: the discovery of the self in a postconventional world. *Daedalus* **100**: 1051-1086.

Kohlberg, L., and Turiel, E. 1971. Moral development and moral education. In G. S. Lesser (Ed.), *Psychology and educational practice*. Glenview, Ill.: Scott Foresman & Co.

Kohlberg, L., and Zigler, E. 1967. The impact of cognitive maturity on the development of sex-role attitudes in the years 4 to 8. *Genetic Psychology Monographs* **75**:89-165.

Kohn, M. 1977. *Social competence, symptoms and underachievement in childhood: a longitudinal perspective*. New York: John Wiley & Sons, Inc.

Kohn, M., and Rosman, B. L. 1973a. Cognitive functioning in five-year-old boys as related to social-emotional and background variables. *Developmental Psychology* **8**:277-294.

Kohn, M., and Rosman, B. L. 1973b. Cross-situational and longitudinal stability of social-emotional functioning in young children. *Child Development* **44**:721-727.

Kohn, M., and Rosman, B. L. 1974. Social-emotional, cognitive and demographic determinants of poor school achievement: implications for a strategy of intervention. *Journal of Educational Psychology* **66**:267-276.

Krasner, L., and Ullman, L. P. 1965. *Research in behavior modification*. New York: Holt, Rinehart & Winston, Inc.

Kuhlen, R. G. 1952. *The psychology of adolescent development*. New York: Harper & Brothers.

Langford, W. S. 1961. The child in the pediatric hospital: adaptation to illness and hospitalization. *American Journal of Orthopsychiatry* **31**:667-684.

Lavatelli, C. S., and Stendler, F. 1972. *Readings in child behavior and development*. New York: Harcourt Brace Jovanovich, Inc.

Lazarus, R. S. 1966. *Psychological stress and the coping process*. New York: McGraw-Hill Book Co.

Lazarus, R. S. 1969. *Patterns of adjustment and human effectiveness*. New York: McGraw-Hill Book Co.

Lazarus, R. S. 1975. The healthy personality—a review of conceptualizations and research. In L. Levi (Ed.), *Society, stress and disease* (Vol. 2). London: Oxford University Press Ltd.

Lee, L. C. 1976. *Personality development in childhood*. Monterey, Calif.: Brooks/Cole Publishing Co.

Lefcourt, H. E. 1966. Internal versus external control of reinforcement: a review. *Psychological Bulletin* **65**:206-220.

Levenson, S., and Kendrick, W. 1967. *Readings in foreign language for the elementary school*. Waltham, Mass.: Blaisdell Publishing Co.

Levi, L. (Ed.). 1975. *Society, stress and disease: childhood and adolescence* (Vol. 2). London: Oxford University Press.

Levitt, M. (Ed.). 1959. *Readings in psychoanalytic psychology*. New York: Appleton-Century-Crofts.

Levy, D. M. 1945. Psychic trauma of operations in children. *American Journal of Diseases of Children* **69**:7-25.

Liebert, R. M., Neale, J. M., and Davidson, E. S. 1973. *The early window: effects of television on children and youth*. New York: Pergamon Press, Inc.

Liebert, R. M., Poulas, R. W., and Strauss, G. D. 1974. *Developmental psychology*. Englewood Cliffs, N.J.: Prentice-Hall, Inc.

Lindgren, S. 1976. Height, weight and menarche in Swedish urban school children in relation to socioeconomic and regional factors. *Annals of Human Biology* **3**:510-528.

Lipsitt, L. P., and Spiker, C. C. 1965. *Advances in child development and behavior*. New York: Academic Press, Inc.

Lorenz, K. 1935. Der Kumpan in der Umwelt des Vogels. *Journal für Ornithologie* **83**:137-213, 289-413.

Lourie, R. S., and Schwarzbeck, C. 1979. When children feel helpless in the face of stress. *Childhood Education* **55**:134-140.

Lowrey, G. H. 1978. *Growth and development of children* (7th ed.). Chicago: Year Book Medical Publishers, Inc.

Lynn, R. 1978. Ethnic and racial differences in intelligence: international comparisons. In R. T. Osborne, C. E. Noble, and N. Weyl (Eds.), *Human variation: the biopsychology of age, race, and sex*. New York: Academic Press, Inc.

Maccoby, E. E. 1966. *The development of sex differences*. Stanford, Calif.: Stanford University Press.

Maccoby, E. E., and Jacklin, C. N. 1974. *The psychology of sex differences*. Stanford, Calif.: Stanford University Press.

Macfarlane, J. W., Allen, L., and Honzik, M. P. 1954. *A developmental study of the behavior problems of normal children between twenty-one months and fourteen years*. Los Angeles: University of California Press.

Macht, J. 1975. *Teaching our children*. New York: John Wiley & Sons, Inc.

Magnusson, D., Duner, A., and Zetterblom, G. 1975. *Adjustment: a longitudinal study*. New York: John Wiley & Sons, Inc.

Mahler, M. S. 1967. On human symbiosis and the vicissitudes of individuation. *Journal of the American Psychoanalytic Association* **15**:740-763.

Maier, H. W. 1965. *Three theories of child development*. New York: Harper & Row Publishers, Inc.

Marantz, S. A., and Mansfield, A. F. 1977. Maternal employment and the development of sex-role sterotyping in five- to eleven-year-old girls. *Child Development* **48**:668-673.

Marshall, W. A. 1971. Evaluation of growth rate in height over periods of less than a year. *Archives of Disease in Childhood* **46**:414-420.

Marshall, W. A., and Swan, A. B. 1971. Seasonal variation in growth rate of normal and blind children. *Annals of Human Biology* **43**:502-516.

Marshall, W. A., and Tanner, J. M. 1969. Variations in patterns of pubertal changes in girls. *Archives of Disease in Childhood* **44**:291-303.

Marshall, W. A., and Tanner, J. M. 1970. Variations in patterns of pubertal changes in boys. *Archives of Disease in Childhood* **45**:13-23.

Martin, B. 1975. Parent-child relations. In F. D. Horowitz (Ed.), *Review of child development research* (Vol. 4). Chicago: University of Chicago Press.

Mash, E. J., Handy, L. C., and Hamerlynck, L. A. (Eds.). 1976. *Behavior modification approaches to parenting*. New York: Brunner/Mazel, Inc.

Mason, E. A. 1965. The hospitalized child—his emotional needs. *New England Journal of Medicine* **272**:406-414.

Masse, N. P. 1975. Parental deprivation—hospitalization, working mothers and day care. In L. Levi (Ed.), *Society, stress and disease* (Vol. 2). London: Oxford University Press.

Masters, J. C. 1972. Social comparison by children. In W. W. Hartup (Ed.), *The young child* (Vol. 2). Washington, D.C.: National Association for the Education of Young Children.

Mattsson, A. 1972. Long-term physical illness in childhood: a challenge to psychosocial adaptation. *Pediatrics* **50**:801-811.

McAnarney, E. R. 1975. Adolescent pregnancy—a pediatric concern? *Clinical Pediatrics* **14**:19-22.

McAnarney, E. R., Pless, I. B., Satterwhite, B., and Friedman, S. B. 1974. Psychological problems of children with chronic juvenile arthritis. *Pediatrics* **53**:523-528.

McCandless, B. R. 1969. Childhood socialization. In D. A. Goslin (Ed.), *Handbook of socialization theory and research*. Chicago: Rand McNally & Co.

McCandless, B. R., and Evans, E. D. 1973. *Children and youth: psychosocial development*. Hinsdale, Ill.: The Dryden Press.

McCay, J. B., Waring, E. B., and Kruse, P. J. 1940. Learning by children at noon-meal in a nursery school: ten "good" eaters and ten "poor" eaters. *Genetic Psychology Monographs* **22**:491-555.

McDermott, J. F. 1976. Parental divorce in early childhood. In R. H. Moos (Ed.), *Human adaptation: coping with life crises*. Lexington, Mass.: D. C. Heath & Co.

McGraw, M. 1946. Maturation of behavior. In L. Carmichael (Ed.), *Manual of child psychology*. New York: John Wiley & Sons, Inc.

McKinney, F., Lorion, R. P., and Zax, M. 1976. *Effective behavior and human development*. New York: Macmillan Publishing Co.

McKinney, J. P., Fitzgerald, H. E., and Strommen, E. A. 1977. *Developmental psychology: the adolescent and young adult*. Homewood, Ill.: The Dorsey Press.

Mead, M. 1973. *Coming of age in Samoa*. New York: William Morrow & Co., Inc.

Mellish, R. W. P. 1969. Preparation of a child for hospitalization and surgery. *Pediatric Clinics of North America* **16**:543-553.

Mesibov, G. B., Schroeder, C. S., and Wesson, L. 1977. Parental concerns about their children. *Journal of Pediatric Psychology* **2**:13-17.

Miller, D. R. 1969. Psychoanalytic theory of development: a re-evaluation. In D. A. Goslin (Ed.), *Handbook of socialization theory and research*. Chicago: Rand McNally & Co.

Miller, J. B. M. 1972. Children's reactions to the death of a parent: a review of the psychoanalytic literature. In S. Chess and A. Thomas (Eds.), *Annual progress in child psychiatry and child development*. New York: Brunner/Mazel, Inc.

Miller, N. E., and Dollard, J. 1941. *Social learning and imitation*. New Haven, Conn.: Yale University Press.

Minuchin, P., Biber, B., Shapiro, E., and Zimiles, H. 1969. *The psychological impact of the school experience*. New York: Basic Books, Inc., Publishers.

Minuchin, S. 1974. *Families and family therapy*. Cambridge, Mass.: Harvard University Press.

Minuchin, S., Baker, L., Rosman, B. L., et al. 1975. A conceptual model of psychosomatic illness in children. *Archives of General Psychiatry* 32:1031-1038.

Mischel, W. 1968. *Personality and assessment*. New York: John Wiley & Sons, Inc.

Money, J., and Ehrhardt, A. A. 1972. *Man and woman, boy and girl: the differentiation and dimorphism of gender identity from conception to maturity*. Baltimore: The Johns Hopkins University Press.

Montessori, M. 1964a. *The Montessori method*. New York: Schocken Books, Inc.

Montessori, M. 1964b. *Spontaneous activity in education*. Cambridge, Mass.: Robert Bentley, Inc.

Moore, T. 1969. Stress in normal childhood. *Human Relations* 22:235-250.

Moore, T. 1975. Stress in normal childhood. In L. Levi (Ed.), *Society, stress and disease* (Vol. 2). London: Oxford University Press.

Moriarty, D. M. 1967. *The loss of loved ones: the effects of death in the family on personality development*. Springfield, Ill.: Charles C Thomas, Publisher.

Moss, H. A. 1974. Early sex differences and mother-infant interaction. In R. C. Friedhuar, R. M. Richart, and R. L. VandeWiele (Eds.), *Sex differences in behaviors*. New York: John Wiley & Sons, Inc.

Mowrer, D. H. 1960. *Learning theory and behavior*. New York: John Wiley & Sons, Inc.

Muller, P. 1969. *The tasks of childhood*. New York: McGraw-Hill Book Co.

Munsinger, H. 1975a. The adopted child's IQ: a critical review. *Psychological Bulletin* 82:623-659.

Munsinger, H. 1975b. Children's resemblance to their biological and adoptive parents in two ethnic groups. *Behavior Genetics* 5:239-254.

Murphy, L. B. 1962. *The widening world of childhood: paths toward mastery*. New York: Basic Books, Inc., Publishers.

Murphy, L. B., and Moriarty, A. E. 1976. *Vulnerability, coping, and growth: from infancy to adolescence*. New Haven, Conn.: Yale University Press.

Mussen, P. H. (Ed.). 1970. *Carmichael's manual of child psychology*. New York: John Wiley & Sons, Inc.

Mussen, P. H., Conger, J. J., and Kagan, J. 1979. *Child development and personality* (5th ed.). New York: Harper & Row, Publishers, Inc.

Muuss, R. E. 1975. *Theories of adolescence* (3rd ed). New York: Random House, Inc.

Nader, P. R., Bullock, D., and Caldwell, B. 1975. School phobia. *Pediatric Clinics of North America* 22:605-619.

Nagy, M. H. 1948. The child's view of death. *Journal of Genetic Psychology* 73:3-27.

National Center for Health Statistics, U.S. Department of Health, Education, and Welfare. 1974. Teenagers: marriages, divorces, parenthood, and mortality. *Vital and Health Statistics*, Series 31, p. 18.

Neligan, G. A., and Prudham, D. 1976. Family factors affecting child development. *Archives of Disease in Childhood* 51:853-858.

Newman, J. 1971. Psychological problems of children and youth with chronic medical disorders. In W. M Cruickshank (Ed.), *Psychology of exceptional children and youth*. Englewood Cliffs, N.J.: Prentice-Hall, Inc.

Niemark, E. 1975. Intellectual development during adolescence. In F. D. Horowitz (Ed.), *Review of child development research* (Vol. 4). Chicago: University of Chicago Press.

Oremland, E. K., and Oremland, J. D. 1973. *The effects of hospitalization on children*. Springfield, Ill.: Charles C Thomas, Publisher.

Parke, R. D. 1977. Punishment in children: effects, side effects, and alternative strategies. In H. L. Hom and P. A. Robinson (Eds.), *Psychological processes in early education*. New York: Academic Press, Inc.

Pattson, R. G., and Gardner, L. I. 1969. Short stature associated with maternal deprivation syndrome: disordered family environment as a cause of so-called idiopathic hypopituitarism. In L. I. Gardner (Ed.), *Endocrine and genetic dis-*

orders of childhood. Philadelphia: W. B. Saunders Co.

Pearson, G. H. J. 1941. Effect of operative procedures on the emotional life of the child. *American Journal of Diseases of Children* **62**:716-729.

Peskin, H. 1967. Pubertal onset and ego functioning. *Journal of Abnormal Psychology* **72**:1-15.

Peterson, D. R. 1961. Behavior problems of middle childhood. *Journal of Consulting Psychology* **25**:205-209.

Petri, E. 1935. Untersuchungen zur Erbbedingtheit der Menarche. *Zeitschrift für Morphologie und Anthropologie* **33**:43-48.

Petrillo, M., and Sanger, S. 1980. *Emotional care of hospitalized children* (2nd ed.). Philadelphia: J. B. Lippincott Co.

Piaget, J. 1926. *The language and thought of the child*. New York: Harcourt, Brace & Co., Inc.

Piaget, J. 1959. *Judgment and reasoning in the child*. Ames, Iowa: Littlefield, Adams & Co.

Piaget, J. 1962. *Play, dreams and imitation in childhood*. New York: W. W. Norton & Co., Inc.

Piaget, J. 1969. The intellectual development of the adolescent. In G. Caplan and S. Lebovici (Eds.), *Adolescence: psychosocial perspectives*. New York: Basic Books, Inc., Publishers.

Piaget, J. 1972. Development and learning. In C. S. Lavatelli and F. Stendler (Eds.), *Readings in child behavior and development* (3rd ed.). New York: Harcourt Brace Jovanovich, Inc.

Piaget, J. 1976. *The child's conception of the world*. Totowa, N.J.: Littlefield, Adams & Co.

Piers, M. W. (Ed.). 1972. *Play and development*. New York: W. W. Norton & Co., Inc.

Pizzo, P. D. 1977. Counseling parents about day care. *Pediatric Annals* **6**:67-82.

Pless, I. B., and Pinkerton, P. 1975. *Chronic childhood disorder: promoting patterns of adjustment*. Chicago: Year Book Medical Publishers, Inc.

Pless, I. B., and Roghmann, K. J. 1972. Chronic illness and its consequences: observations based on three epidemiologic surveys. In S. Chess and A. Thomas (Eds.), *Annual progress in child psychiatry and child development*. New York: Brunner/Mazel, Inc.

Powell, G. F., Brasel, J. A., and Blizzard, R. M. 1967. Emotional deprivation and growth retardation simulating idiopathic hypopituitarism. I: Clinical evaluation of the syndrome. *New England Journal of Medicine* **276**:1271-1278.

Powell, G. F., Brasel, J. A., Raiti, S., and Blizzard, R. M. 1967. Emotional deprivation and growth retardation simulating idiopathic hypopituitarism. II: Endocrinologic evaluation of the syndrome. *New England Journal of Medicine* **276**:1279-1283.

Ralston, N. C., and Thomas, G. P. 1974. *The adolescent: case studies for analysis*. New York: Chandler Publishing Co.

Raph, J. B., Goldberg, M. L., and Passow, A. H. 1960. *Bright underachievers*. New York: Teachers College Press.

Reed, E. L. 1970. *Helping children with the mystery of death*. Nashville,Tenn.: Abingdon Press.

Rest, J. 1968. *Developmental hierarchy in preference and comprehension of moral judgment*. Unpublished doctoral dissertation, University of Chicago.

Rest, J., Turiel, E., and Kohlberg, L. 1969. Level of moral development as a determinant of preference and comprehension of moral judgments of others. *Journal of Personality* **37**:225-252.

Rexford, E. N. 1966. *A developmental approach to problems of acting out: a symposium*. New York: International Universities Press, Inc.

Richardson, S. A. 1975. Physical growth of Jamaican school children who were severely malnourished before 2 years of age. *Journal of Biosocial Science* **7**:445-462.

Ricks, D. M. 1977. Bringing up disabled children. *Proceedings of the Royal Society of Medicine* **70**:28-30.

Riester, A. E., and Zucker, R. A. 1968. Adolescent social structure and drinking behavior. *Personnel and Guidance Journal* **47**:304-312.

Risley, T. R., and Baer, D. M. 1973. Operant behavior modification: the deliberate development of behavior. In B. M. Caldwell and H. N. Ricciuti (Eds.), *Review of child development research* (Vol. 3). Chicago: University of Chicago Press.

Robertson, J. 1970. *Young children in hospitals*. London: Tavistock Publications, Ltd.

Roche, A. F. 1979. Current issues in physical development. Presented at the biennial meeting of the Society for Research in Child Development, San Francisco, March.

Roedell, W. C., Slaby, R. G., and Robinson, H. B. 1977. *Social development in young children*. Monterey, Calif.: Brooks/Cole Publishing Co.

Rohwer, W. D., Ammon, P. R., and Cramer, P. 1974. *Understanding intellectual development*. Hinsdale, Ill.: Dryden Press.

Root, A. 1973. Endocrinology of puberty. I: Normal sexual maturation. *Journal of Pediatrics* 83:1-19.

Rosen, B. C., and D'Andrade, R. 1959. The psychosocial origins of achievement motivation. *Sociometry* 22:185-218.

Rosenberg, C. M. 1969. Young alcoholics. *British Journal of Psychiatry* 115:181-188.

Rosenthal, R., and Jacobsen, L. 1968. *Pygmalion in the classroom: teacher expectation and pupils' intellectual development*. New York: Holt, Rinehart, & Winston.

Rothstein, A. A. 1978. Adolescent males, fatherhood, and abortion. *Journal of Youth and Adolescence* 7:203-214.

Rutter, M. 1972. Normal psychosexual development. In S. Chess and A. Thomas (Eds.), *Annual progress in child psychiatry and child development*. New York: Brunner/Mazel, Inc.

Rutter, M. 1979. Separation experiences: a new look at an old topic. *Journal of Pediatrics* 95:147-154.

Sameroff, A. J. 1975. Early influences on development: fact or fancy? *Merrill-Palmer Quarterly* 21:267-294.

Sarason, S. B., Davidson, K. S., Lighthall, F. F., Waite, R. R., and Ruebusch, B. K. 1960. *Anxiety in elementary school children*. New York: John Wiley & Sons, Inc.

Sarnoff, C. 1976. *Latency*. New York: Jason Aronson, Inc.

Satterwhite, B. B. 1978. Impact of chronic illness on child and family: an overview based on five surveys with implications for management. *International Journal of Rehabilitation Research* 1:7-17.

Satterwhite, B. B., Belle-Isle, J., and Conradt, B. 1978. Parent groups as an aid in mourning and grief work. In O. J. Z. Sahler (Ed.), *The child and death*. St. Louis: The C. V. Mosby Co.

Schmitt, B. 1971. School phobia—the great imitator: a pediatrician's viewpoint. *Pediatrics* 48:433-441.

Schopler, E., and Reichler, R. 1976. *Psychopathology and child development*. New York: Plenum Publishing Corp.

Schowalter, J. E. 1970. The child's reaction to his own terminal illness. In B. Schoenberg, A. C. Carr, D. Peretz, and A. H. Kutscher (Eds.), *Loss and grief: psychological management in medical practice*. New York: Columbia University Press.

Scott, J. P. 1962. Critical periods in behavioral development. *Science* 138:949-958.

Sears, P. S., and Sherman, V. S. 1964. *In pursuit of self-esteem: case studies of eight elementary school children*. Belmont, Calif.: Wadsworth Publishing Co.

Sears, R. R. 1951. A theoretical framework for personality and social behavior. *American Psychologist* 6:476-483.

Sears, R. R., Maccoby, E. E., and Levin, H. 1957. *Patterns of child rearing*. Evanston, Ill.: Row, Peterson & Co.

Sears, R. R., Whiting, J. W. M., Nowlis, V., and Sears, P. S. 1953. Some child-rearing antecedents of aggression and dependency in young children. *Genetic Psychology Monographs* 47:135-234.

Selye, H. 1956. *The stress of life*. New York: McGraw-Hill Book Co.

Senn, M. J. E. 1977. *Speaking out for America's children*. New Haven, Conn.: Yale University Press.

Shaw, M. C. 1968. Underachievement: useful construct or misleading illusion? *Psychology in the Schools* 5:41-46.

Sherif, M., and Cantril, H. 1947. *The psychology of ego-involvements*. New York: John Wiley & Sons, Inc.

Short, J. F. 1966. Juvenile delinquency: the sociocultural context. In L. W. Hoffman and M. L. Hoffman (Eds.), *Review of child development research* (Vol. 2). New York: Russell Sage Foundation.

Shuttleworth, F. K. 1937. Sexual maturation and the physical growth of girls age six to nineteen. *Monographs of the Society for Research in Child Development* 2:1-253.

Shuttleworth, F. K. 1939. The physical and mental growth of girls and boys age sixteen to nineteen in relation to age at maximum growth. *Monographs of the Society for Research in Child Development* 4:1-291.

Signell, K. A. 1976. Kindergarten entry: a preventive approach to community mental health. In R. H. Moos (Ed.), *Human adaptation: coping with life crises*. Lexington, Mass.: D.C. Heath & Co.

Silber, E., Hamburg, D. A., Coelho, G. V., Murphey, E. B., Rosenberg, M., and Pearlin, L. I. 1976. Adaptive behavior in competent adolescents: coping with the anticipation of college. In R. H. Moos (Ed.), *Human adaptation: coping with life crises*. Lexington, Mass.: D. C. Heath & Co.

Simmons, R. G., Bulcroft, R., Blyth, D. A., and Bush, D. M. 1979. The vulnerable adolescent:

school context and self-esteem. Presented at the biennial meeting of the Society for Research in Child Development, San Francisco, March.

Simon, W., and Gagnon, J. H. 1969. On psychosexual development. In D. A. Goslin (Ed.), *Handbook of socialization theory and research*. Chicago: Rand McNally & Co.

Singer, J. L. 1973. *The child's world of make-believe*. New York: Academic Press, Inc.

Skodale, H., and Skeels, H. M. 1949. A final follow-up of one hundred adopted children. *Journal of Genetic Psychology* **75**:85-125.

Smart, M. S., and Smart, R. C. 1978. *School-age children: development and relationships* (2nd ed). New York: Macmillan, Inc.

Smith, C. P. 1969. *Achievement-related motives in children*. New York: Russell Sage Foundation.

Smith, L. 1975. Effects of brief separation from parent on young children. *Journal of Child Psychology and Psychiatry* **16**:245-254.

Smith, R. B. 1968. A study of personality variables associated with discrepant achievement. *Psychology in the Schools* **5**:75-77.

Smoyak, S. 1977. Symposium on parenting. *Nursing Clinics of North America* **12**:447-533.

Solnit, A. J. 1960. Hospitalization: an aid to physical and psychological health in childhood. *American Journal of Diseases of Children* **99**:155-163.

Solnit, A. J., and Green, M. 1963. The pediatric management of the dying child. II: The child's reaction to the fear of dying. In A. J. Solnit and S. A. Provence (Eds.), *Modern perspectives in child development*. New York: International Universities Press, Inc.

Spear, P. S. 1970. Motivational effects of praise and criticism on children's learning. *Developmental Psychology* **3**:124-132.

Spinetta, J. J. 1978. Communication patterns in families dealing with life-threatening illness. In O. J. Z. Sahler (Ed.), *The child and death*. St. Louis: The C. V. Mosby Co.

Stacey, M., Dearden, R., Pill, R., and Robinson, D. 1970. *Hospitals, children, and their families: the report of a pilot study*. London: Routledge & Kegan Paul Ltd.

Starr, B. D. 1970. *The psychology of school adjustment*. New York: Random House, Inc.

Steinhauer, R., Mushin, D., and Rae-Grant, Q. 1974. Psychological aspects of chronic illness: symposium on chronic disease in children. *Pediatric Clinics of North America* **21**:825-840.

Stocking, M., Rothney, W., Grosser, G., and

Goodwin, R. 1973. Psychopathology in the pediatric hospital—implications for community health. In S. Chess and A. Thomas (Eds.), *Annual progress in child psychiatry and child development*. New York: Brunner/Mazel, Inc.

Stringer, L. A. 1973. Children at risk. I: The unready for school. *Elementary School Journal* **73**:364-373.

Strommen, E. A., McKinney, J. P., and Fitzgerald, H. E. 1977. *Developmental psychology: the school-aged child*. Homewood, Ill.: Dorsey Press.

Strupp, H. H. 1967. *Freud and modern psychoanalysis*. Woodbury, N. Y.: Barron's Educational Series, Inc.

Stuart, I. R., and Abt, L. E. 1972. *Children of separation and divorce*. New York: Grossman Publishers.

Sullivan, H. S. 1953. *The interpersonal theory of psychiatry*. New York: W. W. Norton & Co., Inc.

Susanne, C. 1975. Genetic and environmental influence on morphological characteristics. *Annals of Human Biology* **2**:279-288.

Sutton-Smith B. (Ed.). 1976. *The psychology of play*. New York: Arno Press, Inc.

Swift, C. R., and Seidman, F. L. 1964. Adjustment problems of juvenile diabetes. *Journal of the American Academy of Child Psychiatry* **3**:500-515.

Swinger, H. K., and Sandler, A. P. 1977. Parenting problems and the mental health referral. *Pediatric Annals* **6**:97-107.

Szybist, C. 1976. The subsequent child. U.S. Department of Health, Education, and Welfare Publ. No. (HSA) 76-5145. Washington, D.C.: U. S. Government Printing Office.

Szybist, C. 1978. Thoughts of a mother. In O. J. Z. Sahler (Ed.), *The child and death*. St. Louis: The C. V. Mosby Co.

Szybist, L. A. 1978. Thoughts of a sister, In O. J. Z. Sahler (Ed.), *The child and death*. St. Louis: The C. V. Mosby Co.

Tagliacozzo, D. M., and Kenju, I. 1970. Knowledge of illness as a predictor of patient behavior. *Journal of Chronic Disease* **22**:765-775.

Talbot, N. B., Sobel, E. H., Burke, B. S., Lindemann, E., and Kaufman, S. B. 1973. Dwarfism in healthy children: its possible relation to emotional, nutritional and endocrine disturbances. *New England Journal of Medicine* **236**:783-793.

Talbot, T. 1974. *The world of the child*. New York: Jason Aronson, Inc.

Tanner, J. M. 1962. *Growth at adolescence* (2nd ed.). Oxford, England: Blackwell Scientific Publications Ltd.

Tanner, J. M. 1971. Sequence, tempo, and individual variation in the growth and development of boys and girls aged twelve to sixteen. *Daedalus* **100**:907-930.

Tanner, J. M. 1975. Growth and endocrinology of the adolescent. In L. I. Gardner (Ed.), *Endocrine and genetic diseases of childhood and adolescence* (2nd ed.). Philadelphia: W. B. Saunders Co.

Tanner, J. M. 1978. *Fetus into man*. Cambridge, Mass.: Harvard University Press.

Task Force on Pediatric Education. 1978. *The future of pediatric education*. Denver: Hirschfield Press.

Thomas, A. 1979. Learned helplessness and expectancy factors: implications for research in learning disabilities. *Review of Educational Research* **49**:208-221.

Thomas, A., and Chess, S. 1973. Development in middle childhood. In S. Chess and A. Thomas (Eds.), *Annual progress in child psychiatry and child development*. New York: Brunner/Mazel, Inc.

Thomas, A., Chess, S., and Birch, H. G. 1968. *Temperament and behavior disorders in children*. London: University of London Press Ltd.

Thomas, A., Chess, S., Birch, H. G., Hertzig, M. E., and Korn, S. 1964. *Behavioral individuality in early childhood*. New York: New York University Press.

Thomas, E. D., Letchworth, C. J., Rogers, G. A., Jones, M., Akin, M., and Levy, J. 1973. The diagnosis of learning disabilities. *Southern Medical Journal* **66**:1286-1293.

Thomson, A. M. 1959. Maternal stature and reproductive efficiency. *Eugenics Review* **51**:157-162.

Tietz, W., and Vidmar, T. 1972. The impact of coping styles on the control of juvenile diabetes. *Psychiatric Medicine* **3**:67-74.

Tomlinson-Keasey, C. 1972. Formal operations in females from eleven to fifty-four years of age. *Developmental Psychology* **6**:364.

Tulkin, S. R., and Konner, M. J. 1973. Alternative conceptions of intellectual functioning. *Human Development* **16**:33-52.

Vaillant, G. E. 1977. *Adaptation to life*. Boston: Little, Brown & Co.

Vaughn, G. F. 1957. Children in hospital. *Lancet* **1**:117-120.

Vernon, D. T. A., Foley, J. M., Sipowicz, R. R., and Schulman, J. L. 1965. *The psychological responses of children to hospitalization and illness: a review of the literature*. Springfield, Ill. Charles C Thomas, Publisher.

Vygotsky, L. S. 1962. *Thought and language*. Cambridge, Mass.: The M.I.T. Press.

Waechter, E. H. 1977. Children's awareness of fatal illness. In L. Wilkenfeld (Ed.), *When children die*. Dubuque, Ia.: Kendall/Hunt Publishing Co.

Waelder, R. 1960. *Basic theory of psychoanalysis*. New York: International Universities Press, Inc.

Waldfogel, S., Coolidge, J. C., and Hahn, P. B. 1972. The development, meaning and management of school phobia. In C. Lavatelli and F. Stendler (Eds.), *Readings in child behavior and development*. New York: Harcourt Brace Jovanovich, Inc.

Wallerstein, J. S. 1980. Children and divorce. *Pediatrics in Review* **1**:211-217.

Wallerstein, J. S., and Kelly, J. B. 1974. The effects of parental divorce: the adolescent experience. In E. J. Anthony and C. Koupernik (Eds.), *The child in his family: children at psychiatric risk*. New York: John Wiley & Sons, Inc.

Wallerstein, J. S., and Kelly, J. B. 1976a. The effects of parental divorce: experiences of the child in later latency. *American Journal of Orthopsychiatry* **46**:256-269.

Wallerstein, J. S., and Kelly, J. B. 1976b. The effects of parental divorce: experiences of the preschool child. In S. Chess and A. Thomas (Eds.), *Annual progress in child psychiatry and child development*. New York: Brunner/Mazel, Inc.

Warshak, R., and Santrock, J. W. 1979. The effects of father and mother custody on children's social development. Presented at the biennial meeting of the Society for Research in Child Development, San Francisco, March.

Wattenberg, W. W., and Clare, C. 1964. Relation of self-concept to beginning achievement in reading. *Child Development* **35**:416-467.

Weiner, B. 1979. A theory of motivation for some classroom experiences. *Journal of Educational Psychology* **71**:3-25.

Weiner, I. B. 1970. *Psychological disturbance in adolescence*. New York: Interscience Publishers, Inc.

Weiner, I. B., and Elkind, D. 1972. *Child development: a core approach*. New York: John Wiley & Sons, Inc.

Weininger, O. 1977. The disabled and dying children: does it have to hurt so much? In L. Wilkenfeld (Ed.), *When children die*. Dubuque, Ia.: Kendall/Hunt Publishing Co.

Wellington, C. B., and Wellington, J. 1965. *The underachiever: challenges and guidelines*. Chicago: Rand McNally & Co.

Wenar, C. 1971. *Personality development: from infancy to adulthood*. Boston: Houghton Mifflin Co.

Werner, H. 1972. The concept of development from a comparative and organismic point of view. In C. Lavatelli and F. Stendler (Eds.), *Readings in child behavior and development*. New York: Harcourt Brace Jovanovich, Inc.

Werry, J. S., and Wollersheim, J. P. 1968. Behavior therapy with children: a broad overview. In S. Chess and A. Thomas (Eds.), *Annual progress in child psychiatry and child development*. New York: Brunner/Mazel, Inc.

White, E., Elsom, B., and Prawat, R. 1978. Children's conceptions of death. *Child Development* 49:307-310.

Whiting, B. B. 1963. *Six cultures: studies of child rearing*. New York: John Wiley & Sons, Inc.

Wiedeman, G. H., and Matison, S. 1975. *Personality development and deviation*. New York: International Universities Press, Inc.

William-Olsson, I. 1975. Some problems confronting the child in the industrial society. In L. Levi (Ed.), *Society, stress and disease* (Vol. 2). Oxford, England: Oxford University Press.

Williams, F. S. 1977. Parenting the adolescent. *Pediatric Annals* 6:48-58.

Williams, T. F., Martin, D. A., Hogan, M. D., et al. 1967. The clinical picture of diabetic control, studied in four settings. *American Journal of Public Health* 57:441-451.

Wilson, R. S. 1972. Twins: early mental development. *Science* 175:914-917.

Wilson, R. S., and Harpring, E. B. 1972. Mental and motor development in infant twins. *Developmental Psychology* 7:277-287.

Wolfenstein, M. 1966. How is mourning possible? *Psychoanalytic Study of the Child* 21:93-123.

Wolff, S. 1969. *Children under stress*. London: Allen Lane the Penguin Press.

Woody, R. H. 1969. *Behavioral problem children in the schools*. New York: Appleton-Century-Crofts.

Woolsey, S. F., Thornton, D. S., and Friedman, S. B. 1978. Sudden death. In O. J. Z. Sahler (Ed.), *The child and death*. St. Louis: The C. V. Mosby Co.

Yudkin, S. 1977. Death and the young. In L. Wilkenfeld (Ed.), *When children die*. Dubuque, Ia.: Kendall/Hunt publishing Co.

Zelnick, M., Kim, Y., and Kantner, J. F. 1979. Probabilities of intercourse and conception among U.S. teenage women, 1971 and 1976. *Family Planning Perspectives* 11:177-183.

Zigler, E., and Child, I. L. 1973. *Socialization and personality development*. Reading, Mass.: Addison-Wesley Publishing Co., Inc.

INDEX

INDEX